Albert Fytche

Burma

Past and Present. Vol. 2

Albert Fytche

Burma
Past and Present. Vol. 2

ISBN/EAN: 9783337248000

Printed in Europe, USA, Canada, Australia, Japan

Cover: Foto ©Andreas Hilbeck / pixelio.de

More available books at **www.hansebooks.com**

BURMA, PAST AND PRESENT.

THE SHWÉ DAGON PAGODA, RANGOON

BURMA

PAST AND PRESENT

WITH

PERSONAL REMINISCENCES OF THE COUNTRY

BY

Lieut.-Gen. ALBERT FYTCHE, C.S.I.

LATE CHIEF COMMISSIONER OF BRITISH BURMA, AND AGENT TO THE VICEROY
AND GOVERNOR-GENERAL OF INDIA.

'Ἤδη μὲν πολίων κεκορήμεθ᾽ ἀέθλων.

IN TWO VOLUMES.

VOL. II.

WITH ILLUSTRATIONS

LONDON:
C. KEGAN PAUL & CO., 1, PATERNOSTER SQUARE.
1878.

CONTENTS.

CHAPTER I.

LANGUAGE AND LITERATURE.

PAGE

The Burmese the standard language of the country.—The Talaing little used.—The Burmese and Talaings received their religion and alphabet from India.—Description of the Burmese and Talaing languages. —Great reverence paid to the numerals III. and IX.—Use made of the numeral V.—Burmese metaphysical works are in the Pali language. —Books, how formed.—Writing of the Burmese.—Burmese literature. —Their sacred books.—The Bee-da-gat-thoon-bon and the Baideng. —Secular literature.—The disputed wife.—The Burmese drama.— Description of a Burmese theatre.—Dress of the actors.—The orchestra.—Plots of the plays.—A ballet at the Palace at Mandalay.— Burmese great lovers of both vocal and instrumental music.—Translation of a Burmese drama, The Silver Hill 1

CHAPTER II.

PHYSICAL DESCRIPTION, AND HABITS AND CUSTOMS OF THE BURMESE.

Physical characteristics of the Burmese race.—Male costume.—Tattooing. —Its absence considered a mark of effeminacy.—Female dress and ornaments.—Ear-tubes.—Universality of smoking.—Singular custom. —Burmese altogether a different people from the inhabitants of Hindostan.—Absence of caste prejudices.—Their pleasing manners. —Happiness of the people.—Absence of pauperism.—Affection of parents for their children.—Fondness for amusement and excitement. —As a rule not laborious.—Marriage customs.—Perfect freedom of marriageable girls.—Marriage purely a civil rite.—Hla-pet.—Curious custom pursued by a bridegroom's bachelor friends.—Privileges of

PAGE

the female sex.—Code of divorce.—Polygamy.—Sensitiveness to
raillery.—Tendency to suicide.—Suicide of a bridegroom.—Attempted
suicide of a girl.—Food.—Description of a Burmese banquet.—Their
treatment of disease.—The devil dance.—Disease caused by witchcraft.—Funerals.—Boat races.—Peculiarity of the boats.—Mode of
rowing.—Description of the goal.—"Palmam qui meruit *ferit.*"—
Vaunting songs, and grotesque attitudes of the winners.—Subscription purses.—Game of football.—Boxing and wrestling.—Admirable
temper of the combatants.—Description of the Ta-soung-doing festival.—Weaving the sacred cloth.—Relays of workers.—Working
and courting.—Floating lights.—Water festival on New Year's Day.
—Meaning of the observance.—Mythological legend   .   59

CHAPTER III.

FOUR YEARS' ADMINISTRATION OF BRITISH BURMA, 1867-1871.

Our commerce with China confined to sea-ports.—Ancient overland commerce between Burma and Western China viâ Bhamo.—Brought to a
close in 1855.—Early history of the Panthays or Chinese Mahommedans.—They establish a Mahommedan kingdom in Yunnan.—
Monopoly of trade between Burma and Yunnan confined to Chinese
inhabitants of Mandalay and Bhamo.—Their jealousy regarding it.—
Despatch of a Mission under Major Sladen to Western China viâ
Bhamo.—Burmese suspicion of it.—The King ultimately sends the
expedition in his own steamer to Bhamo.—Hill ranges and valleys
occupied by Kakhyens and Shans.—Description of these tribes.—
The Governor of Bhamo defeated and slain by the Kakhyens.—Difficulties of the Mission in consequence.—The Mission starts for
Momein.—Secret agencies at work to stop the Mission.—Mission
delayed at Ponsee.—Delay profitable in some ways.—Valuable collection of specimens of natural history made by Dr. Anderson.—Bambusicola Fytchii.—Kakhyen ideas of marriage.—Their superstitious
observances.—Communication opened with the Governor of Momein.
—The Chinese freebooter Li Hsieh-tai.—Destruction of his stronghold.—Mission escorted by Shans and Panthays to Momein.—
Hospitality of Ta-sa-kon.—All objects of Mission successfully
obtained.—Mission returns to Bhamo.—Return journey quite an
ovation.—Description of Kakhyen oath.—Exposition of the policy in
despatching the Mission.—Objects not political but commercial.—The
tact and gallantry shewn by Major Sladen.—Favourable view taken
by him of the Panthay rebellion.—Policy of the British Government
towards Yacoob Beg, Sultan of Kashgar.—An English political agent

PAGE

appointed to Bhamo.—Large increase of trade.—A Panthay Embassy
proceeds to England viâ Rangoon and Calcutta.—Collapse of Mahommedan power in Yunnan.—Despatch of a second Mission to Western
China.—Its failure.—Murder of Mr. Margary.—Lord Lawrence retires
from the Viceroyalty of India.—Lord Mayo appointed Viceroy.—
Correspondence with Lord Mayo.—Important measures carried out
during my administration of British Burma.—Speech at a public
dinner 95

CHAPTER IV.

BUDDHISM AND EDUCATION IN BURMA.

Shamanism the ancient religion of Burma.—Adoration of nats and other
spirits.—Three religions preceded Buddhism in India.—Buddhism a
wide-spread religion.—Propagated by persuasion alone.—The Buddhas
previous to Gautama.—The Jâtaka fables.—Birth and parentage of
Gautama.—His miraculous conception.—Education of Gautama.—
Gautama's four visions.—He deserts his palace and assumes the garb
of an ascetic.—His trials and temptations in the wilderness.—He
becomes a Buddha.—The sacred Bô-tree.—Gautama proceeds towards
Benares to preach his doctrine.—He visits his father.—Attempts on
his life.—Punishment of Dêwadat.—Gautama's death.—His funeral.
—Gautama's relics.—The Shwé-dagon pagoda at Rangoon.—The
three Synods.—The Pitakatayan, or Buddhist scriptures.—Powers of
memory of Buddhist priests.—Two Buddhist missionaries arrive at
Thatún.—Buddhagosa.—Talaings received their religion and alphabet
from Ceylon.—The Burmese from the Talaings.—Karma and Nirvâna
described.—Buddhism and Brahminism compared.—Dâna, or almsgiving.—Purity of Buddhist ethics.—Singular analogy of Buddhistic
rites and observances to those of Romish Christianity.—Early Roman
Catholic missionaries in the East.—Their opinions regarding Buddhism.—Buddhism existent in the western world previous to the birth
of our Saviour.—Gautama a saint in the Roman calendar.—Phongyees.
—Rules of the Order.—The Novitiate.—Ordination.—Celibacy.—
Diet.—The Habit.—The Order of Nuns.—Funerals.—Monasteries.
—Education in Burma.—Monastic and lay schools.—System of
education lately adopted by the British Government.—Difficulties
regarding it.—How overcome.—Success of the system . . 137

viii

CONTENTS.

APPENDICES.

PAGE

APPENDIX A.—Official reports regarding an expedition against an Arakan Hill Tribe 213

APPENDIX B.—Official documents connected with services in the Bassein district 220

APPENDIX C.—Narrative of the Mission to Mandalay in 1867 . . 252

APPENDIX D.—Memorandum on the comparative progress of the provinces now forming British Burma under British and Native rule . 286

APPENDIX E.—Memorandum on the Panthays, or Mahommedan population of Yunnan 296

APPENDIX F.—Letter of apology from the Emperor of China . . . 304

APPENDIX G.—Memorandum on four years' administration of British Burma, 1867-71 307

LIST OF

MAPS AND ILLUSTRATIONS.

—•—

VIEW OF THE SHWÉ-DAGON PAGODA AT RANGOON . *Frontispiece*

SPECIMEN OF BURMESE WRITING **3**

BURMESE DANCING GIRL AND A BURMESE LADY *To face page* **63**

GAME OF FOOTBALL . . . . . . ,, **86**

BAMBUSICOLA FYTCHII . . . . . ,, **104**

FUNERAL PROCESSION OF A BUDDHIST PRIEST . ,, **201**

INTERIOR OF A BUDDHIST MONASTERY . . ,, **204**

MAP OF BURMA AND ADJACENT COUNTRIES, WITH ROUTES
OF VARIOUS EXPLORERS . . . . *At end of Volume*

BURMA, PAST AND PRESENT.

CHAPTER I.

LANGUAGE AND LITERATURE.

The Burmese the standard language of the country.—The Talaing little used.—
The Burmese and Talaings received their religion and alphabet from
India.—Description of the Burmese and Talaing languages.—Great
reverence paid to the numerals III. and IX.—Use made of the numeral
V.—Burmese metaphysical works are in the Pali language.—Books, how
formed.—Writing of the Burmese.—Burmese literature.—Their sacred
books.—The Bee-da-gat-thoon-bon and the Baideng.—Secular literature.
—The disputed wife.—The Burmese drama.—Description of a Burmese
theatre.—Dress of the actors.—The orchestra.—Plots of the plays.—A
ballet at the Palace at Mandalay.—Burmese great lovers of both vocal
and instrumental music.—Translation of a Burmese drama, The Silver
Hill.

THE Burmese is the standard language of the
country, in which the administration of affairs is
conducted, and is spoken generally by all classes of
natives, including, also, in many instances, the hill
tribes. In a few villages coast-ward, however,
peopled by descendants of the old kingdom of
Pegu, and remote from the main sources of access
to the principal towns, the Talaing, or Mon language
—notwithstanding the efforts of the Burmans during
their rule to stamp out all knowledge of it—is

still taught in the Buddhist monasteries, and the sacred writings expounded in that dialect.

It is, I consider, a source of regret that nationality of language was not restored to the Talaings on our occupation of the country. It would have removed the feeling of degradation of a conquered race, and, together with the grateful sense for such a consideration, have served as a check on any combination by them with the Burmese, which might possibly arise in the future.

The Burmese, as well as the Talaings, received their religion and alphabet from India. Their alphabets differ very slightly, both being a circular variety of the ancient Deva Nagri;* but the two languages have no radical affinity, the Burmese being cognate with the Tibetan, and the Talaing (as stated in the previous chapter) with the aboriginal Indian tribes of the north-east, Monda, or Kól family. The former is labial and soft as the Italian, the latter harsh and guttural as Arabic. In combination of words and sentences and in idiom they are entirely different. In the Talaing language† the subject usually precedes the verb, and the object follows it, as in English; but in a Burmese and Tibetan sentence the order of the words is inverted.

---

* A specimen of Burmese writing, being a transcript of a petition made to me when Chief Commissioner of British Burma, is given on the opposite page.

† The Rev. Dr. Mason, " Burma," p. 126.

အင်္ဂလိပ်မင်းပိုင်၊မြန်မာနိုင်ငံကိုအစိုးရတော်မူသော
မဟာဝန်ရှင်တော်မင်းကြီးသခင်ဘုရား
ထံရှိခိုးသံတော်ဦးတင်ရန်အရွှာ

ဘုရားကျွန်တော်မောင်အောင်။ရှိခိုးသံတော်ဦးတင်ပါသည်အရှင်သခင်မင်းမြတ်ကြီးဘုရား ကျွန်တော်မျိုးသည်။ငယ်ရွယ်စဉ်ကယခုတိုင်။မြေတိုင်းခြင်းပညာ၊အင်းစာရင်းအတွက်၊လက်ရေးလက်သားများကိုသင်ကြားတတ်မြောက်ပြီးသည်နောင်။အစိုးရမင်းရုံးတော်မှာ၂နှစ်စည်မပြတ်အာ ၅ တော်ကိုထမ်းရွက်ရေးပါကိုင်နေပါသည်။ဤသို့ရေးပါကိုင်သည်အတွင်း။ကျွန်တော်မျိုးအပေါ်၌က် ၊ ၅ ဖြစ်တစုံတရာမရှိဘူးပါ။ယခုကျွန်တော်မျိုးမှာအလုပ်မရှိပါသောကြောင့်။အရွှန်ဆင်ရဲပင်ပန်းခွမ်း နယ်ရှိနေပါသည်။ကိုယ်တော်အရှင်သခင်မှတပါး။အခြားကိုးကွယ်ရာအရှင်သခင်မရှိပါသော ကြောင့်။မြေရင်းတော်တွင်အမှုတော်ကိုထမ်းရွက်အသက်မွေးရပါအောင်။တစုံတခုသောနေရာ၊ မှာ။ခန့်ထားသနားတော်မူရန်၊အမိန့်လက်မှတ်ကယ်မသနားတော်မူပါမည်အကြောင်းကို၊ကိုးကွ ကွယ်ရာအရှင်တပါးရှိပါ၍။ရှိခိုးသံတော်ဦးတင်ပါသည်အရှင်မင်းမြတ်ကြီးဘုရား။

၁၈၆၉ ခုနှစ် နိုလ ၂၂ ရက်နေ့…}
ဘုရားခုပဌမဝါဆိုလဆန်း၁၃ရက်နေ့…}

။မောင်အောင်။

SPECIMEN OF BURMESE WRITING.

For instance, in the example given by Csoma de
Koros in his grammar of the Tibetan language,
the translation of "*in a book seen by me*," would
become in both these latter languages "*me by seen
book a in.*"

The Burmese language, according to August
Schleicher's classification * belongs, in common with
the other Indo-Chinese tongues, to the type of the
isolating languages, consisting of mere roots, incapable of forming compounds, and not susceptible
of inflectional change.   With few exceptions all
words are derived from original roots, which, by
being used with affixes or prefixes, are converted
without inflection into different parts of speech.   It
is written from left to right, has no division between the words, and is wholly monosyllabic,
with the exception of polysyllabic words introduced from the Pali dialect, and even these are
pronounced as if each syllable of them was a
distinct word.†

The alphabet consists of ten vowels and thirty-
two consonants.   The vowels are written in their
original character only when they form the initial
syllable of a word of Pali origin.   When combined

* Compendium der Vergleichenden Grammatick der Indogermanischen
Sprachen, von August Schleicher, 8vo. Weimar, 1866.

† From this has arisen the system complained of by Colonel Yule, of
hyphenized aggregation of syllables, when Pali names are written in English.
See "Mission to Ava," p. 106.

with consonants they are represented by symbols.
The vowel *a* is supposed to be inherent in every
consonant that is not furnished with the symbol
of another vowel or marked as final. The first
twenty-five consonants are divided into five classes
of five each, viz., gutturals, palatals, linguals, dentals,
and labials. Of the remaining seven, five may be
considered liquids, one a sibilant, and the other is
the aspirate *h.*

Gender is strictly confined to those appellatives
which imply objects distinguished by sex, and is
usually expressed by affixes referring to the sexual
difference ; such nouns as *virtue, house,* are not held
to be of the neuter gender, but are considered to be
of no gender at all. In combining a numeral with
a noun, the term implying the genus, or essential
quality of the thing spoken of, is added. To render
into Burmese the idea two oxen, it would be necessary to say oxen, two animals : two shillings, shillings, two flat things ; four priests, priests, four
objects of reverence ; and even when the appellative
is used without a numeral, the term implying its
class is often superadded, as tsa-gnhet, a sparrow ;
from tsa, a sparrow, and gnhet, bird.

In the oral language, affixed particles, especially
connective ones, are often omitted : this, with many
words being spelt the same and only differing very
slightly in tone when spoken, but having a widely

different signification; and words declaring any action being frequently not used in expressing a modification * of them; together with other peculiarities, renders the language difficult of acquisition, at first, to those accustomed to the inflecting and more finished structure of the Indo-European languages.

The numeral system of the Burmese is decimal. Most of the names of the numerals have some signification in the language, and two of them bear evident marks of allusion to the tenets of the Buddhist faith. They are *thoon*, " three,"† and *Ko*, " nine." The first typifies the Buddhist triad, or " the three most precious gems," *Buddha, Dhamma, Thengha*. " Buddha, His Law, and the congregation of his Saints."

According to Buddhism, from Buddha proceeded the Law, and from the Law came those who fulfilled it; for, that human intelligence has in itself the power of transcendental perfectibility, is the diagnostic dogma, the foundation-stone of Buddhism as a religion. For this reason, *thoon* implies, likewise,

* For instance, to wash the hands, the face, the body, linen, dishes, &c., are all different phrases, each expressing the action to wash by a different verb.

† Great reverence is also paid to the number three by the Egyptians in their worship of Amounra, Amoun-neu, and Sevek-ra; by the Hindús of Brahma, Vishna and Siva, and by the ancient Greeks of Jupiter, Neptune, and Pluto. Number *seven* is held among Semitic nations as a sacred and perfect number, evidently in allusion to the seven epochs of creation: or, possibly, to the seven stars (the Pleiades) in the constellation of Taurus. See footnote to page 91.

so to perform one's moral exigencies, as, by becoming enrolled in the latter member of the triune Three (the Thengha) to become also a component part of the Supreme Triad, the *Thărănagŏon*, "the Supreme and final attributes, beyond which there is no passing." The number *nine*, in the same manner, is a *triple* combination of three ; a trebly expressive symbol, therefore, of the expressive *three ;* and, being the product of that number into itself, it emblematises the active energy of the Supreme Triad teeming in itself : hence *Kŏ*, "nine," implies likewise, to "reverence, worship, trust in," &c.

It is usual, in epistolary writing, to make a mark or pause, as a sort of starting point : the figure *five* is often used in this way, because it refers to *Pegnytseng*, "the five commandments ;" and its use in this instance implies that the writer has kept in mind these commandments while writing his letter, as also that the reader should do the same, and not put an evil interpretation on any part of it. *

On the introduction of the Buddhist religion and literature, numerous admixtures of terms from the Pali dialect were introduced ; but they remain as distinctly extraneous now as they did on their first admission, and are seldom made use of in common conversation. All the Burmese metaphysical works

* "Grammar of the Burmese Language," by Lieutenant Thos. Latter, pp. 89, 90.

are in the Pali language,* in copying which recourse
is had to the vernacular alphabet, the ancient square
Pali character being seldom adopted, except in one
instance, in which it is invariably used, and that is
for the sacred *Kambhawa,*† or rules to be observed
at the ordination of priests. These ordinances
are supposed to have been promulgated and sanctioned by Gautama himself, and are held in profound
veneration by all Buddhists.

Burmese books are composed of leaves ‡ of the
Palmyra palm, through the ends of which a string is
passed, and are bound between a couple of wooden
covers, gilt, and lacquered in coloured devices. The
letters are engraved on the leaves with an iron
stylus, held nearly perpendicular by the two forefingers and thumb of the right hand, and steadied

---

* It has long been a disputed point whether the Pali or the Sanskrit is the
most ancient language. The Buddhists hold that Pali is the root of Sanskrit,
and the primitive language from which all others are descended. Whereas
their rivals, the Brahmans, declare that it is a derivation from the Sanskrit ; but
polluted like cow's milk in a dog's skin by the unholy contact of Buddhist
heretics.

European philologists appear generally to agree that Pali represents one of
the oldest Prākritic dialects of Northern India, which has been handed down
to us, and was the popular dialect of Māgadha and Central India at the time
of Gautama ; and if not a derivation from Sanskrit in an early stage of its
development, that the two dialects were contemporaneously evolved from a
kindred source, the traces of which cannot be discovered at the present day.
See Muir's "Sanskrit Texts," pp. 53—103, vol. ii. ; Lotus de la Bonne Loi.
App. Burnouf.

† I have in my possession two very beautiful manuscripts of this work in the
old square Pali character ; one written in letters of gold on ivory leaves, and
the other on gilt, and highly varnished palm leaves.

‡ The process of preparing these leaves has been given in the preceding
chapter.

by the thumb-nail of the left hand, in which a nick is often cut to receive it. The writing is rendered visible by the application of charcoal ground with eng-tway, a fragrant gum procured from *Diptero-carpus grandiflora*, and which latter preserves also the leaves from the attacks of insects. Every Buddhist monastery contains a library of these books, kept in carved and lacquered cabinets.

The literature of the Burmese, both sacred and profane, has mostly an Indian origin. Their two great metaphysical works are the Bee-da-gat thoon-bon, or Pittakatayan * (the three baskets), and the Baideng. The former contains the three great divisions of the Buddhist scriptures, the Thuttan, Winiya, and Abhidhamma, and is very voluminous. The first, Thuttan, or the line,† contains the nume-rous sermons and discourses of Gautama; the ex-cellent precepts contained in some of which would do honour to a Christian teacher of the present day.

In one of these sermons, for instance, Gautama prescribes the manner in which religious festivals should be observed. "Whoever," he says, "wishes

---

* The King is having the entire Bee-da-gat engraved on white marble slabs, which are to be placed round the temple he has built near Mandalay. When at Mandalay I visited the place where they were being engraved. A large number of stone-cutters were employed, and busily engaged on the work.

† It is like a rule or line, because as the line (thuttan) is a mark of definition to carpenters, so is the Thuttan a rule of conduct to the wise. In the same way that flowers strung together upon a thread are neither scattered nor lost, so the precepts contained herein are united by this line (thuttan). Turnour's "Mahawanso." Hardy's "Eastern Monachism," p. 168.

to acquire great merit, must not limit himself to the customary adorations and offerings on these days, but must spend them in meditating on the favours of God, and the excellence of his law. He must be contented with one simple dish in the morning, and with little or no sleep at night, which should be passed in prayer, and in reading good books. As it is, moreover, forbidden to do any work on these days, everyone must be careful to despatch all necessary business the day before, that so he may be free from all cares and distractions."

In another, he thus accosts a young disciple who had gone astray. "A man should refrain from the six things that are called ruinous, viz.: love of intoxicating liquors ; the custom of wandering about the streets ; too great passion for dancing ; games and spectacles ; gambling ; frequenting vicious company ; and lastly, slothfulness and negligence in the performance of one's duties. Drunkenness is the cause of the loss of goods and reputation, of quarrels, diseases, immodesty of dress, disregard of honour, and incapacity for learning. Unseasonable wanderings expose a man to great dangers and temptation, and leave his family and possessions unprotected. A passion for games and shows draws a man from his occupations, and hinders him from gaining his livelihood. A gambler has no friends. In gaming, success is followed by intrigues and quarrels : loss,

by bitterness and sorrow of heart, as well as dilapi-
dation of fortune.   Finally, frequenting the company
of the vicious, idleness, and neglect of one's proper
duties, lead to debauchery, deceit, robbery, and all
kinds of wickedness."

In speaking of false friends, he describes them
"as always making show of friendship without its
reality, professing a love which they do not feel,
giving little that they may receive much, and being
friends with a man only because he is rich, or
because they have need of his favour.   Those, too,
are false friends, who give a promise in words, but
are far from fulfilling it in their actions : and, finally,
those who are ever ready to assist a man in doing
evil, but never in doing good.   Real friends, he
adds, are of four kinds; firstly, those who are
such both in adversity and prosperity ; secondly,
those who give good advice on proper occasions,
even at the peril of their lives ; thirdly, those who
take care of whatever belongs to him they love ;
and fourthly, those who teach a man what is good,
who are delighted in his prosperity, and sorrowful
in his misfortunes."

The second division,* Winya, or discipline, is
subdivided into five books, and contains the regula-
tions of the priesthood.   It "is said to be the life of
the Buddhist religion, as where discipline is at an

* Hardy's "Eastern Monachism," p. 168.

end, religion is at an end." The third division,
Abhi-dhamma, or pre-eminent truths, was addressed
by Gautama to the Brahmas and Déwas, and contains seven sections, not in the form of sermons, but
specifying terms and doctrines of dogmatic philosophy,
with definitions and explanations.

The Baideng is divided into four parts, one, however, of which has been lost. It is the great Pali
work on mathematics and astronomy, or rather
astrology.

Of secular literature there are works on subjects
such as chronological history, medicine, topography,
ballads, and romances ; the latter two of which are,
to the credit of the Burmese, free from the gross-
ness and indelicacy of similar productions in India.
I will here extract a tale from the Thoo-dhamma-
tsarie, translated by the late Colonel Sparks, which
will serve to illustrate the general character of the
latter kind of literature.

THE DISPUTED WIFE.

In the olden time, during the era of Thermaydha,*
in the country of Kaytoomatee, the son of a certain
man who was possessed of countless wealth, and the
daughter of another rich man named Thanga, were

* The sixteenth Buddh, who lived 90,000 years, and was eighty-eight cubits
in stature.

married to each other, with the consent of their parents. The rich man's son said to his wife, " Our parents are in the enjoyment of vast wealth, but we have nothing ; therefore, I shall embark on board ship, and go with others to Lankha Deepa.*

His wife, on hearing these words, spoke to him affectionately, saying, " My husband, if you leave me to go trading, I have no other protector ; it is the poor only that go to sea ; both your parents and mine are in the enjoyment of all that wealth can bestow ; go not, I beseech you." Her husband replied, " It is good to have riches which have been gained by our own industry, and even if I am drowned in the attempt, such a death will be honourable. A man without substance is base and contemptible. Sitting still, and eating and drinking, are disgraceful to a man. The wise have said, therefore, that they who, setting no value upon their lives, embark upon the ocean in search of wealth, even although they should be disappointed in their aim, are deserving of praise ; † so I am determined to go." Thus saying he took some stock in trade with him and departed.

He had not been gone long before his wife formed an intimacy with a servant named Payta, who said to her one day, " We are living together

* The Pali name of Ceylon.
† These manly sentiments are expressed at much greater length, and with more force, in the Zanekka, one of the ten Daats which contain the history of Gaudama in a former transmigration.

now, but how shall we be able to continue to do so, when your husband returns?" The rich man's daughter desired Payta to bring a corpse from the burying ground, and to place it on the roof, and set the house on fire, saying, "People will think that I have been burnt to death, and then we can go to some other place, and live together." Payta did as he was told, and they removed to another part of the country.

The parents thinking that it was in reality their daughter who had been burnt, mourned for her bitterly, and performed the funeral rites over the corpse.

Payta and the rich man's daughter, being without the means of subsistence in their new place of abode, the latter said, "We are in a miserable condition here, let us return, and my parents, on seeing me, will be struck with my resemblance to their daughter, and give us something with which we shall be able to procure clothes and food." They returned accordingly, and arriving at her parents' garden, sat down to rest under the shade of a flowering tree, by the side of a bank. The rich man's servants came down to draw water for a libation to the memory of their master's daughter, and on seeing her cried out, "If it were not that she has a husband with her, we could declare that this is our master's daughter."

So taking up their golden pitchers, they returned

and reported to their mistress what they had seen. The rich man's wife hastened down to the garden, and on looking upon her daughter, with difficulty refrained from weeping ; as she asked her who she was, she answered, " Madam, your servants are travellers, and are about to depart immediately." " Go not away from us," said the lady, " you shall be to us in the place of the daughter we have lost." So saying, she made them both return to the house with her, and gave them a pavilion to dwell in with a pinnacled roof.*

About this time the husband returned, and, on inquiring for his wife, was informed that she had perished in her house, which had been destroyed by fire.   Restraining his tears, he chanced to enter the pavilion which his mother-in-law had built, where, seeing his wife, he exclaimed, " What do people mean by saying that my wife is dead, when here she is all the time ? "   So he applied to the village judge, who, on the testimony of the complainant's mother-in-law, and many other persons, threw out the case.   Being dissatisfied, he appealed to the governor of the district, who confirmed the previous decision.   He then went to the King, who, not being much versed in the law, the nat's daughter, the guardian of the white umbrella, cried

---

* A roof of several stages, rising one above another, the use of which is confined in Burma to religious edifices, palaces, and the houses of men of rank.

out, " O King, this case is not one for the ignorant
to meddle with.   Is not your chief noble skilful in
the disposal of suits?"   The King, on hearing this,
sent for the chief nobleman, and told him that,
unless he settled the case, he would degrade him
from his rank.

The nobleman's daughter observing that her
father was dejected, inquired the reason; whereupon
he repeated to her the King's order.   She said,
" Let not my father distress himself, but let him
cause the three parties to appear before me, and
let him erect a building for the purpose, and place
them in the three corners thereof, whilst I will
remain in the centre and examine them."

All having been done as she desired, the nobleman's daughter called the rich man's son and thus
addressed him, " O excellent man, adorned with
all perfection, every one says that after, regardless
of life, you embarked upon the ocean, your wife
perished here in the flames which consumed your
dwelling.   Your parents abound in riches, and you
have acquired much wealth besides by your voyage.
It is unbecoming in a person of your condition to be
engaged in such a contest as this, where two men
are quarrelling for the possession of one woman.
This young lady also says that she is your adver-
sary's wife, and he declares the same thing, consequently all, from the King downwards, have decided

against you. If she were really your wife, why should she deny the fact?

"You had better follow my counsel which I am about to unfold to you; but how will you receive it, or how shall I utter it?" Being asked to explain herself further, she continued, "You are the son of a rich man, and I am the daughter of a great noble; if we are both but of one mind, what sorrow can ever befall us for the rest of our lives?" *
The rich man's son replied, "How can I give up a wife who was betrothed to me by her parents before she was able to walk alone, and before she ceased to be allowed to go without clothes on? The nature of man ought to be incapable of doing a cruel or heartless action, and what good can ever result from the breach of a solemn compact?" The nobleman's daughter, on hearing these words of this man of honour, expressed her astonishment and dismissed
. him.

The nobleman's daughter then called Payta, and said to him, "It is not meet for two young men, who are endowed with every perfection, to quarrel for one woman. I have no husband, and I desire to live with you; great will be our love; and, I being

---

* I cannot help noting the delicacy with which this proposal is made. Indeed, there are several passages in this story, which are calculated to give a favourable idea of Burmese literature. How simple, for instance, and yet how noble, is the young man's reply. Mark also the different styles of her address to Payta, with whom there was no occasion for much refinement. She tempts the former with her love, the latter with her riches and her rank.

a nobleman's daughter, shall not we enjoy the pleasures attending upon rank and wealth?" Payta, on hearing this, considering that it would be wise to follow her advice, replied, "Women are by nature fertile in devices for the accomplishment of their ends; they are full of deceit, and their minds disposed to treachery. My life is like water in the hollow of the hand of this woman.* Therefore I will do as you desire." "If you agree to my plan," answered she, "we must elope together, and live in some other part of the country; on this condition only will I trust you." To this also he consented, and she desired him to return to his place.

After this she sent for the rich man's daughter, and thus examined her. "My sister, the circumstances of your husband are humble, whilst the position and means of happiness enjoyed by this rich man's son are great. If you were to live with him, you would know no sorrow during the rest of your life; why then do you refuse?" She replied, "You, lady, are a woman, and so also am I; the nature of woman is like fruit upon a tree, and her husband is like the tree itself. The nature of fruit is this; first a shoot sprouts out, which gives forth

---

* His paramour,—either because she was his accomplice, and he feared that she might betray him, or because it occurred to him, that as she had suggested the means by which she had rid herself of her husband, she would not be wanting in an expedient to put himself out of the way hereafter, should she entertain the wish to do so, and would not scruple to use violent means, if necessary, to effect her purpose.

one or two leaves, and then grows into a branch; on the branch is formed a bud; this in time expands into a blossom, which changes into fruit; the fruit ripens, and then falls off, and is cast away among the refuse. Can the fruit be re-attached to the stalk from which it has fallen? or can a child, after it has once been born, re-enter its mother's womb from which it came forth?" *

When the nobleman's daughter had heard this she exclaimed, "Now I comprehend the treachery of which this woman has been guilty." So saying, she dismissed them all three, and having dictated to the secretaries all that each of them had said, and caused them to record it, she had it read to her father. He, rejoicing exceedingly, took the three parties to the suit before the King, and on questioning them [they confessed the truth].

The King thus passed sentence: "The servant Payta, not being the true husband, deserves to suffer death; nevertheless, I spare his life. The rich man's son turned merchant, who, although he had acquired vast wealth, would not break his troth, is the original husband. The rich man's daughter is also worthy of death, because she denied her husband; but, in consideration of her having indicated the truth, by the

---

* An elegant and touching picture of the lost and fallen state of a wife, who by her unfaithfulness has forfeited the love and respect of her husband, to which she feels her too late repentance can never hope to restore her.

metaphor of the ripe fruit, which after it has fallen
from its stalk cannot be united to it again, and of the
child, which having once been born, cannot re-enter
its mother's womb, she is cautioned and released."

Then the nat's daughter, the guardian of the
white umbrella, testified her approval, and the King
made the nobleman's daughter his Queen.

Therefore let wise judges carefully consider and
inquire into all cases of fraud, deceit, and treachery,
before they pass a decision.

Another of their romances, called " Apau-radza-
bon," treats of the principles of political science, and
shows peculiar shrewdness in many of its precepts.
I will quote one of these precepts, and which may
yet be applicable to the present great war raging
between Russia and Turkey.

" Once upon a time two Kings, whose territories
bordered on Burma, declared war against each
other, and both had recourse for assistance to the
Burmese monarch, who sent for the Minister, in
whom he placed much confidence, for advice as to
what he was to do under the circumstances ; and
which was given in the following manner :—

" In the presence of a countryman, who was
working in his field, two cocks ran out of the jungle
and commenced fighting together, and after con-
tinuing the combat for some time with great
bravery and determination, they became so over-

come with their exertions, that they became exhausted and could fight no longer, when he sprang upon them and seized them both. Do you therefore, O King! do likewise. Remain quiet. Let these two Kings fight with each other until their resources are exhausted, and then dictate peace to them, and annex such portions of their territories as your Majesty may desire."

The drama in Burma is a national institution, exercising a wide-spread and powerful influence on the minds of the population : and one of the first impressions which strike a stranger is the universal passion that exists among the people for dramatic performances. It is a strange and curious sight to see the large crowds of Burmese assembled for the night to witness the performance of a *pooay*, or play, and the delight and perfect good order which they manifest. Their attention appears wholly absorbed by the performance, and the sympathy shown for distressed virtue, and rattling peals of laughter caused by the comic parts of the play, are very natural.

Except for the dresses of the actors and actresses, which appear rich and handsome, the *mise-en-scène* and stage accompaniments are rude and simple. A structure of bamboos, supporting a roof of trellis work, lightly thatched with grass, and picturesquely draped with bright-coloured silks and cloths, suffice for a theatre. The stage is in the centre, and in its midst, around a green bough unhesitatingly accepted as a substitute for a wood scene, are grouped the footlights, consisting of earthen bowls placed on plantain stems, and fed with petroleum oil. Raised bamboo platforms, on one or more sides for distinguished visitors, supply the place of boxes ; and pit and gallery are represented by the orderly crowd seated close together in a circle on the ground. At the back is the orchestra, and behind it the *corps dramatique*, surrounded with dragon wings, masks, and other stage properties, change their dresses, and have their " exits and their entrances."

The plots of the different plays bear a great resemblance to each other. The *dramatis personae* generally representing the adventures of a prince, first in quest of, and then in the courtship of a princess, a " heavy father " in the shape of a king, oppressively wise ministers, humble courtiers, and maids-of-honour for the princess. There are court receptions, processions, and dances as interludes. The prince is invariably accompanied by a servant, a *loo-byet*, or " sort of Shakespearian Lance," whose jokes with the maids-of-honour and others, often improvised, and bearing on matters of local gossip and scandal, give rise to peals of laughter. The tones and cadences of the Burmese language, giving a different meaning to words whose alphabetic forms are the same, lends itself readily to puns and *double entendre*, and the jokes of the *loo-byet* are not always of the most delicate nature ; though seldom or ever anything said at these plays exceed the average licence of an English stage.

The dialogue is chiefly recitative, interspersed with solos, chorus, and dancing. The music and singing are by no means dissonant and inharmonious, many of the airs being very sweet and pleasing. In dancing they observe time accurately, not only with their voices, but every joint in their bodies appear obedient to the sound of the instruments, displaying that litheness and flexibility of fibre, which distinguish natives of a tropical climate from those of a temperate region.

When I was at Mandalay the King invited the Mission to a ballet at the palace. The performance commenced by the entrance of about thirty young girls in single file, who arranged themselves in a semi-circle, and kneeling down bowed to his Majesty. They wore the ordinary *hta-mien*, or Burmese petticoat, but the jacket was more of the fashion after that worn by princes in the plays. The *hta-miens* were all red and green, the jackets white satin, with circular pieces of silver stitched on, so as somewhat to resemble armour. On their heads the girls wore peaked helmets, such as are used by male performers in the ordinary plays.

The girls, rising, first performed a slow graceful dance round the theatre to the accompaniment of the band, varying the step and pace from time to time, and again kneeling down; one of the number, taking up her position in the centre, then sang or chanted a slow hymn in honour of his Majesty, describing his greatness and goodness.

This was acknowledged by all of us to be one of the most effective exhibitions we had ever witnessed in the East. The dead silence of the whole assembly, the clear and exceedingly sweet tone of the girl's voice, and the peculiar measure of the air, half-recitative, half-melody, made the whole scene most striking and beautiful. The hymn consisted of three verses; at the end of each, the girls, still kneeling, bowed low to his Majesty. They then resumed the dance, which they accompanied with a low chant, and varied it by beating time with two ornamental sticks which they now carried. This, too, being ended, the King rose and left. During the performance the Nanmadau Phura, or chief Queen, entered, and seated herself close to his Majesty on a sofa placed for her reception.

The people are great lovers of both vocal and instrumental music, and many Englishmen and other foreigners, who have merely a superficial knowledge of the language, are under the impression that the songs of the people are wholly, or chiefly amatory ones. But such is not the case ; they delight in those of a domestic nature, also ; and many a time when on my tours in the interior of the country, I have heard villagers singing charming little songs of children playing, flowers, birds, the merry sunshine, the working in the rice-fields, and such-like subjects.

Their war-boat songs are stirring and lively.* The recitative of the *pai-neng*, or steersman, and then the swell of voices when the boatmen, often sixty or eighty in number, join in the chorus, keeping time with their oars, is very striking. I landed Lord Dalhousie in one of these boats on his visit to Bassein shortly after the last Burmese war, and he was very much struck with the men's song, remarking that it reminded him of the boat-songs he used to hear in Canada in the days of his youth.

As some of my readers can have possibly no conception of what a Burmese play really is, the following drama, called " The Silver Hill,"† which is a good type of this vein of Burmese literature, and one of their popular plays, will give a good idea of their general plot and dialogue.

---

* This part is often taken by the *pai-kheit*, or stroke oar, in place of the steersman, and he is chosen for this post on account of his good voice, as well as his skill with the oar.

† This play was translated by Lieut. Sladen (now Lieut.-Col. Sladen) and the late Colonel Sparks in 1856, and the original thoughts and imagery of the vernacular has been well and carefully preserved.

THE SILVER HILL.

A BURMESE DRAMA.

Dramatis Personae.

THE KING OF PINZALA.
PRINCE THOODANOO, his son, heir to the throne.
DOOMARAJAH, King of the Silver Hill in Fairy-land.
MOZALINDA, a hunter.
PAMOUK, a hermit.
MOKA, a soothsayer.
Another Hermit.

Ministers of State, Officers, a Beloo,* Guards, Attendants, &c., &c.

PRINCESS DWAYMENAU, daughter of King Doomarajah.
Six Princesses, her sisters.
MALA, chief of the Ladies of the Palace of Pinzala.
MANINGYA, wife of Mozalinda.

Virgin Attendants, &c.

ACT I.

SCENE I.—A HALL IN THE PALACE OF PINZALA.

The KING *surrounded by his* Ministers of State. *In a recess the* PRINCE *sleeping on a couch of gold;* Attendants *watching over his slumbers.*

KING.

My faithful Ministers, who constant pay
To me your cheerful homage, as the stars
Rejoicing circle round the glorious moon
Enthroned in splendour on Eugandia's mount ;

---

* An ogre, who possesses certain superhuman powers and whose favourite food is human flesh.

Say, since the day when first Pinzala's realm
Bowed 'neath our sceptre, have its people known
One hour of fear, one cause of discontent?

MINISTERS.

Not one, O King !

KING.

        Attend, then, while I ask
Your counsel on a matter which concerns
Not us alone, but all our subjects' weal.
You know the Prince ; albeit green in years,
To Zamboodeepa's * farthest boundary
Extends the fame of his transcendant worth.
Speak, wise and trusty nobles, know ye cause
Why this our son, who, as the orb of heaven,
Shines forth in radiant glory, should not be
Straightway installed successor to our crown?

FIRST MINISTER.

Joyfully, sire, your servants acquiesce
In this your royal purpose.   Our young prince,
Sprung from the race of Maha Thamada,—
Before whom kneels the mighty elephant,
Who, like a warrior, curbs his fiery steed,
Bends the tough bow, and every weapon wields,—
Excels the greatest monarchs of the world.
Why then delay ?—With fitting pomp and state,
Let this day see him heir apparent made.
               [*Exeunt* KING *and* Ministers.

PRINCE (*awaking from sleep*).

In vain upon this diamond couch recline
My weary limbs.   Vain is my princely birth,
My high estate.   With sorrow's weight oppressed,

          * The world of man.

Nor pomp, nor power, can calm my tortured breast.
See, at yon lattice, 'midst her shining train
Of beauteous handmaids, my beloved stands.—
Ah me! I do but dream ;—the vision melts
Away, and mocks my waking loneliness.
Methought I lay upon a golden couch,
Thick studded o'er with gems, and by my side
Reposed the Princess,—but in sleep alone
E'er knows this heart one moment's happiness.—
As fades the lily when the sun departs,
So do I pine and droop, whom cruel fate
Divides for ever from the one I love.·

ATTENDANT.

Dear master, weep not.   E'en the fairy maids,
Who love to twine amidst their golden hair
The blossoms of the sweet Mezoothaka,
Must wait to cull their floral favourites ·
Till spring returning calls them into life ;
So, in due season, shall possession cool
The fiery torment of your passion's flame.   [*Exeunt.*

SCENE II.—A FOREST.

Enter MOZALINDA.

MOZALINDA.

O you love of a black lily! as a poet would say. O you very
reverse of grace and beauty ! O you frizzle-haired, crook-backed,
dirt-begrimed, thick-lipped, paunchy, beetle-browed, pug-nosed,
pig-eyed, black beetle ! O you dear little Maningya, get up, will
you, and give your darling husband, who is as good as a father to
you, something to eat and drink ; for he is off to the hills with
his bow, to pick up some game. Come, look sharp, you dearest
of wives, and don't be dawdling there all day.

Enter MANINGYA.

MANINGYA.

You lump of calamity ! You quintessence of selfishness ! What is all this hurry-skurry about? Don't you see that I am shaking with the cold, with nothing on me but this rag of a petticoat to keep out the cutting wind—and midnight too !—What are you after? I'll not stand any more of your behaviour. I'll kick you with these two legs of mine till you learn better manners, you five-broken-ribbed fool ! Here, take this jar of water and bundle of rice, and be off with you to the jungle, and mind what you are about, for, if you return again without some game worth eating, I'll abuse you till you don't know whether you are standing on your head or your heels. [*Exit.*

MOZALINDA.

Behold the noble hunter Mozalinda,
At the soft bidding of his beauteous dame,
Armed with his bow of horn and glitt'ring arrow—
Defence sufficient against ev'ry foe—
Off to the forest wends his way. (*To the orchestra.*) What, ho!
As with its million wheels the Ship of Fire
Strikes with loud noise the extremest firmament,
Making the world as with an earthquake tremble,
So let the thunder of your drums resound.

[*Loud music. Exit* MOZALINDA. *After a pause,*
re-enter MOZALINDA. *Soft music.*

MOZALINDA.

How sweet to wander through these shady groves,
Where star-like jasmine flowers their incense breathe,
And the bright Engyin blooms on every side.
In amorous couples rainbow-tinted birds
Flit through the branches. Here my weary feet
Shall rest awhile.—(*Starts.*) Hark ! from yon sloping hill
The tiger's roar comes floating down the breeze.
Alas ! my Maningya, in this lone spot

My heart is heavy when I think on thee.
I still must onward, if I would escape
The savage beasts that in these hills abound.

[He arrives at the Lotus Lake.

Ha ! what bright scene is this ?   I surely stand
On some enchanted ground.   See ! here the frequent prints
Of various animals who throng the brink
Of this fair lake to quench their burning thirst.
The zephyr, laden with the blended scent
Of jasmine, lily, and unnumbered flowers,
Cools my hot brow ;—gay flocks of parroquets,
In circling flight, like shooting emeralds, wheel ;
The song of birds makes pleasant melody.
My Maningya ! O, would that you were here,
To share the enjoyment of this paradise !
Here, by the margin of the limpid wave,
Whose waters gleam like diamonds in the sun,
Upon whose bosom float the lotus buds,
Purple and white, like amethysts and pearls,
I'll lay me down beneath th' umbrageous boughs
Of this wide-spreading banyan, and court
The soft approaches of refreshing sleep.

[He sleeps.   Scene closes.

SCENE III.—Fairy-land, or the Country of the
Silver Hill.

The King Doomarajah *on one side of the stage, and his*
Seven Daughters *on the other.*

FIRST PRINCESS.

Dear sisters, and companions, who with me
Share the calm quiet of our blest abode
In Fairy-land ;—once more the time is come
That we, as is our custom, should descend
To earth, and in the lovely Lotus Lake

Sport 'midst the lilies we alone outvie.
Come, let us ask our royal father's leave.

SECOND PRINCESS.

O lovely daughter of a kingly sire,
Whose glory that of other kings excels,
As thou all other maidens dost surpass
In beauty ; go, and to your father kneel ;
We, your six sisters of one mother born,
Who love you as our lives, will follow thee.

[*They cross over to the* KING.

FIRST PRINCESS.

O King and Father ! greatest of thy race,
Lord of this palace and of Fairy-land,
Whose might, like Meru's Mount, no power can shake ;
Behold your daughters suppliant at your feet.
We crave permission to descend to earth
To enjoy our pastime 'midst the shady bowers
That fringe the Lotus Lake, and, when fatigued,
Our glowing bodies in its waves to cool.

KING.

Go, if it please you, but, my daughters dear,
Remember that the world where mortals dwell,
Is not, like ours, exempt from accident.
Be careful then ;—that bright intelligence
Which to our highly gifted race belongs
Exert, I charge you ; well each action weigh,
And with all speed to this your home return.

FIRST PRINCESS.

Thanks, generous father ;—in the world of men
No lingering stay our nimble feet shall make,
But hasten back to Fairy-land and thee.
[*Exeunt.*

SCENE IV.—The Lotus Lake.

Mozalinda asleep under a banyan tree.

Enter the seven Fairy Princesses.

FIRST PRINCESS.

O lovely lake, what sweet and tender thoughts
Thy emerald waters in my breast awake !
O fount of rapture !   Here the balmy wind
Is but the sigh of incense-breathing flowers ;—
What god, or fairy, first created thee ?
(*To her sisters.*) Come, let us doff our costly ornaments,
Our necklaces and chaplets set with gems,
And, as we sport amidst the crystal waves,
Our lovely forms, but half concealed, shall gleam
Like summer lightning through a silvery cloud.

> [*They bathe.* Mozalinda *awakes.*

MOZALINDA.

Sure I was born 'neath some auspicious star !
Happy the hour in which I first drew breath !
Yes, now I feel the proverb's homely truth
" Who wins a Beauty needs desire no more."
No fabled beings of inferior race
Are these, but fairies of the first degree.
Behold the dazzling lustre of the gems
And pearls that glisten, like the morning dew,
On their rich necklaces and earrings rare.
Not lovelier is the moon, when all the sky
Reflects the splendour of her argent rays.
I faint with ecstacy ;—a sight like this
Is more than poor humanity can bear.

> [*He falls back insensible, then slowly recovers.*

These sweet perfections mock the limner's skill.
O could I one of these fair bathers seize,
And to our Prince present my peerless prize,

Such bounteous largess would my guerdon be,
That care or want I never more should know.
I have it.—Near this lake a holy man,
Pamouk, the Hermit, dwells. He has, 'tis said,
A magic noose, which if I can obtain,
One of these birds of paradise I shall
With ease secure.—To him I will repair.   [*Exit.*

SCENE V.—THE HERMIT'S CELL IN THE FOREST NEAR THE
LOTUS LAKE.

Enter the Hermit PAMOUK *and* MOZALINDA.

PAMOUK.

There is one way, and only one, my son,
To gain the end you seek. A magic noose
The King of Dragons gave himself to me.
The worthless gift, in yonder alms-bowl cast,
Neglected lies ;—nor will I now defile
My hands by touching the unhallowed thing ;—
But take it, if you list, and snare your bird.

MOZALINDA.

Kind Hermit, deign to accept a poor man's thanks.
                            [*Takes the noose and exit.*

SCENE VI.—THE LOTUS LAKE.

Fairies bathing. Enter MOZALINDA, *who casts the lasso and catches
the Princess* DWAYMENAU. *Exeunt the other* Six Fairies,
who fly off to Fairy-land.

DWAYMENAU.

Ah me ! what unforeseen calamity
On me has fallen ? Help, dearest sisters, help !

And free me from this horrible distress !
In vain I struggle, all my limbs are cramped,
And like a statue's, stiffen into stone.
Help, or your sister dies !—

MOZALINDA.

                       Nay, beauteous Queen
Of Fairy-land, such idle words as these
Become not those fair lips.   What now you deem
Misfortune, rather is the sure reward
Of works of merit in a former state.
The Prince of this great country, to whose sire,
Lord of the Tsuddan Elephant, and raised
Above the influence of Destiny,
A hundred kings submissive homage pay,
Still needs a wife his loneliness to cheer :—
You, therefore, have I thus, by magic art,
Ensnared, to make you sharer of his throne.

DWAYMENAU.

Kind Hunter, whom men Mozalinda call,
In me behold a daughter of the King
Of Fairy-land, Lord of the Silver Hill :—
Reflect, I pray thee, whether such as I
Can stoop to be the bride of mortal man.
You will not then this hateful union press,
But rather free me from these cruel bonds.

MOZALINDA.

Grieve not, most beautiful of fairy queens,
For some good action done in ages past,
'Tis now your happy destiny to share
The heart and fortunes of this puissant Prince.
Come, my fair captive, you must follow me
Straight to the palace of your future lord.
           [*Exit* MOZALINDA, *leading off* DWAYMENAU.

SCENE VII.—HALL IN THE PALACE OF PINZALA.

Enter PRINCE *and* MOZALINDA.

MOZALINDA.

Great Prince, whose majesty surpasses all
Th' united glory of the hundred kings
Who at thy footstool bow their lowly heads,
As thy rare beauty in itself contains
The several attributes of every flower
That glads the eyes of earth's inhabitants;
As I was wandering through the pleasant woods,
Where dappled deer and antelope abound,
I came by chance upon the Lotus Lake;
There I beheld, descending from the sky,
Seven beauteous damsels like a flock of birds
Alight upon the margin of the pool:
One of these seven I, with a magic noose,
Secured, and with due reverence, O Prince,
My peerless prize I humbly now present;—
Deign to accept the lovely Dwaymenau
A Fairy Princess, pure as virgin gold.

PRINCE.

My worthy Mozalinda—quick—your gift
Bring to our presence.   [*Exit* MOZALINDA.

Re-enters, leading in DWAYMENAU.

                    Ha! what do I see?
Before that face, the moon abashed would veil
Herself in clouds; Thooza, the Fairy Queen,
With envy pale;—more beautiful than gold
Wrought into fairest forms by artist hands;
Pure as a lily, or the morning dew;
Soft is her cheek, as down on insect's wing;
Her mouth breathes incense, and her flowing hair

D 2

Is dark as night.   How musical her voice !
How graceful every movement !   She indeed,
And she alone, is meet my Queen to be.

COURTIERS.

The Princess is in truth most fair, and seems
As good as she is fair.—

PRINCE.

O charming nymph,
Daughter of Fairy-land, whose blushing cheek
Glows like a petal of the lotus bud ;
Some work of merit in a former state
Which we have done, now bears its fated fruit,
And in one lot our destinies unites.
Still am I free : but thy consent accord,
And, to my father's throne when I succeed,
Thou, dearest Dwaymenau, with me shall sit—
My Queen.

DWAYMENAU.

O mighty Prince, this may not be ;
Our races differ, and our countries lie
Wide as the poles asunder.—I was born
In Fairy-land, a daughter of the king
Who reigns in splendour o'er the Silver Hill ;
I with no earthly monarch e'er will mate :
Therefore, I pray your Highness, give me leave
Back to my home and father to return.

PRINCE.

Nay ! lovely gem, thou precious composite
Of all things beautiful, thou shalt not thus
My proffered love reject.   With life alone
Will I so rare a pearl consent to lose !

No! grieve not dearest, though I still persist
To win and wear thee ever near my heart.

[*He takes her hand.*

END OF ACT I.

In the interval between the 1st and 2nd Acts the PRINCE *marries* DWAYMENAU *and she becomes pregnant. Pinzala is invaded by a hostile army.*

ACT II.

SCENE I.—HALL IN THE PALACE OF PINZALA.

KING *surrounded by his* Ministers of State.

KING.

Nobles and Ministers, well versed in all
The arts of war, attend! These men of Gyoon
Have dared Pinzala's borders to invade.
Therefore our will is that our Rôyal Son
Shall head our army, and make instant march,
These boasting rebels to exterminate;
So that not one be left to carry back
The fearful tidings of his comrade's doom.   [*Exit* KING.

Enter PRINCE.

FIRST MINISTER.

O Prince, as noble as the lion king,
Presumptuous foes, regardless of your might,
Within the confines of our realm unfurl
The standard of revolt. Our lord, your sire,
Has therefore sent us to inform your Highness,
It is his pleasure that you take command
Of all our forces, and, with utmost haste,
March forth and make an end of these his foes.

PRINCE.

Gladly will I the king's behest obey.
Foot, cavalry, and elephants prepare,
And see the army thoroughly equipped
With all this expedition may require ;
Then not an instant will we loiter here.   [*Exeunt* Ministers.

Enter DWAYMENAU.

Fair as the moon, and soon to reign a Queen,
Stern duty calls me hence against our foes :—
Grieve not, beloved, whose perfection needs
No aid of ornament or glittering gems,
Whose every movement in its grace excels
The lily waving gently to the breeze ;
Safe in the palace, dearest wife, remain,
Surrounded by your faithful handmaidens.

DWAYMENAU.

Pity ! my lord, you surely must forget
That I, no mortal, but a fairy, am.
If you forsake me, whither shall I turn
For comfort or support ?   It cannot be ;—
I will not leave thee, but, where'er you go,
There will I follow thee, though forced to cling
In humble desperation to thy robe.
Ah ! cruel one, to choose this time to leave
Your Dwaymenau, who bears your own dear babe
Within her womb ; a little while at least
Delay ;—if you desert me now, the world,
Ten times consumed by fire, less hot would be
Than the fierce flame of anguish that will burn
This tortured breast.   O would that I were dead !
My heart is in my mouth and chokes my speech. [*She weeps.*

PRINCE.

It must be, dearest ;—dry these bootless tears,

And let me see thee smiling say, Farewell.
Grieve not for me ;—our enemies o'erthrown,
I soon shall from the battle-field return.
Whilst I am absent, daily offer, love,
Prayers and libations to our God for me.

DWAYMENAU.

O come kind Death, and free me from this load
Of grief ; my heart has sunk within my breast,
As o'er-ripe fruit falls from the laden tree.
[She falls fainting on a couch.

Re-enter Ministers, *with* Officers *and Standards.*

FIRST MINISTER.

All is prepared, my Lord, in strict accord
With the wise precepts of our Sacred Books
That treat on War.   The Forces are drawn up.
And wait impatient for the word—Advance !
Away then, mighty Prince, and lead them on.

PRINCE.

'Tis well, I go to head this fierce array
Of million warriors whose heavy tread
Will shake the balance of the trembling Earth.
Let the loud cannon instantly proclaim   [farewell,
Our coming, and march on ! (*To* DWAYMENAU.) Dearest,
I will return before one little sigh
Has time to travel 'twixt your heart and lips.   [*Exeunt.*

SCENE II.—CAMP IN THE JUNGLE.

PRINCE *surrounded by his* Officers.   *Enter* Ministers.

FIRST MINISTER.

Good tidings bear I to my Lord the Prince ;—
On the same day your prosperous march began,

The flower you left put forth a tender bud,
And your fair Princess to a son gave birth,
Who, lovely as the nine most precious gems,
Shall live exempt from all calamity.

PRINCE.

Thanks, noble friends.   Let this our Infant Heir
Moung Kyau be called.   To your fidelity
I with implicit confidence intrust
The welfare of my absent wife and Son.   [*Exeunt.*

SCENE III.—HALL IN THE PALACE OF PINZALA.

KING surrounded by his Ministers.

KING.

Right trusty Friends, to whose experience
And practised wisdom ever I resort
In times of trouble or perplexity;
As on my diamond-studded couch I lay,
I saw ten thousand sharp and threatening blades,
Like forked lightning, flash on every side :
I also saw my entrails thrice infold,
Like a huge serpent, high Pinzala's walls :—
The Soothsayer Moka to our presence bring
To interpret what this vision may portend.

[*Exeunt* Ministers.

Re-enter with MOKA.

MOKA.

(*Aside.*) O happy chance, at length I see a way
To avenge the insults which that haughty Prince
Has heaped on me.   He loves his dainty wife ;—
Her life my debt with interest shall pay.—
(*To the* KING.) Illustrious Monarch of the Universe,
Pardon your servant, if, by Truth compelled,

His tidings sound unwelcome to your ear.
Thus do I read, O King, your fatal dream.
Against your throne shall enemies conspire,
And dire misfortunes in a ceaseless train
Your steps pursue, till death shall lay you low.

KING.

Must it indeed be so?   Is there no way
By which I may these fearful ills avert?

MOKA.

O King, inexorable Fate ordains
One only terrible alternative.
A hundred fowls, as many goats and swine,
Must on the altar of the Yeetnat * bleed,
And the fair Consort of your Royal son
Crown with her life the costly sacrifice.

KING.

It is in vain to strive with Destiny :
To avert these threatened dangers from our head,
Whate'er the price demanded we must pay :
Therefore, for this great hecatomb prepare
Goats, fowls, and swine ;—a gilt Pavilion raise,
And in the midst an Altar dedicate
To the all-powerful Yeetnat Deity ;
Then let our daughter, beauteous Dwaymenau,
The Fairy Princess of the Silver Hill,
Who, as Queen Thooza's golden image, shines
In radiant loveliness, thereon be laid.   [*Exeunt.*

* A demon, supposed to exercise a special influence on the fortunes of Kings.

SCENE IV.—Apartment of the Princess in the Palace
of Pinzala.

The Princess *seated on a couch with her infant in her arms.*

Enter Ministers.

FIRST MINISTER.

We come, by order of our Lord the King,
Fraught with sad tidings which we fear to tell.
It is his sovereign will that you, sweet Lady,
Fairer than mortals, pure as virgin gold,
Shall on the Yeetnat's altar offered be.

DWAYMENAU.

Do I hear rightly?   You must needs mistake
You cannot mean that I, whom he so loves,
Am by my Royal Father doom'd to die?

MINISTERS.

Alas! too faithfully have we discharged
Our solemn duty.

DWAYMENAU.

                O what fate is mine!
My grief is wider than the boundless sea,
The Prince, regardless of his wretched wife,
Deserts and leaves me for the tented field;
And now they bid me for my death prepare,
So I shall never see my husband more.   [*She weeps.*
Alas! what deadly sin can I have done,
That this calamity should me o'ertake?
Wo worth the day that I, a Fairy born,
Came down to earth 'midst mortal men to die!
(*To her child.*) Sweet innocent, cling closer to my breast,
And, e'er we part for ever, draw once more
From nature's fount the bland maternal stream.

How can I leave thee, and thy father dear?
As when fierce flames in one vast blaze unite,
So burns my anguish.   O ye Powers that be,
Why have ye thus against me all conspired?
Must I, who love them both so fondly, leave
My babe, more beauteous than the pearls I wear,
And my dear Lord, without one fond adieu,
Abandoning, return to whence I came?
Cry not, my darling, ere I quit your side,
From this full bosom I will draw a cup
Of mother's milk, and leave it, sweet, for thee.
When your dear father, who, in these fond eyes,
Is fairer than the flowers from which I weave
Chaplets amidst my tresses to entwine,
Returns, and for his Dwaymenau inquires,
Tell him what I have suffered for his sake.
Now I must tear myself away, my child.
Dark clouds are gathering in the distant sky,
And long the journey that before me lies.—
My fairy robes once more I must resume,
Then, spreading my long idle pinions, soar
High up amidst the rainbow-tinted clouds
Which, by the gentle zephyr drawn aside,
Shall, like a curtain, part to let me through.
(*Aside to the* ⎰ With a soft strain of tender melody,
Musicians.) ⎱ As I ascend, my flight accompany.
Farewell, once more farewell, my darling babe,
And you, my husband.   Ah! that you could see
Your wretched wife, and her last kiss receive.—
I cannot go—and yet 'tis death to stay.

[*Exit, after slowly retiring and three times returning
to embrace her child.*

SCENE V.—HERMIT's CELL IN THE FOREST.

Enter HERMIT *and* DWAYMENAU.

HERMIT.

Art thou the lovely Beranee, new fallen
From Fairy-land, who thus appearest, decked
With bracelets, necklaces, and chains of gold,
And pearly chaplets 'midst thy tresses twined?
The greedy eyes that once have looked on thee
From the rich feast, refuse to turn away.
Say, from what region of celestial bliss
Hast thou descended, and what cruel fate
Has one like thee conducted to my cell?
It cannot be that you, a fugitive,
Are flying from a cruel husband's wrath;
Or art thou some unfortunate Princess
Compelled, in peril of thy life, to flee
Before thy father's conquering foes?   The truth,
Fear not, my daughter, to impart to me.

DWAYMENAU.

Father, in thee I gladly will confide,
And all my tragic history relate.
Know, then, that I was with a husband blest.
Dearer to me than life, a Royal Prince,
Next in succession to his father's throne:
He, called away his country's foes to meet,
Was forced to leave me:—Whilst he was away,
His father, moved by evil counsellors,
Determined to the Yeetnat deity
That I should offered be.   To save my life
I was compelled to fly, and thus am here.
The Prince, my husband, when he learns my loss,
Instant, I know, will follow on my track;
When, in pursuit of me, he comes this way,
Good Hermit, give to him this emerald ring,

And this enchanted drug, whose potent charms
Shall from all evil my dear Lord protect.

HERMIT.

Daughter, I will ; but e'er you go, inform
Me how his future course I may direct.

DWAYMENAU.

First, in the Forest's gloomiest recess,
A fierce Beloo his way will intercept ;
Then, sore entangled, he will struggle long
Through thickets of impenetrable cane ;
This past, a hissing stream of molten brass
Will farther progress bar,—amidst the mass
Of glowing metal, he will see emerge,
With threatening head and crest, a Dragon vast,—
Let him, undaunted, on the monster tread,
He will, subdued, his writhing folds uncoil,
And form a bridge o'er which my Lord shall pass ;
Lastly, a pair of Rocs he will descry,
Perched high in air upon a cotton tree,—
These daily to my father's Palace come
In search of food.   Kind Hermit, these my words,
When to thy cell my noble husband comes,
To him convey, and say that, by the charm
Of this enchanted drug, he will surmount
In safety all the perils that beset
His way to me, and that his every wish
Will, with its aid, accomplishment attain.

HERMIT.

Doubt not, my daughter, all you ask of me
I will perform.

DWAYMENAU.

Thanks, reverend sir, farewell !   [*Exit.*

SCENE VI.—PALACE OF THE KING OF THE SILVER HILL.

The KING.   *Enter* DWAYMENAU *to the sound of soft music.*

KING.

What ! do I see my Dwaymenau again ?
Tell me, dear daughter, all that has befallen
You whilst a captive 'midst the haunts of men,
And how your efforts to escape were crowned
With this successful issue.

DWAYMENAU.

                O my father,
For some good deed which in a former state
I must have done, in concert with the son
Of him who o'er Pinzala's realm is King,
My fate decreed that I the happy wife,
On earth, should be of good Prince Thoodanoo.
But brief my joy, my gallant husband, called
To head his troops against his country's foes,
Left me ;—no sooner his protecting arm
Was from his wife withdrawn, than, lending ear .
To some malicious Brahmin's treacherous tongue,
His sire, the King, his pleasure signified
That I should on the Yeetnat's altar die :—
This when I heard, I deemed it time to fly,
And hastening home, in all humility,
Behold me prostrate at your Royal feet.

KING.

Attendant Nobles, let it be your care
That all arrangements speedily are made
To lodge the Princess as befits her rank ;
See that a band of slaves obedient wait
To minister to e'en her slightest wish.

MINISTERS.

Sire, your commands we hasten to obey.   [*Exeunt.*

SCENE VII.—EXTERIOR OF THE PALACE OF PINZALA.

Enter MALA, *at the head of a band of female* Attendants.

MALA.

O Royal maidens, virtuous as fair,
Our Prince victorious from the war returns,
Let us of betel and choice food prepare
Our humble offerings, and haste to lay
Them with congratulations at his feet.

Enter PRINCE *and* Officers.

PRINCE.

Our foes subdued by my resistless might,
I count the moments till in my embrace
I fold once more my dearest Dwaymenau.
Ha! Mala, welcome,—but say, how is this?
Your Royal Mistress was not wont, methinks,
To be the last to greet her Lord's approach;
What holds her prisoner in her Palace walls?
Our little friend Moung Kyau, too,—is not he
Crying to spring into his father's arms?—
But you look sad, and your once cherished locks
I see neglected and dishevelled hang.

MALA.

Alas! our noble Master must prepare
For evil tidings.   Scarcely were you gone,
'Ere certain Brahmins, with malicious spite,
Prevailed upon our sovereign Lord the King
To sacrifice the blameless Dwaymenau
Upon an altar to the Yeetnat raised:

She, hearing this, her fairy wings unfurled,
And left, for ever, this too dangerous home.

PRINCE.

O dearest Mala, tell me what befell
My boy, when thus abandoned to his fate.

MALA.

Blame not the Princess,—so reluctantly
Did she depart, that, like a new-fledged bird,
She hovered long with hesitating wings ;
At last, a cup, with her own milk she filled,
Like molten pearls, and mingled with her tears,—
This leaving for her child, at length she soared
On high, and disappeared amidst the skies.
We, who remained, have tended on the child,
And, by his golden cradle set with gems,
Continued watch have o'er his slumbers kept.

PRINCE.

Listen, brave warriors, to my words give heed :—
When first the invaders lit the torch of war,
And all Pinzala kindled into flame,
I sallied forth with you, my gallant Chiefs,
To do our duty in our country's cause ;
Scarce had I marched, before our Lord the King,
By some vile, false astrologer misled,
My wife unlawfully condemned to die :—
This fit reward for all my loyalty
Tradition will preserve,—aye, though this earth
Ten times may be destroyed, the tale shall live : —
She, like a bird of Paradise, has flown,
And left a world unworthy her to hold.
But though the universe ten times dissolve
Ere I o'ertake her, nought shall me prevent
Her steps from following.   Wherefore beat to arms,—

The army will pursue its march with me.
Go, tell the King, that I no more return,
Until I bring my Dwaymenau with me.   [*Exeunt.*

SCENE VIII.—THE HERMIT'S CELL.

Enter HERMIT.

HERMIT.

What means this clang of armed warriors
Which strikes my ears?   Ha! hitherward they come,
A mighty host, with helmet, sword, and shield,
Horses and elephants,—the trembling earth
Quivers beneath their tread.

Enter PRINCE.

                    Illustrious Prince,
From what far country, and with what intent,
Has this vast army here arrived with you?

PRINCE.

Most reverend sir, I am Prince Thoodanoo,
The next successor to Pinzala's throne,—
A realm as glorious as the rising sun,—
Whilst I, a hostile army to repel,
Led forth our troops, some traitor knave beguiled
The King, my Princess to condemn to die.
She fled, and I, impelled by love and hope,
Am hastening onward to the Silver Hill.
Charmed with the beauty of your calm retreat,
I turned aside more near the scene to view,
And so approached your cell.

HERMIT.

                    But two days gone,
A creature beautiful as Thooza's self,

And graceful as a young gazelle, was here,
Calling herself a daughter of the King
Of that same place you name, the Silver Hill,—
Mayhap that you, from some good deed long past,
Some slight acquaintance have enjoyed with her,
But the effect of that good deed, be sure,
Whate'er it was, has now exhausted ceased,
And with it your good fortune. O my son,
Consider what a difference exists
Between a Fairy's nature and our own,—
And how unsuitable must ever be
Association, therefore, 'twixt the two.
Blinded by passion now, you undertake
This toilsome journey ;—pray, what recompense
Can you for all your pains anticipate ?
A youth like you, so noble and so fair,
Should seek a wife as perfect as the Queen
Of Tsekya Meng, the King of Nats, herself,
To share the glory of your future throne ;
Wherefore, be wise,—relinquish this pursuit,
And, ere it be too late, your steps retrace.

PRINCE.

Your counsel, holy father, I admit,
Becomes the prudence of a sage like thee :
But I can never for an instant cease,—
Aye, though the heavens and earth should pass away,—
From following, till at last I overtake
The Fairy mistress of my heart and soul.
Therefore, I am resolved, if need there be,
Through my next ten existences I still
Will persevere undaunted, e'en although
The Tsekya Meng should with his thunderbolts
Oppose, and hurl me to destruction.   Now,
Stay me no longer, only show the road
Which she was pleased to take.

HERMIT.

If go you will,—
Why go,—but ere you leave,—here, take this ring,
A perfect emerald, which your Princess
Gave me for you, and this enchanted drug,
Which from all evil will preserve you safe,
And all your wishes with fruition crown.
Long is your way, and as you journey on,
A fierce Beloo will your first danger be ;
The next, a forest of impervious cane ;
And last of all, a stream of molten brass,
O'er which a Dragon keeps perpetual guard :
When these are past, far off you will descry,
Perched on the summit of a cotton-tree,
A pair of Rocs,—these follow in their flight,
And they will lead you to the Silver Hill.
Thus said fair Dwaymenau, and as she charged
Me strictly, I her very words repeat.
Now, go, my son, success attend your hopes !

PRINCE.

Accept my thanks, good father.—Fare thee well.   [*Exit.*

SCENE IX.—A DARK FOREST.

PRINCE *resting under a banyan tree.   Enter a* Beloo.

BELOO.

Haugh ! here I am,—of all my mighty race
The most terrific monster.—It is time
I to the Himalayan forests should repair.—

[*Aside to musicians.*

Strike up, and let your martial strains create
Such a sensation, that all eyes shall turn

To gaze on me, as though upon my head
The Sun's ten thousand rays concentred shone.
(*Sees the* PRINCE.) Ha ! ha ! a dainty dinner I espy.

> [*Approaches him threateningly.   Loud music.*

PRINCE (*rising*).

Vile, miserable monster ! dost thou dare
With me, descended from the Sun, to fight ?
This golden arrow, with a diamond head,
Launched from my bow shall end thy worthless life.

> [*Shoots at the* Beloo *and kills him.   Flourish on the
> drums.   The* PRINCE *proceeds, and becomes en-
> tangled in the cane forest.*

I can no more,—exhausted nature fails :
Turn where I will, the matted creepers form
A net whose meshes round me interlaced,
All progress bar.   Ah ! the enchanted drug,—
Let me invoke its aid, and try once more.

> [*He emerges from the cane forest and proceeds.*

O lovely Fairy of the Silver Hill,
What pangs do I for thy dear sake endure !
Yet as I journey up the mountain side,
Or through the gloomy forest, I defy
Beloos, whose favourite food is human flesh,
And tigers, scarce less terrible than they.
My precious Pearl, for thy dear sake alone
Your poor devoted husband struggles on.

> [*He comes to the river of molten brass.*

O what is here ?   Above a bubbling mass
Of liquid metal a huge dragon rears
His head, and gapes at me with threatening jaws ;—
Once more the magic drug must me befriend,
And guide me safely o'er the monster's back.

> [*He crosses the stream over the* Dragon's back, and
> arrives at a cotton-tree, on which are a pair of
> Rocs.*

FEMALE ROC.

My brother dear, from whom, since we were hatched,
I ne'er have been divided, and with whom
I share the shelter of the same soft nest,
Say, whither shall we fly for food to-day?

MALE ROC.

What, sister, know you not that from the land
Of men the daughter of King Doomarajah
Has safe returned ; the which to celebrate
A royal festival this day is held?
Let us then to the Silver Hill repair,
And be partakers of the sumptuous feast.

> [*The* PRINCE *spreads some of the enchanted drug over
> his body, which renders him invisible. He
> mounts between the wings of one of the* Rocs.
> *They fly away.*

SCENE X.—A WELL IN THE COURT-YARD OF THE PALACE
OF THE SILVER HILL.

Seven Female Attendants *of the Palace drawing water.*

Enter PRINCE.

PRINCE.

Ye Powers divine, vouchsafe to me a sign,—
If I am destined ever more to see
My much loved Dwaymenau, then let the last
Of these fair maidens try without success
To draw her golden pitcher from the well.

> [*Six of the maidens draw up their pitchers, the
> seventh is unable to do so.*

FEMALE ATTENDANT.

Here, gentle youth, your courteous help I crave
To raise this pitcher, which my strength exceeds.

> [*The* PRINCE *draws up the pitcher, and drops into it
> the emerald ring.*   [*Exeunt.*

SCENE XI.—APARTMENT OF THE PRINCESS DWAYMENAU.

DWAYMENAU, *attended by her maidens, washing her head, finds her ring in the pitcher.*

DWAYMENAU.

Ah me! I faint,—my thoughts are all confused,—
Body and mind alike are paralyzed.
The father of my child, as beautiful
As these my tresses, has at last arrived.
Brave heart! thus fearlessly to persevere,
And conquer all the dangers that beset
His way to me.   What has he not endured!
My heart is melting at the dreadful thought.

Enter KING DOOMARAJAH.

KING.

Why, how now, daughter,—wherefore lie you thus,
As though a thunderbolt had struck you down?

DWAYMENAU.

O dearest father, this, my favourite ring,
Which, as you know, my finger never left,
And which I parted with not long ago
For a most special purpose, has returned.
From out this pitcher as my hand I drew,
I found it to its former place restored;—
This is to me a sign infallible
That my dear husband has indeed arrived.
Now, can you wonder that this sweet surprise
Was more than I, at first, could calmly bear?

KING (*to* Attendants).

Which of you brought this pitcher from the well?

FEMALE ATTENDANT.

Great King, forgive your slave, this slender arm

In vain a task beyond its strength essayed,—
A courteous youth, who stood beside the well,
I asked to help me, and his aid he gave.

KING.

Bring him before me in the Audience Hall.   [*Exeunt.*

SCENE XII.—Audience Hall of the Palace.

KING *on his Throne. Enter* PRINCE, *escorted by* Ministers.

KING.

O thou who art o'er all pre-eminent
In beauty, with all qualities endowed
Which man adorn, and as a lion brave,
Whence art thou, and what strange adventures led
Thee to the country of the Silver Hill?
Without concealment let us briefly hear.

PRINCE.

I will, O King.—In me behold the son
Of him who o'er Pinzala reigns supreme,
And next successor to my father's throne;
For some good deed which in a former state
I must have done, it was my rich reward
To win your lovely daughter for my bride,
And to complete our happiness a son
Our union blessed.   But brief are all our joys;—
A hostile force advancing to repel,
Our arms I led,—one march I scarce had ta'en,
When, by a Brahmin's artful tongue beguiled,
My royal father issued a decree
That your dear daughter should a victim bleed
Upon the Yectnat's altar.   Hearing this
She fled for safety to her native land.
I, counting life as but a grain of dust

When cast into the scale against my love,
Have followed her, and thus you see me now
A suppliant kneel before your royal feet.

KING.

Listen, my Ministers : this gentle youth,
Urged on, he tells us, by the love he bears
Our daughter Dwaymenau, has hither come.
If he so high a prize expects to win,
He must convince us that his love is true,
And undergo a trial of his worth.
Therefore, from out our armory bring forth
The famous bow, whose string uncurved sustains
A ton suspended ;—let this stranger try
If he can bend this tough unyielding bow.   [*Exeunt.*

SCENE XIII.—LISTS IN THE COURT-YARD OF THE PALACE.

Enter KING, Ministers, *and* PRINCE.

FIRST MINISTER.

Here is the bow on which our Lord the King
Has willed that you make trial of your strength.
                              [PRINCE *takes the bow.*

PRINCE.

Now is the crisis of my fate.   Succeed,—
And Dwaymenau is mine for ever.   Fail,—
And all is lost.   [*He tries the bow and bends it.*

FIRST MINISTER.

Your Majesty,
The stubborn bow curved like the eagle's wing,
And hard as steel, is, in his hands, a reed.

KING.

He has done well ; but to a further test

We needs must subject him, before the hand
Of our Princess we can on him bestow.
Bring from the stables our most vicious steed,
And a wild elephant that ne'er has felt
The driver's goad, whose glaring eye proclaims
A spirit unsubdued ;—these let him mount,
And in our presence to subjection tame.

MINISTERS.

You hear the royal order, will you dare
This last, and worst, ordeal to essay?

PRINCE.

Is't not enough that I the bow have bent,
And must I still new trials undertake?
Well, be it so ;—I never can draw back,—
Bring the wild horse and wilder elephant !
                    [*The horse and elephant are led on.*
(*To the orchestra.*) Now thunder forth a bold inspiring strain,
Whose echoes, spreading far and wide, shall shake
The earth to its foundations.
            [*He mounts the wild horse, and rides it round the
                Lists, after which he dismounts.*
                            On the neck
Of this fierce brute I plant my royal foot,
                        [*He mounts the elephant.*
And thus obedient to my armed heel,
He turns whichever way I please to guide.   [*He dismounts.*

FIRST MINISTER.   (*To the* KING.)

The second trial, which the King ordained,
Has but confirmed the presage of the first.

KING.

Before my daughters let a seven-fold screen
Of silk inwrought with gems suspended be,

And from within let each of them, in turn,
One taper finger carefully expose.
If he, who claims the lovely Dwaymenau,
By this can single her from all the rest,
I will admit his title to her hand.

> [*A screen is dropped. The* Princesses *in turn put
> forth a finger.*

PRINCE.

O all ye Powers, vouchsafe your gracious aid,
Grant me some sign my choice to guide aright.

> [*As* DWAYMENAU *puts forth her finger, a bee settles
> on it.*

I hail the omen (*takes the finger*).   Ah! the thrill I feel,
As this dear hand I touch once more, confirms
My happy choice.   Now, King, my prize I claim.

KING.

Well hast thou earned it, true and gallant Prince.

> [*Leads forward* DWAYMENAU *from behind the screen.*

Embrace your blushing wife, and happy be
The reign of Thoodanoo and Dwaymenau.

CHAPTER II.

PHYSICAL DESCRIPTION, AND HABITS AND CUSTOMS OF THE BURMESE.

Physical characteristics of the Burmese race.—Male costume.—Tattooing.—Its absence considered a mark of effeminacy.—Female dress and ornaments.—Ear-tubes.—Universality of smoking.—Singular custom.—Burmese altogether a different people from the inhabitants of Hindostan.—Absence of caste prejudices.—Their pleasing manners.—Happiness of the people.—Absence of pauperism.—Affection of parents for their children.—Fondness for amusement and excitement.—As a rule not laborious.—Marriage customs.—Perfect freedom of marriageable girls.—Marriage purely a civil rite.—Hla-pet.—Curious custom pursued by a bridegroom's bachelor friends.—Privileges of the female sex.—Code of divorce.—Polygamy.—Sensitiveness to raillery.—Tendency to suicide.—Suicide of a bridegroom.—Attempted suicide of a girl.—Food.—Description of a Burmese banquet.—Their treatment of disease.—The devil dance.—Disease caused by witchcraft.—Funerals.—Boat races.—Peculiarity of the boats.—Mode of rowing.—Description of the goal.—"Palmam qui meruit *ferit*."—Vaunting songs, and grotesque attitudes of the winners.—Subscription purses.—Game of football.—Boxing and wrestling.—Admirable temper of the combatants.—Description of the Ta-soung-doing festival.—Weaving the sacred cloth.—Relays of workers.—Working and courting.—Floating lights.—Water festival on New Year's Day.—Meaning of the observance.—Mythological legend.

THE physical characteristics of the Burmese are those which distinguish the Mongolian race generally. The shape of the skull is globular, and seen from the front has a peculiar pyramidal, or lozenge form,* owing to a great lateral extension of the zygomatic arches, coupled with a narrow forehead,

* Cunningham's "Ladak," p. 297.

causing great breadth of face below the eyes, narrowing upwards and downwards. The face is broad and flat with high cheek-bones. Mouth moderate in size, with fine vertical teeth, and showing no symptom of prognathism in the jaws. Lips often fleshy and somewhat intumescent, and chin short. Eyes, black, wide apart, and generally oblique, which latter appearance is caused, not by the shape or position of the orbits,* but by the structure of the lids, and is produced by the tension of the skin over the projecting cheek-bones, under the outer angles of the eyes, and by the flatness of the space between the eyes. The nose is broad, with little or no bridge, generally short, with broad nostrils, and flattened towards the forehead. Hair black, long, straight, and abundant. No beard or whiskers, and moustache small and slight. Facial angle about 77°. Colour of skin, bright pale brown, or isabelline hue, approaching to yellow.

They are a fine, robust, athletic race, but not tall, the men averaging about five feet four inches in height. Their bodies are well proportioned ; but somewhat long in the trunk, and arms relatively to the legs. Head well set on, shoulders square, chest wide and deep, and legs showing great muscular development. As a race, they are very healthy ; and idiotcy and deformity of body are of unusually

* Pritchard's "Natural History of Man," vol. i., p. 214.

rare occurrence. Their demeanour is marked by elasticity of step, and the composure of their countenance denotes great confidence in themselves.

They wear their hair tied in a knot on the top of the head, and wound round or intertwined with it is a piece of muslin or gay silk handkerchief; a jacket of cotton or broadcloth, according to the season, hangs loosely from their shoulders over the hips ; and a *potso* of bright silk or cotton wound round the waist, extending to the ankles, and with one end often thrown jauntily over the shoulder, in the fashion of a Highlander's kilt, forms their dress.

From the waist to the knees nearly every male amongst the Burmese is tattooed with a black or blue pigment in figures of lions, tigers, elephants, nats, birds, and beloos, enclosed in a groundwork of fine tracery and flowing lines. This operation commences as early as the age of six years, and is done gradually until completed, often extending over several years. The operation, performed by needles and an instrument shaped like a mathematical steel pen, is a very painful one, and during the process the patient is drugged with opium to render his feelings less acute. Portions of the arms and upper part of the body are also often tattooed in vermilion with cabalistic and mystic characters, as charms against an enemy, evil spirits, and disease. These squares are subdivided into several small ones, with figures in each, so arranged by arithmetical progression, that whether added up horizontally, transversely, or perpendicularly, the sum-total is always the same. The following are examples :—

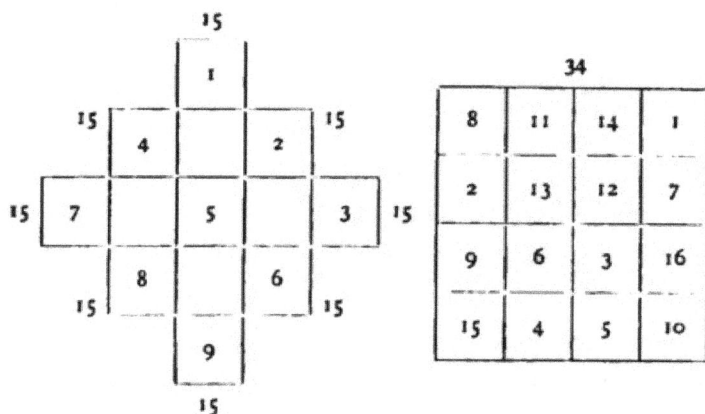

```
                    15
                    |
                    1
        15 ┌────┬────┐ 15
           │ 4  │ 2  │
   15 ┌────┼────┼────┤ 15
      │ 7  │ 5  │ 3  │
      └────┼────┼────┤
        8  │    │  6
     15 └────┴────┘ 15
                9
                |
               15
```

34

8	11	14	1
2	13	12	7
9	6	3	16
15	4	5	10

Herodotus (v. 6) mentions the Thracians as being tattooed (ἐστύχθαι) which was considered an emblem of rank, and the want of it showing meanness of descent. With the Burmese it is not a sign of rank, as mostly all are more or less tattooed, and its absence is considered as a mark of effeminacy.*

The Burmese women are much fairer in complexion than the men, and their features more delicate. They have good figures, with small

---

* William of Malmesbury mentions tattooing as being one of the English vices at the time of the Norman conquest ; but, according to Cæsar, their bodies were merely stained with woad, the pigment not being inserted under the skin, as in the case of the Burmese.

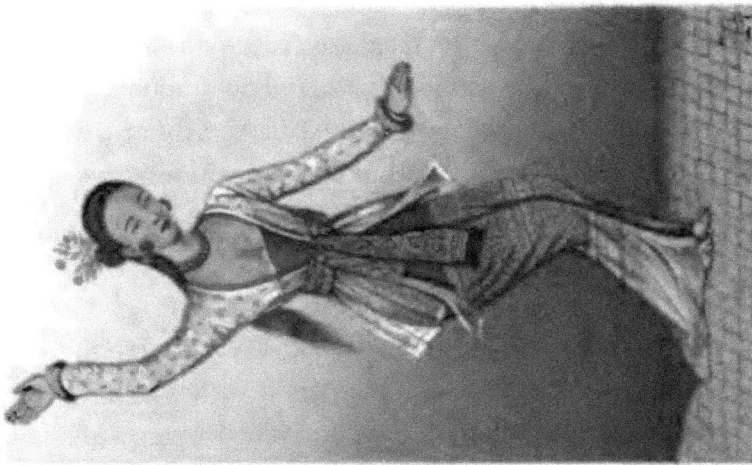

BURMESE DANCING GIRL.

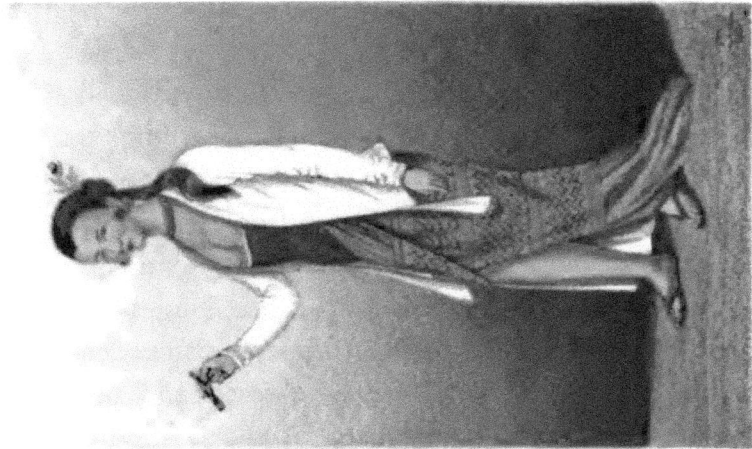

A BURMESE LADY

hands and feet, and limbs well proportioned. They are not handsome, perhaps, according to European ideas of beauty ; but they are, nevertheless, often very comely, as much from expression, as feature, or more so. They pay great attention to the adornment of their persons. Their long black tresses (frequently like their European sisters, enriched with false tails), carefully dressed and perfumed, are gathered at the back of the head, *à la Madonna*, and gracefully adorned with fresh flowers, usually an orchid, a jasmine, or a chumpac.

Their petticoat, or *hta-mein*, is of silk from the native loom, woven in vandyke, cable, or serpentine patterns of the brightest dye and varied hues, but always blended with great taste. This is wrapped round the body, and the bust covered by a bodice generally of Turkey-red cloth, folded in under the left arm. The petticoat is tucked in tightly at the waist, and falls down in front to the ankles ; but merely slightly lapping over discloses a portion of the leg when walking, one limb being visible at a time, according to the forward step.

To the petticoat is attached a skirt of a different pattern, most generally of a pale pink, with horizontal narrow stripes of dark colours, interwoven with gold or silver threads. This skirt trails behind some ten inches to a foot on the ground, and its graceful management, in either walking or dancing, is one of the accomplishments of a Burmese belle. An *engyce*, or jacket, of muslin, silk, or satin, worn open ; a *ta-bet*, or shawl, thrown over the shoulders, and red sandals, complete the habiliments of the sex. When in full-dress they are in the habit of powdering their faces with *tha-nat-kha*—a cosmetic prepared from the *Murraya exotica*, having a somewhat similar fragrance to sandal-wood—pencilling their eyebrows and rougeing their lips.

Their necklaces and ornaments, of pure gold, set with rubies and other precious stones, are handsome and in good taste. But their most remarkable ornaments are their ear-tubes*—for they cannot be called earrings, which are introduced into a large orifice made in the lobe of the ear. The boring of the lobe of the ear is common to both sexes. It is pierced in the ordinary manner, and the aperture gradually enlarged by introducing small slips of bamboo, increasing in number by slow degrees. The ear-tubes most commonly in use are cylinders of gold, about one-and-a-half inches long, and three-quarters of an inch in diameter, and into which is often thrust a half-smoked cigar. Men, women, and children are all great smokers ; and even infants at the breast, incredible as it may appear to those who have not seen them, are occasionally observed having a pull at the fragrant weed.

* Na-doungs.

The ceremony of boring* a child's ears is kept as a great festival, and all the relations and friends of the parents are invited. The invitations are not made by notes or cards, but, according to Burmese custom, by sending round small conical packets of pickled tea (*let-phet-dhok*). After the completion of the ceremony a dinner is given, and a Burmese play, open to all comers, is generally performed under a temporary theatre in front of the house.

A singular practice prevails of accustoming girls, from the earliest age, to turn the inside of the elbow outwards, as if dislocated, and, by constant working, the joint is rendered so flexible that it moves with equal facility either way. When the arm is extended the elbow is inverted, the inside of the joint being protruded, and the external part bending inwards. This is considered the *ne plus ultra*

---

* The custom of enlarging the lobe of the ear, so as to enable it to carry ear-tubes of large size, appears to be a very ancient custom, and is supposed to be connected with sun worship. Spanish historians mention that elaborate religious ceremonies were held at the Temple of the Sun at Cuzco, on the occasion of boring the ears of the young Peruvian nobles, and in the case of princes of the blood, the Inca himself pierced the ear-lobes with a golden pin.

The image of Gautama is always portrayed with long pendant ear-lobes reaching to his shoulders, "characteristic of his pre-eminence over all men."

In Pinkerton's "Voyage" (vol. xi., p. 375) it is related that Pigafetta, who sailed with Magellan in 1519, heard from an old pilot that there was an island where a race of diminutive stature existed, with ears as long as their bodies, so that they lay on one ear, and used the other for a coverlid. They were said to be Troglodides. A similar story is told by Strabo, on the authority of Megasthenes. Pliny also states that in the "Isles of the Scythians" there were reported to be natives with ears of similar dimensions, and used for the same purpose. See article in the "Journal of the Anthropological Institute," vol. ii., No. 11., by J. Park Harrison, M.A.

of elegance, and in all Burmese drawings women are represented in this posture.

The people of Burma, whether Arakanese, Talaings, or Burmese properly so called, are altogether a different people from the inhabitants of India. They are not trammelled by hereditary priests, like Brahmins, or hedged round with caste * distinctions, compelling them to live on in the same narrow grooves as their forefathers from generation to generation. Unlike the distrustful and suspicious Hindus and Mahommedans, woman holds a position amongst them of perfect freedom and independence, and their children are free to come and go. They are open-hearted and merry in disposition, and no European has ever entered into free and kindly intercourse with them without being more struck with their virtues than their faults. They are free from traditional and conventional dogmata, and are by nature and habit far less imbued with the *odium*

* The Hindus recognise four distinct castes : Brahmans, Kshatriyas, Vaisyas, and Sudras. The "Jatimala," a Sanskrit work, gives the following tradition respecting the origin of each caste. "In the first creation by Brahma, Brahmanas proceeded, with the Veda, from the mouth of Brahma. From his arms Kshatriyas sprung ; so from his thigh Vaisyas, from his foot Sudras, were produced : all with females."

The word caste is derived from the Portuguese word *casta*, "race" or "lineage ;" in Sanskrit they are called *varnas*, that is, "colours." Heeren supposes that the origin of the institution was founded upon conquest ; the first three tribes being a foreign race who subdued the aborigines of the country and reduced them to an inferior caste ; while others trace it "as the result of that fondness for perpetuating, like heirlooms, by descent from father to son, certain offices, or the exercise of certain arts or professions, which is so peculiarly characteristic of almost all nations of the Indo-Germanic race."

theologicum, or that contemptuous abhorrence of all creeds and customs, other than their own, than is the case with the ordinary Asiatic of whatever creed or denomination.

Their manners are distinguished by a pleasing mixture of courtesy and freedom. They possess great *aplomb;* and even the poorest, while frank, are well bred. In their intercourse with each other they are good-humoured and considerate, and the observer cannot but be struck with the enjoyment, contentment, and happiness of the people. All appear well off. None are very rich, or poor ; two days' labour suffices for three days' bread, and destitution is quite unknown. There is neither pauperism nor poor-law in the province.

If a family should happen to be in want, they are at once assisted by their neighbours, and " the stranger within their gates," of whatever creed, has never to ask twice for food. The affection of parents for their children is very great. Filial piety is inculcated as a sacred precept and its duties religiously observed. Much respect is shown by the young to the old, and there are two forms of address which are always used by the young to the middle-aged, and by both to the old. Mendacity, so characteristic of Orientals, is not a national defect amongst this people, and my experience has shown that the chances are greatly in favour of truth when evidence is sought.

They are fond of amusement and excitement, and
as a rule are not laborious.   All have enough for their
wants, and they are content with that sufficiency,
They act fully up to the maxim—which is Buddhist
as well as Christian—"sufficient for the day is the
evil thereof."   Strong, patient, and good-tempered,
they are utterly without the restless energy of
Europe.   Their repose is perfect, yet it is that of
placidity, rather than that of indolence, the quies-
cence which is the root of the Buddhist creed, which
forms their idea of happiness, and which is "the
only expression in the features of their motionless
god."   They do not, like the Europeans, convert the
world into a workshop, because their world is not
yet darkened with the pressure of over-population
and competition ; neither is their desire to possess
great wealth stimulated by the painful contrast of
extreme luxury with squalid poverty and humiliating
dependence.

The social condition of the people is largely
affected by their marriage customs.   In India,
though betrothals take place at a very early age—
even in infancy—no one ever sees a young man
and a young woman walking together as companions,
friends, or lovers.   In Burma such a sight is common.   On these, and when they meet on other
occasions, the blind god is allowed to have his
sway, and there is a freedom of manners, a fre-

quent interchange of wit and raillery, and interchange of sentiment, which would horrify a native of India. About eight o'clock in the evening is " courting time,"* when the young ladies " receive " their bachelor acquaintances, and a lamp placed in their casement is a signal that they are "at home."

Women are generally married about seventeen or nineteen years of age, to the man of their choice of about the same age or older, the parents very seldom interfering, more than to advise. The Buddhist law forbids opposition in such cases, leaving young people, in a great measure, to follow their own inclinations, and marriages are occasionally contracted without the consent of the parents of either party; and sometimes even in direct opposition to their wishes.

When a couple have agreed between themselves to marry, the mother of the man, or his nearest female relation, is generally first sent to sound the mother of the girl privately, and if she appears to approve of the match, some of the suitor's elderly friends are sent to propose the marriage formally to the girl's parents, and adjust the settlement. On

---

* *Loo-byo lai-thee kala.* In this happy land, *loo-byo hoing* or *apyo-hoing* (old bachelors and old maids) are unknown, and the widowed seldom remain long in that state. It may not be out of place here to observe that the Burmese do not kiss each other in the western fashion, but apply the lips and nose to the cheek, and make a strong inhalation, which they express by the term *nan-shok-thee*, to sniff up a scent.

the parents giving their consent to the marriage, the *corbeille de noce* is furnished by the bridegroom according to his means,* and the marriage takes place almost immediately.

A feast is prepared, accompanied with the inevitable *pooay*, or play ; the happy couple eat out of the same dish before the assembled guests ; after which the bridegroom presents the bride with *hla-pet* † (pickled tea), the compliment is returned, and the ceremony is practically brought to a close. The marriage is thus purely a simple civil rite, to which religion lends not its holy aid ; for marriage is looked upon by the Buddhist priesthood as a concession to human frailty, of the earth earthy, and opposed to the ideas of religious contemplation and abstraction which govern their order.

A curious custom prevails of the bridegroom's bachelor friends and others assembling on the night of the marriage round his house, and throwing

---

* Dowries are seldom ever given by parents to their daughters at the time of marriage ; almost everything is expected to be furnished by the bridegroom. A Burmese, therefore, cannot say with the Latin poet :—

"Pars minima est ipsa puella sui."

† *Hla-pet*, or pickled tea, is used on many festive occasions by the Burmese, and is imported chiefly from Thein-nee, in the Shan states, bordering on China. It is made up into balls of different sizes, by means of a glutinous substance, which unites the leaves together without injuring their qualities. I have also seen it in the form of small pressed cakes ; and also packed in hollow bamboos of about three feet in length, with the ends stopped up with clay. This latter comes from the Kubo valley, on the borders of Munipúr.

The Burmese serve up the tea-leaves dressed with sesamum oil, garlick, and assafœtida, and thus prepared look upon it as a great delicacy, and a good promoter of digestion.

stones on its roof and at the doors, and which is
kept up often for many hours. It is not done as
a protest against the marriage, or in the way of
what an English lad would call "*fun;*" but as
following out an immemorial custom, and though
the practice must, one would think, be an incon-
venient one to the " happy couple," still they would
think that a proper compliment had not been paid
them if it was omitted.

I have already remarked that the position of
woman amongst the Burmese is a much higher and
independent one than amongst Mahommedans* and
Hindus. She is with them, not the mere slave of
passion, but has equal rights, and is the recognized
and duly honoured helpmate of man, and, in fact,
bears a more prominent share in the transaction of
the more ordinary affairs of life than is the case,

* A Mahommedan woman has neither social rank nor civil rights. She is
not even permitted to enter their ideal paradise, but sighs at the portals of
Heaven, a mere spectator of that happiness which she can never hope to share.
"Woman," by G. N. Cresswell, p. 45.

In ancient times a much purer morality existed in the East. In the laws of
Menu, said to have been composed 1280 B.C., we read (Book iii., § 58):
"Women are to be esteemed and honoured by their fathers, brothers, husbands, and fathers-in-law, if the latter wish to be happy themselves. The
gods rejoice when women are honoured; where it is not done, sacrifices avail
nothing. When the women are ill-treated the whole family goes to ruin;
when the contrary happens, it flourishes for ever."

In the Maha-bharata King Dushmanta expresses himself in the following
beautiful language:—"The woman is the honour of the family; she, who
gives the children; the woman is the life of man; she, who is ever faithful.
The woman is the half of the man, she is his best friend, the source of all
happiness. The woman, with her sweet language, is the friend in solitude,
the mother of the oppressed, refreshment on the journey through the wilderness
of life." (Digest of Hindu Law, translated by Coleman.)

perhaps, with any other people, either eastern or
western.   To give a very striking instance, even in
a matter the most remote from the ordinary expected
duties and conventionalities of womankind, I may cite
a case where the wife of a Myo-ok (head judicial
and revenue officer of a township) came before me
in open court, when I was Deputy Commissioner of
Bassein, having nine notorious dacoits or robbers in
her custody, and stating that her husband would
follow with the record of the proceedings in the
case.

The retail business of the country is mostly carried
on by women, and a large proportion, also, of the
wholesale description.   A Burmese seldom does
anything without first consulting his wife.   In fact,
she possesses the "key of the house," and of the
household establishment.   She is no "*purdah
nasheen*" (hidden behind a screen), or wears no
boorkhah, or Mahommedan veil, for she has no
cause to hide her face ; her legal rights are admitted
as maid, wife, or widow; the sole right in her
property before, and that acquired after marriage is
acknowledged, and only under rare and peculiar
circumstances can property, left her by her parents
or ancestors, become her husband's during her lifetime ; she can hold real property in her own right,
and even obtain legal possession of her husband's if
he forsakes her.

A code of divorce is provided for ill-assorted unions, which has been pronounced by Father Bigandet, the Roman Catholic Bishop of Rangoon, as "a damnable laxity." Amongst its other provisions are, where a desire for a separation is mutual, from " incompatibility of temper," or other causes, parties can divorce each other by an equal division of goods ; or if one of them is unwilling, the other is free to go, provided all property except the clothes in wear are left behind. A woman can demand a divorce for ill-treatment, or if her husband cannot properly maintain her, and he from her in case of barrenness or infidelity. Another method which is not unfrequently resorted to is that of the aggrieved parties turning priests or nuns, which at once dissolves the matrimonial bond. They may return to a secular life at any time, and marry another ; but, for the sake of appearance, their return to the world is usually deferred some months.

Serious connubial quarrels appear rarer amongst the Burmese than most communities ; and apart from their natural good temper, the easy severance of the nuptial knot may, notwithstanding its sweeping condemnation by the good bishop, have something in its favour, namely, that of rendering husband and wife mutually forbearing.

Buddhism disapproves of polygamy ; but does

not wholly disallow it. Few Burmese have, however, more than one wife, and in the case of a
second or more being taken, the *Ma-ya-gyee*, or
first wife, always holds the highest rank in the
household.

Burmese women are as a rule prolific, and have
the ordinary proportion of male and female children.
As soon as a child is born, whatever the season
may be, it is the custom to light a large fire in
the mother's apartment, and place her before it,
which treatment is continued for seven days. This
roasting not unfrequently injures the health of the
patient, and though English medical officers have
often pointed out its absurdity, and tried to combat
the system, all their efforts have proved in vain, so
universal is the custom and so strong the prejudice
in its favour. The usage is associated, I believe,
with some ideas of purification, which, on such
occasions, prevail in different forms in other parts
of the world; but I never heard any satisfactory
reason given for the practice. Mothers suckle their
children for a long period, extending occasionally
to two or three years, gradually weaning them on
boiled rice and plantains.

The Burmese are very sensitive to raillery, and
have a peculiar delicacy of feeling, or dread of what
they call *a-shet*, or shame, to use the English translation of the expression, which does not, however,

hardly convey its full meaning, and show a great disregard of life by committing suicide for the most trifling causes. The nature of this feeling is well shown by Colonel J. P. Briggs, in his interesting work on Heathen and Holy Lands, in the two following cases with which he became acquainted in his official capacity.

Two young women, both much admired, resided near each other; and though a good-natured rivalry existed between them, they were great friends, and often used to meet together, and relate mutually their conquests and girlish secrets. This occurred more particularly in the evening time at the village well, where they met to draw water. Here they were wont to laugh and joke with one another on that most important of all subjects, which of them would be married first, and what sort of husbands they would get.

After a time one of these girls married a good respectable man, a sawyer by occupation, and had been living in her husband's house but a few days, when her old companion with others paid her a friendly visit. Her husband was not present, and the visitors commenced teasing and joking with her about her husband.

"Ah!" said her friend, "you are married first, but only to a sawyer! I would not marry a sawyer! much you have got by your good looks, and your family that looked so high!" The young wife good-naturedly joined in the laugh against herself, and did not think it necessary to defend her husband, whose good qualities were well known. So her thoughtless visitors began pitying her for not having made a better match. The husband, who was in the garden at the back of the house overheard all the conversation, and was so ashamed at not being thought good enough for his pretty young wife, and annoyed at her not taking his part, that he forthwith went away and hung himself.

Any momentary annoyance, or shock to their pride, furnishes them with sufficient cause for self-destruction, and opium is one of the means often employed for the purpose.

A girl of about fifteen years of age, being sent to market by her mother to sell some oranges gathered from her garden, met a female friend there of about the same age, and employed in a similar manner. The market was not full, and the trade not sufficiently brisk to keep them employed, and the two good-for-nothings commenced gambling for the oranges, by playing odd and even with the small dried flowers attached to the fruit. One of them lost nearly all her oranges to the other, and returned home without the computed number of coppers, the sale of the missing fruit ought to have realised.

On her mother discovering that her daughter had
lost her oranges by gambling, she boxed her ears,
and scolded her in the presence of some neighbours,
when the girl left the house, purchased some opium,
enough to poison two or three people, and swal-
lowed it ; she then returned to her mother, and
quietly told her what she had done, and that she
would never have the power to ill-treat her again.
The mother greatly alarmed, and in the wildest
grief hugging her child to her bosom, rushed off
with her to the Government Hospital, where the
surgeon, being fortunately present at the time, was
enabled to save her life.

Rice, as in all the countries of Southern Asia,
takes the position of "the staff of life," and is the
universal food, so much so as to tint the language.
Breakfast is called the morning, dinner the noon,
and supper the evening rice. It is usually accompanied by a ragout of fish of different kinds, meat,
and vegetables, which are eaten with it. Besides
these, are salads of sliced cucumber, and on the
sea-coast oysters and other shell fish, and several
chutneys ; amongst the latter, and without which
no Burmese considers he has made a good dinner,
is *nga-pee*, a potent preparation, somewhat resembling anchovy paste, composed of prawns and
fish fry, pounded with chillies, garlic, and other
condiments. A soup composed of the nests of the

small sea-swallow (*Hirundo esculenta*) closely resembling isinglass, which are found on the rocky
islands of the coast, occasionally accompany their
meals, and is much prized by old men for its
supposed recuperative powers.

Their meals are served up in circular red
japanned trays, fitting successively into a conical
apparatus tapering to a point, called an *ŏk*. The
lowest and largest receptacle contains the rice, and
the others china cups and platters holding the fish,
meat, etc. When several are partaking of the
same meal, they assemble round the large tray
containing the rice, each helping themselves to it
with their hands, and seasoning the rice with the
materials taken with a spoon from the attendant
trays, which are passed round. Their beverage is
water.

The tenets of the Buddhist religion forbid them
wilfully to deprive animals of life. Any, even the
most strictly religious amongst them, however,
have no scruples in eating the flesh of an animal
killed by another person; as then, they consider,
the sin of its destruction does not rest upon them,
but on the person who actually caused it. They
are very hearty eaters, and are not particularly
choice in the description of the food they eat.
The lower classes, especially, will eat anything.
They eat vermin, such as rats, and reptiles like

lizards and snakes. They will eat animals, even, that have died a natural death. In fact, they are the same foul feeders as their Mongol ancestors, the rude Tatar warriors who fought in the armies of Jenghis Khan.

The Burmese know nothing of anatomy; and their treatment of disease is mixed up with ignorance, superstition, and prejudice. Anyone is allowed to practise medicine. No license or diploma is necessary, and the members of the profession are, generally speaking, rogues and charlatans. Their classical work on medicine (Baideng) teaches that the human body is composed of the four elements, and the symptoms of disease manifested in the five senses. That there are ninety-six genera of diseases, which are caused by evil spirits, passions, or humours seated in the blood and nerves by climate and by food.

One of their most esteemed remedies is mercury; but their prescriptions are chiefly confined to aromatic ingredients, such as cardamums, nutmegs, chillies, etc.; and to barks, and particularly various roots, the virtue of which latter is supposed greatly to depend on the periods when they are gathered, such as the changes of the moon, and during eclipses. They have singular ideas regarding diet. During fevers and other acute disorders far from diminishing the quantity of food to be taken by

the patient, they rather increase it : the idea being
that the more that is eaten the stronger the patient
will be, and consequently better able to withstand
the disease.

If all the physician's remedies fail to check the
disease, it is then often declared that the malady
has been caused by an evil spirit, who must be
propitiated by offerings and the devil dance.* For
this purpose a strong-minded female of middle age,
accustomed to hire herself out on such occasions,
and of whom every large village contains at least
one, is sent for, and under the name of the wife of
the *Nat-tso,* or evil spirit, in a shed erected for the
purpose near the patient's house, filled with votive
offerings, she goes through sundry violent con-
tortions to the sound of a drum and brass trumpet,
and ends by feigning syncope. When in this state
she is questioned regarding the sick person, and if
her replies are unfavourable, all hope of the patient's
recovery is given up.

There is one disease in particular that is much
dreaded by the Burmese, called *a-peng* (peng means
a wedge in the vernacular) which they suppose to
be caused by a substance formed of bones, flesh,
and sinews produced by magic, and forced into the

---

* This is not a Buddhist rite, and is doubtless a remnant of Shamanism.
The festival is called by the Burmese *Nat-pan,* or that of the "possessing
spirit."

stomach, or some other part of the body by witches. This disease is considered to be not unfrequent and incurable. I had a favourite servant, named Shwégyau, who had long been in my service, and is supposed to have died of it. After the cremation of his body, his widow brought me a hard, irregularly formed substance found amongst his ashes, and which she gravely declared was the cause of death, and through the power of the Tson-ma, or witch, was the only portion of the body that had resisted the flames.

Burmese funerals are solemnized with great religious parade, and external demonstration of grief. Immediately the breath has left the body, all the people in the house, more especially the female portion, raise the most frightful shrieks, and messengers are despatched with information of the mournful event to the connections and friends of the deceased, who attend as speedily as possible to offer their condolences, and make arrangements for the funeral ; the expenses of which they help to defray by voluntary contributions amongst them.

After the corpse has been washed, and a coin called *kadho-akha,* or ferry-hire—the obolus for the Buddhist Charon—placed in the mouth, it is wrapped in a clean white sheet, and laid on an open bier in a front room of the house, where it remains, generally, for about three days, when it is removed in a wooden coffin to the place of cremation.

First in the funeral procession, slung on poles and carried on men's shoulders, are alms for the priest-hood and for the poor, following which are nuns carrying pickled tea, pawn and betel ; and then come priests carrying their broad-leafed palm-fans on their shoulders, and attended by their disciples, walking two and two ; a band of music precedes the coffin, borne by the friends of the deceased, and imme-diately after it are the nearest relations of the deceased, dressed all in white * — the Buddhist mourning. Attached to the coffin is often a piece of cloth, which is extended over the shoulders of the mourners.

On the arrival of the coffin at the cemetery, it is placed on the ground near the funeral pyre, the priests sitting† at the head of it, with the mourners and others in the same attitude in front of them.

---

* Just the reverse of the custom of the ancient Romans, with their "white days," and their holiday-dress of white clothes, "et populus festo concolor ipse suo ; " indeed, generally in every country at the present day white is considered a festive colour. I am not aware of the reason for the Buddhists adopting white as their mourning colour.

† The sitting posture is the attitude of respect in Burma ; and it is the only one in which an inferior can remain in the presence of a superior. In squatting down they are particularly careful to turn the soles of their feet behind them. When presenting anything to a superior, they do it in a crouching position, with averted head, showing every symptom of awe and respect. In the event of their having to address him, they first join their hands, and touch the forehead.

Instead of an assembly rising when a great man makes his appearance, as is the custom in Europe, it *sinks* down before him.

The chief priest then recites " the five Commandments," the "three kinds of worship," or Buddhist creed, and is followed by the other priests repeating the "ten good works." At the conclusion of these the chief mourner pours out water* from a cup or a cocoa-nut shell upon the cloth attached to the coffin; or, in its absence, on the ground, pronouncing at the same time, after the chief priest, " Let the deceased and all present partake of the merit of the ceremonies now performing," the assembly replying, "We will." They then all retire to a distance, the coffin is placed on the funeral pyre by those whose office it is to burn the dead, and set fire to.

Before leaving the cemetery, the alms are distributed to the priests, and to the poor; and the pickled tea, and the pawn and betel, is partaken of by all who have attended the funeral. On the third day after the funeral, the relations of the deceased return to the cemetery and gather the ashes, which they place in an urn, and bury in the earth.

* This ceremony of pouring out water on the earth is of Indian origin, and adopted by the Burmese with their religion. It is performed on the presentation of a monastery to the priesthood, and on other important occasions; and is done with the intention of calling the guardian nat of the earth as a witness to the donation. When it is performed some such formula as that given in the text is pronounced—the donor not being satisfied with receiving himself the sole benefit of the *Koung-hmo*, or "good-work," wishes also others to reap the merits of his pious liberality; thus showing a great amount of liberallity and brotherly love.

Amongst the wealthier class, until the ninth day after the death, receptions are held nightly at the house of the deceased, with a view of diverting the attention of the relatives, and preventing them from brooding over their bereavement, and concluded on the tenth day by a great feast given to the priests, and all those who have assisted in any way at the funeral.

The ceremonies connected with the cremation of the bodies of priests differ from those of the laity, and will be described in a subsequent chapter.

The Burmese are very fond of amusements of all kinds. One of their most manly and national sports is that of boat-racing, and nowhere are they seen at greater advantage than in their boats, in the management of which they show great skill. In rowing they almost always sing, keeping time with their oars, and the swell of voices (*yä-läy-athän*) appears very melodious when wafted down the broad stream of the Irawadi by the breeze.

The annual boat-races take place on the full moon of October, and every village of any size, and each division of a town, have generally a public racing boat with a picked crew. These boats, which have slightly peaked bows and sterns, and a wash-board about ten inches high, are from forty to sixty feet long, scooped out of a single tree. They are gaily painted, and often gilt, and the largest of them carry crews of from sixty to eighty men, who all sit facing the bow. In racing they do not use oars, but paddles about four feet long, with which, in spurts, they attain great speed.

The course is from a mile to a mile and a half in length, and a boat containing the umpire, with a flag flying at the mast-head, is anchored in mid-stream, and forms the goal. Athwart the bows of this boat, and extending for some distance on either side, is fixed a hollow bamboo, through which a loose cord is passed with a bunch of palm leaves fastened at each end, and projecting from the bamboo. Only two boats race at a time, and to prevent fouling, they have to pass on opposite sides of the goal. As the leading boat shoots past the goal, a man, stationed in the bow for the purpose, seizes the bunch of leaves on his side, and the other, being attached to it, is instantly pulled through the bamboo. By this simple device, dead heats, and all possibility of disputes, are avoided, for " palmam qui meruit *ferit,*" and wins the race.

On the race being won, the winning crew jump up in their boat, throw themselves into grotesque attitudes, gesticulating and shouting wild songs of triumph, in which they are joined by many of their friends and backers on the banks of the river; and this wild state of excitement is often prolonged until the commencement of the next race.

The Burmese are very clannish in their feelings, coupled with a strong itch for gambling, especially at these annual races ; and the purses for the races being raised in the districts to which the contending boats belong, are, consequently often heavy ones. A good deal of money, also, changes hands in outside bets ; but all are ready-money transactions, paid down on the spot, and amongst this light-hearted people, those who lose look for better luck next year, and losses are soon forgotten.

The youth of Burma show great agility in their game of foot-ball (*khyay-lon*), which differs, however, very considerably from the European game, and is played by six or eight young men formed in a circle. The ball, a hollow sphere formed of wicker-work, is tossed up in the air in the centre of the group, and the object is to pass it from one to the other, and keep it from falling to the ground as long as possible. It must not be struck with the hand— but foot, ankle, knee, elbow, shoulder, and any other part of the body may be used. No little skill is required in keeping the ball in motion, and they seldom miss their stroke, or fail to give the ball the direction intended. To have their limbs free, they " gird up their loins," and their tattooing becomes very apparent, as may be observed in the engraving

BURMESE GAME OF FOOTBALL.

on the opposite page. The game causes much merriment and laughter, and is pursued with great spirit. A similar game is played in Cochin China,[*] but with a shuttlecock made of dried skin rolled round and bound with strings, into which feathers are inserted.

Most young men learn to box and wrestle, and a proficient in them is always held in high esteem and respect. In boxing, "tripping up," and striking with the knee and foot,[†] as well as the fist, are allowable. Wrestling is pursued in the same manner as with us, throwing on the back constituting the victory.

On holidays or festive occasions the most common diversions are boxing and wrestling. Ground for the ring is prepared and made soft with moistened sand, and around it the spectators sit or stand, a scaffolding being erected on one side for the umpires and "heads of the people." As is the practice at every festival, a band of music is in attendance, and plays during the combats. No severe or cruel punishment is allowed, and " the first drop of claret tapped," or blood drawn from a cut lip, or elsewhere, decides the fight. To determine this point, curious

* See Macartney's " Embassy to China," vol. i., p. 339.

† It must be remembered that they wear no boots or shoes on these occasions. I have seen a severe fall given by the foot being caught in an attempt at a high kick, and a very awkward blow given under the chin by the knee.

and minute examinations are often set on foot by the umpires, those having cut lips or other trifling mishaps, endeavouring to conceal them, and the detection of which calls forth bursts of laughter from the spectators.

Their first attitude of defence is not good, the principal object appearing to be to plant the first blow, and leave the rest to chance; but the agility and rapidity with which they dodge a blow and return it, would be considered good anywhere. When a match is made up, the two competitors, dressed in a similar fashion to that shown in the "game at foot-ball," after exchanging a friendly word or two, take up a position in the centre of the ring, each being accompanied by a second, who is generally an old professor and teacher of the art. The following description is not unlike that which then happens.

As the combatants advance, each carefully watches his opponent's eye, with one arm in reserve, and the other put out and withdrawn, as if feeling the distance, the music playing as they draw near each other: gradually the measure quickens, the muscular motions of the combatants seem to keep time to it—a feint, a blow dodged, a right and left home—the music faster and faster—a cross-buttock cleverly escaped, and another blow home. The kettle-drums dance madly in their circular frames—the combatants close—hug and trip; and as they come to the ground the seconds rush in and separate them; the music dies away, the musicians perhaps more exhausted than the combatants themselves. Then prizes of gay silks or muslin turbans are distributed to the "gladiatori," the winners' share being more costly than the losers.

The combatants on these occasions show admirable temper throughout, and I have never heard of anyone being seriously hurt, or a case of bad blood arising from a boxing-match.

During the day of the full moon of Ta-soung-mon, corresponding with our month of November, an interesting festival takes place called Ta-soung-doing; when pieces of yellow cloth are presented to the priesthood for their dresses; and, also, as offerings to the pagodas, round the sacred sides of which they are rolled. These pieces of cloth must be made from the raw cotton, and dyed within *one night*.*

The evening before the festival, after the cotton is picked and the thread spun, the looms—with at least one of which every Burmese dwelling is

---

* This is not an ordinance of Gautama. The custom for this rapid manufacture of cloth is said to have proceeded from Maia, Gautama's mother (see the following text). It is more practised on the seaboard than in the interior of Burma. The Egyptian priests had a garment woven in one day when they observed the festival in memory of the return of Rampsinitus from the infernal regions.—Herod. ii., 123. The magic standard of the Danes was also woven and embroidered by royal hands in one noon-tide.—See "Monachism," p. 122.

furnished—are brought outside, and placed in front
of the houses, and lines of them may be seen down
each side of a street, with the women hard at work
weaving, at which they remain all night ; several
reliefs being told off for each loom.   The piece of
cloth furnished by each loom must be fifteen feet
long, by one and a half broad, and there is great
rivalry as to who shall complete the first piece.
Notwithstanding a great deal of flirting among the
younger portion of the weavers, all the cloth is
ready by morning, and the following day is chiefly
spent in visiting the monasteries and presenting the
cloths to the priests.

The origin of the custom for this rapid manufacture of cloth is said to have proceeded from Maia,*
the mother of Gautama, causing a priest's dress to be
instantly woven, and conveyed to her son, on her
perceiving from the realms of bliss that he had fled
from his palace to the desert, and divested himself
of the royal robes with the intention of becoming a
Recluse.†

In the evening the pagodas are illuminated from

* Maia, by virtue of her great merits, migrated after death to the happy
abode of the nats, and became a daughter of the nat Too-tseet-ta. She was
fifty-six years old when she died ; and her decease took place seven days after
her confinement of Gautama. Her death, it is said, " was not the result of her
delivery," but she departed this world because the term of her life had come.

† According to Bishop Bigaudet (" Life of Gautama," p. 60) this dress, and
the other priestly requisites, were miraculously presented to Gautama by a great
Brahma named Gatigara, who had been an intimate friend of Gautama in a
former state of existence.

top to bottom by means of small oil-lamps, and
owing to these religious edifices being always built
on commanding sites, the general effect of them
is very beautiful. Opposite the door of every
house is also suspended a lamp on a lofty pole,
which is lighted every day at sunset, and continued until the close of the month. From this
latter feature the festival takes its designation—
Ta-soung, the name of the month, and *doing*, a pole
or post.*

On the night of the full moon, in addition to
the above lights, where a river or large stream
exists in the vicinity of the town or village, small
fire-boats and rafts are launched, each with a number
of lights on them ; and as they float down the
current, forming brilliant lines of fantastic shapes
and figures, waning away in the distance, are
anxiously watched by the people who launch them ;

* This festival is no doubt connected with the great festival of the Pleiades,
or "feast of first fruits and of the dead," held in ancient times in the month of
November ; and which is still held, during this month, in some form or other
in Asia, America, Polynesia and Europe. It lingers with us in the festivals of
All Halloween, All Saints, and All Souls. The rising of the Pleiades on an
evening of the month of November, culminating at midnight, and setting in
the morning, is supposed to have marked the commencement of the primitive
new year, which was siderial or astral, and regulated by the seven stars in the
constellation of Taurus. The Bull and the Seven Stars are also associated
with the tradition of the deluge. The deluge is supposed to have commenced on the 17th November, at the moment of the culmination of the
Pleiades. (See "Life and Work at the Great Pyramid," by C. Piazzi Smith,
p. 370 *et seq.*). I may add also that the "Feast of Lanterns," or "Feast of
Ancestors," is held by the Chinese inhabitants of Burma at the same time as
the Burmese festival of Ta-Soung-doing.

for they are looked upon as offerings to the river
nat, and it is a token of good luck if the lights burn
long.*

On the first day of the new year commences
the "water festival," which lasts for four days.
At daybreak the people proceed to the pagodas
which they sprinkle with water, offering up at the
same time prayers for a plentiful season. They,
also, present jars of water to the priests, and ask
forgiveness for any wickedness they may have committed by thought, word, or deed during the past
year.

After these religious ceremonies are over, a
kind of Burmese carnival begins, reminding one
of the showers of *confetti*, and *mázzi di fióri* that
salute the revellers during the carnival at Rome ;
only here, instead of sweetmeats and nosegays, water
is thrown, sometimes indeed scented, or having
flowers in it. The fronts of the houses are decorated
with green leaves and flowers, and all hands, particularly the young men and women, send showers of
water on the passers-by, bursts of laughter succeeding

---

* A somewhat similar custom exists in Hindústan, where floating lights may
be often seen at night on the river Ganges ; and they are looked upon there
also as votive offerings to the spirit of the stream. The ceremony, however,
is not confined to any particular night, and the offerings are made for the safe
return of relations, friends, or lovers, who have gone on long journeys. If the
lamp meets with an accident and sinks, or goes out, the omen is disastrous ;
but if it continues burning until it disappears in the distance, the safe return of
the beloved one is believed certain. The custom is alluded to by Moore in
"Lalla Rookh," p. 317.

each well directed volley :—or parading the streets
armed with earthen jars of water and silver cups
duck everyone they meet. Occasionally these bands
meet and have regular contests, drenching each other
with water. No one, whatever his rank, escapes the
liquid salutation. The licence gives rise to much
harmless merriment, and it is considered very ill-
bred for any one to object to these "compliments
of the season;"—and bad luck is sure to ensue to
those who are not wet at least once during the
day.

It is a quaint wild sight to see a bevy of
maidens rushing wildly about with their long wet
hair streaming down their backs, and their light
dress drenched and clinging to each curve of the
figure, loudly shouting, *Ma-tsō-boo! Ma-tsō-boo!*
(not wet, not wet), much in the same spirit that
an Italian girl calls *Sénza moccoletti! Sénza moccoletti!* after having just dashed the lighted taper
out of an unwary hand on the last night of the
carnival.

The original idea of this festival is, I believe, that
of washing away the sins and impurities of the past,
together with any ill feelings that may have sprung
up during the year that has just faded away, and
commencing the new one free from all stain. There
is also a mythological tale of its typifying the washing of a king's head by the seven nats that watch

over time,* and who pass on the head to each other's
laps as the old year goes out and the new one
comes in.†

* This tradition, also, is not improbably connected with the Pleiades.　See
note at foot of page 91.

† In describing the above festival and the boxing-match, I have, with the
author's permission, drawn largely upon "Heathen and Holy Lands," by
Lieut.-Col. J. P. Briggs, a work containing many good sketches of the habits
and customs of the Burmese.

CHAPTER III.

FOUR YEARS' ADMINISTRATION OF BRITISH BURMA,
1867-1871.

Our commerce with China confined to sea ports.—Ancient overland commerce
between Burma and Western China viâ Bhamo.—Brought to a close in
1855.—Early history of the Panthays or Chinese Mahomedans.—They
establish a Mahommedan kingdom in Yunnan.—Monoply of trade
between Burma and Yunnan confined to Chinese inhabitants of Mandalay
and Bhamo.—Their jealousy regarding it.—Despatch of a Mission under
Major Sladen to Western China viâ Bhamo.—Burmese suspicion of it.—
The King ultimately sends the expedition in his own steamer to Bhamo.—
Hill ranges and valleys occupied by Kakhyens and Shans.—Description
of these tribes.—The Governor of Bhamo defeated and slain by the
Kakhyens.—Difficulties of the Mission in consequence.—The Mission
starts for Momein.—Secret agencies at work to stop the Mission.—Mission
delayed at Ponsee.—Delay profitable in some ways.—Valuable collection
of specimens of natural history made by Dr. Anderson.—Bambusicola
Fytchii.—Kakhyen ideas of marriage.—Their superstitious observances.—
Communication opened with the Governor of Momein.—The Chinese
freebooter, Li Hsieh-tai.—Destruction of his stronghold.—Mission escorted
by Shans and Panthays to Momein.—Hospitality of Ta-sa-kon.—All
objects of Mission successfully obtained.—Mission returns to Bhamo.—
Return journey quite an ovation.—Description of Kakhyen oath.—Exposition of the policy in despatching the Mission.—Objects not political
but commercial.—The tact and gallantry shown by Major Sladen.—
Favourable view taken by him of the Panthay rebellion.—Policy of the
British Government towards Yacoob Beg, Sultan of Kaskgar.—An English
political agent appointed to Bhamo.—Large increase of trade.—A Panthay
Embassy proceeds to England viâ Rangoon and Calcutta.—Collapse
of Mahomedan power in Yunnan.—Despatch of a second Mission to
Western China.—Its failure.—Murder of Mr. Margary.—Lord Lawrence
retires from the Viceroyalty of India.—Lord Mayo appointed Viceroy.—
Correspondence with Lord Mayo.—Important measures carried out during
my administration of British Burma.—Speech at a public dinner.

THE details of four years' administration of a province like British Burma would have but little

interest for English readers. Blue books respecting
remote regions do not constitute the popular reading
of the day, yet measures have been carried out in
Burma which might have engaged the attention of
the empire. The expedition which I sent to China
was of this description. It opened up scenes and
countries which had been for generations a *terra
incognita* to Europeans. It brightened up the hopes
of every merchant in Burma with the prospect of
new markets for British industry, new fields for
British capital and enterprise.

Our intercourse with China has been of growing
importance for more than two centuries, but
hitherto it has been confined to the sea-ports. Few
attempts * have been made to open it up on the
land side, and for all practical purposes the interior
of China has been a sealed book to Europeans.
Yet within the memory of the present generation, a
prosperous trade was carried on between Upper
Burma and Western China.

Burma, amongst other articles of minor importance,
exported cotton, salt, and rubies ; China exported
silk, tea, and gold leaf. The intermediate region
between the two countries consists of hills and
valleys occupied by barbarous and semi-civilized

* The routes surveyed by Major Sladen, as also those by Dr. Richardson,
Captain McLeod, and other explorers in different parts of Burma and the
adjacent countries, are shown in the accompanying map.

tribes known as Kakhyens and Shans. They are as ignorant and credulous as children, but are fully alive to the profits of the carrying trade. This state of things was brought to a close by political revolutions.

About 1855 the Panthays* established a Mahommedan kingdom in the province of Yunnan in Western China. The Chinese failed to crush the movement. The local Chinese authorities ignored it in the eyes of the central authority at Pekin. Indeed, they could have had no desire to draw the attention of the imperial government to their own weakness and incapacity. Meanwhile they tried to harass the Panthay dominion after Chinese fashion. They encouraged the freebooters, who preyed upon the Panthay kingdom from all sides, and so far they succeeded in cutting off the Mahommedan dominion from the world of civilization.

On the side of Burma these freebooters had put an effectual stop to the trade, or only suffered it to pass on the payment of a heavy black mail. The result was that the trade became small but profit-

---

* The Panthays belong to the Sunni sect of the Mahommedans. In physical aspect they are a tall, strongly built, fair-skinned, race, with a type of face differing distinctly from the Chinese. Their dress for the most part resembles the Chinese ; but, unlike them, they wear their hair long, coiled in the folds of large white turbans. In character they are great traders, very industrious and enterprising. A memorandum on their origin and early history, together with other matters connected with the race, read by me before a meeting of the Asiatic Society of Bengal in December, 1867, will be found in the Appendix. (Appendix E.)

able.   It was a monopoly in the hands of the
Chinese of Bhamo and Mandalay, who bribed the
freebooters and did their utmost to keep what little
trade there was entirely under their own control.

The revival of this trade under British auspices
would render Burma the most flourishing province in
the empire of British India.   It would open out a new
market for British manufactures, which in due time
would extend over a greater area than that of India.
But, before this could be attempted, it was necessary
to arrive at the actual facts.   Accordingly, the main
purpose of the expedition of 1868 was to investigate
thoroughly the causes of the cessation of trade : to
discover the exact political condition of the hill tribes
between Burma and China, known as Kakhyens
and Shans : to obtain as much information as possible
respecting the Panthay kingdom in Yunnan : and to
endeavour to interest the local communities in the
restoration and extension of the trade.

It was obvious that the success of any expedition to Western China depended upon its being
cordially supported at starting by the Burmese
government.   All this had been apparently secured
by my treaty of 1867.   The Burmese ministers
issued orders or said they had issued orders to the
Governor of the frontier town of Bhamo, and to the
head men of all the towns and villages on the route,
to make every arrangement in anticipation of the

arrival of the expedition. The King seemed to be enthusiastic on the subject ; he volunteered the services of one of his own steamers to carry the members of the expedition from Mandalay to Bhamo.

Meantime some of the ministers at court began to grow suspicious of the expedition. The Chinese merchants at Mandalay were still more opposed to it ; they were naturally anxious to keep the monopoly of the trade in their own hands. It was whispered that the success of the expedition would bring a large influx of foreigners into Burma, and deprive the King of his independence ; and how the English on their first appearance in India, commenced by asking for leave to trade, and ended by conquering and annexing the country. All these things worked upon the mind of his Majesty. He affected doubt whether the river Irawadi would be navigable between Mandalay and Bhamo during the dry months. At last he said he was afraid to risk his steamer for the conveyance of the expedition.

At this crisis Major Sladen, the Political Agent to the Chief Commissioner at Mandalay, and whom I had appointed leader of the expedition, applied for an English steamer. This step excited the jealousy of the King. He was afraid that an English steamer would have the glory of being the first to go to Bhamo. He withdrew all his objections and again placed his steamer at the disposal of the expedition. Accordingly on the 13th of January, 1868, the expedition steamed away to Bhamo, and reached that place in eight days without any difficulty whatever.

Bhamo is the frontier town towards China. Beyond it are the ranges of hills occupied by the Kakhyens ;* dirty, unkempt, ugly barbarians, armed with bows and arrows, spears and matchlocks; drunken, superstitious, and lawless to the last degree. Beyond the Kakhyen hills are valleys occupied by the Shans ; an industrious people, domestic and pious after Buddhist fashion ; but the chiefs are often as drunken and refractory as their rude neighbours on the hills. The Kakhyens owe a certain amount of allegiance to the King of Burma. The Shans are more independent, and their allegiance is, to say the least, questionable.

The King of Burma is nominally the sovereign of the Kakhyen and Shan tribes up to the Chinese frontier, and in his palace at Mandalay he is induced to believe that his orders are implicitly obeyed and

---

* So called by the Burmese ; but they call themselves *Sheng-paw.* They are a portion of the vast horde of Singphoos that inhabit the mountainous districts of Northern Assam, and stretch round the north of Burma into Western China. Intermixed with Kakoos and other kindred tribes, and the Shans, they extend, not only all along the northern frontier of Burma, but occupy large portions of the hilly tracts on both sides of the Irawadi river, dipping down as far south as the latitude of Tagoung.

respected by all these tribes. Unfortunately, just before the arrival of the expedition at Bhamo, there had been an outbreak amongst the Kakhyen tribes. The Governor of Bhamo had gone out with a force to suppress it, but had been defeated and slain. Such was the unhappy news that greeted Major Sladen on arriving at Bhamo, when he was naturally anxious to start at once for China.

On the day after the arrival of Major Sladen, the two head men or magistrates of Bhamo paid him a visit on board the steamer. They were perfectly courteous, for they knew his rank as Political Agent at Mandalay; but they were strangely reticent about the expedition. They professed to be entirely ignorant of any arrangements for his journey over the Kakhyen hills. They knew of no orders from Mandalay; they had done nothing towards acquainting the heads of villages with the coming expedition. This was not a very promising outlook for Sladen. Moreover, whilst the Burmese officials were friendly and hospitable, they seemed to enjoy his perplexity. Whenever Major Sladen referred to the expedition they moaned over the murder of the Governor of Bhamo, and expatiated upon the lawless character of Kakhyens and Shans. Whenever Major Sladen pressed them to make arrangements, they urged that under existing circumstances nothing whatever could be done. The

Chinese merchants at Bhamo talked in the same strain. They declared that even if the expedition made its way through Kakhyens and Shans, there were freebooters beyond, who would stop all further progress towards Western China.

It is needless to dwell upon the details of the delay. After stopping a month at Bhamo trying to start, but thwarted in every way, the prospects of the expedition began to brighten. A new governor arrived at Bhamo, and the expedition got away. Mule carriage and guides had been furnished by two Kakhyen chiefs, known as Ponlyne and Ponsee. The chiefs engaged to carry the party in safety as far as the Shan states at the foot of the Kakhyen hills.

But from the very first it was evident that secret agencies were at work to stop the expedition, and induce Major Sladen to turn back to Bhamo. Mysterious shots were fired in the distance. Sometimes a bullet whizzed suspiciously near the head of one or other of the members of the expedition. Spears were hurled, nobody knew by whom. Mules were often missing. Sometimes there was a strike amongst the drivers. The Ponlyne and Ponsee chiefs incessantly clamoured for rupees; they exhausted their imaginations in their efforts to find fresh grounds for a renewal of their demands. In all cases of difficulty they got exceedingly drunk,

and were either unable to furnish any explanation, or assumed a threatening attitude which was
extremely provoking. At the same time the authorities at Bhamo were more ready to thwart than to
help the expedition. On one occasion a messenger
arrived with orders for the Ponlyne and Ponsee
chiefs to return to Bhamo; the Governor, it was
said, wanted to consult them about some old silver
mines. This was evidently a mere pretence. Such
obstacles, however, were well calculated to damp
the spirits of the members of the expedition. At
the village of Ponlyne the party was delayed
several days; at Ponsee it was delayed several
weeks. But nothing would induce Major Sladen
to say anything, or make any movement, which
would indicate any intention of returning. He
showed admirable temper and determination throughout.

These delays involved much loss of time, but
they were profitable in other ways. Major Sladen
and his able coadjutor Dr. John Anderson, surgeon
and naturalist to the expedition, were thereby
enabled to collect much valuable information respecting the natural history, products, and manufactures of this unknown region; and, moreover,
become acquainted with the habits and forms of
thought which prevailed amongst its rude inhabitants.

The large collection made by Dr. Anderson, contained many valuable specimens of natural history, some of which are new to science. Amongst these latter is a partridge, which he did me the honour to call after my name. It is figured on the opposite page, and Dr. Anderson's description of the bird, as given by him in the " Proceedings of The Zoological Society of London for February, 1871," is contained in the note below.*

The social and religious life of the Kakhyens, is well deserving of study by all who are interested in the early developments of primitive man.   Their

* *Bambusicola Fytchii.* ♂. Pileo brunneo-ferrugineo : fascia lata superciliari in fronte conjuncta utrinque elongata, albescenti-cinerea ; fascia pone oculos nigra : auchenio cinnamomeo : interscapularibus et tectricibus alarum cinereo-olivaceis, maculis subtriquetris rufo-brunneis, nigro terminatis et plumis brunneo-nigro obscure lineolatis : dorso, uropygio et tectricibus caudæ superioribus cinereo-olivaceis, nigro-brunneo transversim obscure nitideque notatis vel subfasciatis, interdum nigro parce maculatis, maculis triangularibus albescente cinereo terminatis : rectricibus cinnamomeis, duabus mediis nigro-brunneo undulatim fasciatis, fasciis ochraceis pallide marginatis : duabus sequentibus nigro-brunneo obscure lineolatis : loris, mento gulaque pallide ochraceis : jugulo rufo-ochraceo et cinnamomeo longitudinaliter vario : pectore lateribusque ejus cinnamomeis alboque ocellatis et nigro parce maculatis : pectore, ventre crissoque pallide rufescenti-albis, maculis magnis subrotundatis et nigris : hypochondriorum plumarum maculis permagnis et triangularibus : remigibus cinnamomeis, secundariorum marginibus externis brunneo et cinereo obscure marmoratis : remigibus tertiariis rufo-brunneis, apicibus extensis nigris et albescente cinereo tenuiter marginatis : marginibus externis cinereo et albo tenuiter marmoratis.   Long. tota 12, alæ 5·80, caudæ 4·20, tarsi 1·58, rostri a rictu 9·5. a fronte ·86.

♀. Cauda magis brunnea : fascia post oculus cinnamomea : calcari minuto. The structural characters of this bird are decidedly *Bambusicoline* ; but it is related in its colouring to *Arboricola*. Gould describes the spur of *B. sonorivox* as blunt ; but it is very sharp in this species, and is indicated in the female by a small tubercle. The female is also distinguished from the male by the postorbital band being cinnamon instead of black. I procured this bird from the old rice-clearings on the hill sides of I'onsee, at an elevation of 3000 feet.

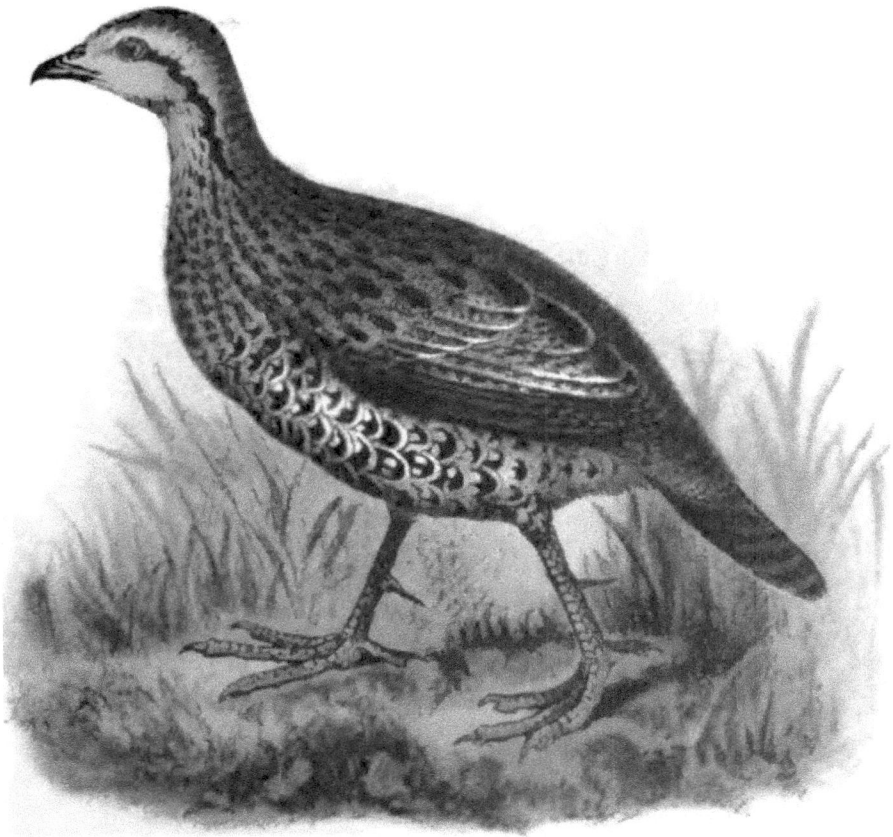

BAMBUSICOLA FYTCHII.

ideas of marriage are specially curious and suggestive. Women are esteemed according to their
ability to bear children. Before marriage, the
utmost liberty is allowed between the sexes. When,
however, the woman has become a mother, she
soon finds a husband; and henceforth, fidelity to
her husband becomes a cardinal virtue. Indeed,
unfaithfulness after marriage is generally punished
by death.

The religion of the Kakhyens is equally primitive.
They propitiate spirits, good and bad, under the
name of nats. They believe that men are sometimes possessed by these spirits. In other words,
they are spiritualists; they believe that certain men
are endowed with the power of expressing the will
of the spirits; and they consult such persons on all
occasions of difficulty or danger.

Major Sladen had several opportunities of forming
a judgment upon these proceedings; for the Kakhyens invariably consulted the nats, when any
doubt arose as regards the expedition. The man
supposed to be possessed went away to a corner of
the house by himself. He crouched down, and
began to work himself into a fury. He shrieked
and groaned; stroked his face with both hands;
tore his hair in his feigned madness. At last, his
legs began to quiver. This was the signal that he
was really possessed. From the moment that his

legs quiver, his utterances are regarded as those of nats and demons. Major Sladen was told to offer a propitiation. He tried to get off by the payment of fifteen rupees. The money was laid on a new cloth, and presented, on a platter of plaintain leaves, to the possessed man. It was rejected by the spirits. A kick from the man possessed, sent the rupees scattering over the floor. Five rupees more were added. The spirits were now propitiated; they proclaimed, through the man possessed, that they regarded the expedition with a favourable eye.

Meantime, Major Sladen made a bold stroke, which ultimately insured the success of his expedition. It will be remembered that his main object was to open up the route as far as Yunnan in Western China, that is, as far as the Panthay kingdom, which the Chinese Mahommedans had established in 1855. This involved the necessity of finding a way, not only through the tracts inhabited by the Kakhyens and Shans, but through the region beyond, which was infested by Chinese freebooters. The Chinese merchants at Bhamo had tried to terrify Major Sladen by stories of the exploits of these Chinese bandits; and especially of one terrible fellow named Li Chên-kuo, alias Li Hsieh-tai.

Major Sladen suspected that the Bhamo merchants were intriguing with this Li Hsieh-tai to cut him off, or at any rate, to stop his expedition.

Accordingly he sent scouts with a letter to the Panthay Governor at Têng-yüeh Chou or Momein, the frontier fortress on the western side of Yunnan, to beg the Panthays to clear the route from all these brigands. The result proved satisfactory. At Ponsee, Major Sladen received letters from the Governor of Momein, to the effect, that he had taken the field against the bandits. Subsequently, the news arrived that the stronghold of Li Hsieh-tai had been captured by the Panthays, and that the Shans were overjoyed at their deliverance from this freebooter.

From this moment, the expedition was a success. The Shans, who were independent of the King of Burma, sent a deputation to Major Sladen at Ponsee. The new arrivals conducted the expedition safely through the whole of the Shan country as far as Mynela. There Captain Sladen was met by a Panthay escort, which conducted the expedition past the ruined stronghold of Li Hsieh-tai, to the frontier fortress of the Panthays at Momein.

Major Sladen was cordially welcomed by Ta-sa-kon the Governor of Momein, and nothing can have exceeded the friendly hospitality with which the mission was treated, both by him, and his people. The three routes by which Momein is approached from Bhamo were surveyed, and the objects for the attainment of which the Mission had been sent fully accomplished, without a single important mishap. Major Sladen would have gone on to Talifu, the head-quarters of the Panthay Government, but found that there were political and other difficulties in the way; and from the circumstances described by him, there can be no doubt he was right in not proceeding beyond Momein.

It would doubtless have been interesting at the time, from some points of view, had the party succeeded in reaching Talifu but the Panthay authorities, whom Major Sladen met at Momein, were of sufficient importance and position to render their views and opinions a safe criterion of the feeling of the Panthay Government. It was evident that on their part there existed a strong desire for the resuscitation of the trade. The long residence of the party among the Kakhyens, and in the Shan States, was productive of the best results.

Apart from some local jealousies—caused by a wish to secure for themselves the advantages of having the route through their individual territories —it appeared that the Shan Chiefs were fully alive to the gain to them of the renewal of trade; while the Kakhyens seemed to have realised the peaceful character of the mission, and the profitable future they would secure, if the route was re-established. Even the physical difficulties of the route proved by no means great, and could be materially modified, whenever considered advisable to do so, by local labour which was only too anxious to be employed.

The mission stayed at Momein from the 28th May until the 13th July, on which latter date they set out on their return to Bhamo, which they reached on 5th September following. Their return journey was quite an ovation, Kakhyens and Shans vying with each other in showing them hospitality. If two routes led to the same place, one Tsanbwa * or Pomaing (chiefs of clans) would almost quarrel with another for the honour of getting them to visit any particular village, or give any particular route preference over others. Thirty-one Kakhyen chiefs, with some two hundred followers accompanied the mission to Bhamo, and there, according to national custom, bound themselves by an oath to protect and afford safe-conduct to all traders and travellers crossing their respective hill ranges.

The taking of the oath is accompanied by peculiar savage solemnities, and is thus described by Major Sladen :

" For each buffalo slaughtered a separate building is constructed, consisting of strong posts sunk into the ground, with cross pieces to which the animal is tied previous to sacrifice.

" A separate altar is also prepared, twenty feet in

* Tsanbwa is a Burmese version of the Shan title Chau-phra meaning Lord-ruler. Pomaing is also a Shan word, signifying Father-noble.

height, with a platform of bamboos some four feet
square, on which the sacrifice is offered.   Kakhyen
deities of every degree and denomination are invited
to attend and bear evidence to the rite about to be
solemnized or oath taken.

" The invocation is repeated twice ; once before
slaughter, and again previous to laying the meat-
offering on the altar.   It is performed by a special
office bearer, whose prayerful intonation is strangely
musical and suggestive of portions of our own
Cathedral service.   The animal to be slaughtered
is firmly bound by its horn to the wooden construction before mentioned, and then thrown on one side.
The whole weight and strain of the body is on the
neck, which is partially twisted.   There is not a
moment's delay : a Kakhyen, specially equipped for
the service, holding a plantain-leaf cup of sacred
water in one hand and a naked sword in the other,
rushes forward.   The water is thrown over the
sacrifice, while the sharp edge of the sword is
brought down with frightful effect on that portion
of the neck where the strain is greatest : the
result is complete.   The savagery of the whole
scene is somewhat atoned for by an absence of
torture or suffering, from which the animal is saved
by its almost instantaneous death.

" The carcase is cut up without loss of time, and
the portion of it alone to which the deities are

known, by Kakhyen experience, to be partial, are
cooked and laid on the altar to be feasted on by the
gods. This is the time, while the deities are being
propitiated with the semblance of a feast, that they
are called upon to witness the oath to which the
whole ceremony leads up.

"A small quantity of the blood of the slaughtered
animal has been caught, and is now mixed in a large
vessel with an abundant supply of raw native spirits.
The whole is stirred up with the points of swords
and spears, which are dipped into the liquor; and
each chief, as he comes up in the supposed presence
of the attendant deities and takes his draught from
the sacred bowl, swears his oath of fidelity in
muttered prayers which imply the most fearful
results as a certain consequence of infidelity.

"The dipping of the spears and swords in the
liquor in which the oath is drank is said to be
typical of the violent death which would of a
certainty be incurred by a departure from the engagements contained in the oath."

Such is the story of the first expedition from
Burma to Western China. It has led to much
controversy, which I believe has chiefly risen
through misconception. It was followed some years
after by another expedition, which was accompanied
by sorrow and disaster, and nearly drifted the
British government into a war with China. I feel,

therefore, that the moment has arrived for making an exposition of the policy by which I was actuated in planning the first expedition, and which I continued to pursue after the return of the expedition, down to the close of my Administration.

The expedition of 1868 had no political object. The leader of the expedition was cautioned to be guarded in allowing the Panthays even to suppose that we had any political aim; or that he was authorized to entertain any propositions of a nature other than commercial. It was undertaken for the purpose of acquiring full information respecting the physical condition of the several trade routes leading from Burma to Yunnan, and how far these might be ameliorated; the causes which had brought about the cessation of the trade since 1855; the exact position held by the different tribes who inhabited the intervening country with reference to that traffic; and the possibility, or otherwise, of re-opening the trade under existing circumstances.

The whole of this information was obtained, and the official narrative of Major Sladen of the proceedings of the mission furnishes the fullest possible details. Nothing is wanting therein in the way of information and explanation. I must at the same time do justice to the tact and gallantry which Major Sladen displayed under various trying circumstances. Occasional misgivings are expressed at different parts of his journal; but no trace of them is to be seen in his actions at any time throughout the expedition. Above all, I have always admired the readiness of his resources in overcoming obstacles purposely placed in his way.

If Major Sladen erred in any way, it was in taking a too favourable view of the strength of the Panthay rebellion, and in intimating to the governor of Momein that the friendly state of our relations with the Court of Pekin might be utilized in bringing about a reconciliation of contending interests in Yunnan.* This, by the proverbial sanguine oriental temperament, may, possibly, have been interpreted to mean really more than was intended.

But in all this, as in everything else, Major Sladen acted in perfect good faith. He was urged on by a generous and chivalrous enthusiasm. He saw the Chinese Mahommedans engaged in a resolute and conscientious struggle against the oppressive government of the Mandarins. His sympathies were powerfully enlisted in the Panthay cause. He believed that the establishment of the independence of the Panthay Sultan, as a friendly power, would prove most advantageous to the British Government. It would solve the great problem of the time, namely, the re-opening of the old trade into Western China, under the most favourable auspices.

* See p. lxvii. of Appendix to Major Sladen's Official Report.

It is due to Major Sladen to say, that this policy was perfectly consistent with the *role* afterwards adopted by the British Government, in dealing with another rebel prince on the side of Western China, namely, Yacoob Beg, the Sultan of Kashgar. How far such proceedings were in accordance with our treaty relations with China is a matter which I leave others to decide; I have only to discuss the nature of our relations with the Panthay Sultan of Yunnan.

I was afraid lest political complications might arise from an early stage of the proceedings; and I did my best to guard against them. After Major Sladen's return, I sent suitable presents and acknowledgments to Ta-sa-kon; for I fully appreciated the help which he had afforded to the Expedition, and the hospitality and kindness with which he had received and entertained Major Sladen and his party. But I took care to explain to him at the same time that the British Government was in treaty alliance with China, and that I could not help him either with arms or men in the Panthay war of independence. All this was perfectly understood between us, and matters remained on this friendly and personal footing until I left the province in 1871.

On the return of the Mission from Momein— with a view to strengthen the belief in the reality of our own intentions to endeavour to resuscitate trade, and to maintain communication with the Kakhyen and Shan chiefs, and the Panthay Government,—an English political agent was at once appointed to Bhamo; which contingency had been provided for in my Treaty of 1867 with the King of Burma.

During 1868–69, the year immediately following this treaty, the customs collection on the trade of the Port of Rangoon increased more than fifty per cent., and the one per cent. duty, leviable under this treaty on all goods *declared for export to Upper Burma and overland to China, upwards of one thousand per cent.*, over that of the preceding year. Owing to this vast increase of trade, I was enabled in 1869 to enter into a contract with an English Steam Company, for a small subsidy, to despatch a steamer weekly to Mandalay, and one once a month to Bhamo; and matters had only to be left alone for trade to further develop itself.

I need not dwell upon the sequel. In 1872 an embassy headed by Hussan, the son of the Sultan of Yunnan, as he was styled, arrived at Rangoon. Help was wanted against the Chinese. The embassy* was very favourably received both at

* A Burmese embassy also left for England about the same time, which was somewhat snubbed, as compared with the reception of the Panthay one. The positions of the two embassies, however, were, very properly, entirely reversed on their arrival in England.

Rangoon and Calcutta, and sent on to England;—
but *there* its status was fully understood, and at once
shewn to be false.

The news of Hussan's embassy having proceeded
to England was carried to China, doubtless with
numerous exaggerations, and the Chinese, who were
even then pressing the Panthays hard, redoubled
their efforts. They concentrated their forces and
surrounded Talifu the capital of Yunnan. They took
the city by storm and committed unutterable horrors.
The Panthay dominion was crushed out with fire
and sword. The embers were still smouldering
when another Mission of peace and commerce was
sent into Western China. Its failure has become a
matter of history. The murder* of Mr. Margary is
one of the saddest events in the story of Chinese
exploration.†

* A copy of the letter of apology for the murder of Mr. Margary from the
Emperor of China, and credentials of the Envoy Kuo Sung-tao on his Mission
to Great Britain, dated October, 1876, is contained in the Appendix.
(Appendix F.)

† From the experience gained in the first expedition, I believe myself that
this second expedition, notwithstanding its questionable opportuneness, would
have successfully made good its way across the vast continent of China, if at the
outset all the members of the Mission, including Mr. Margary, had kept
together, and Colonel Horace Browne, instead of delaying, had pushed
steadily on his way from Bhamo, which, I think, by patience and tact might
have been safely done. Once in communication with any of the responsible
officers of the Chinese Government all petty differences and opposition would
have ceased; in the same way as occurred with the former expedition, when
Major Sladen had succeeded in placing himself in direct intercourse with the
Panthay Governor of Momein.

The Mission had certainly not the difficulties to contend with at first as the
previous one had, and there appears to me to have been no adequate cause for

To return to the story of my own administration. In the beginning of 1869, shortly after the return of Major Sladen from Momein, there was a change in the government of India. Sir John, the present Lord Lawrence, retired from the Viceroyalty, and was succeeded by the late Lord Mayo.

I had, and I have always had, the greatest admiration for the sterling qualities of the famous ruler of the Punjab, who has been generally regarded as the saviour of India. I have always had the utmost respect for the large and varied experiences which he was enabled to bring to bear upon all Indian questions. But his heart was in the Punjab; he never cared much for Burma; he never thoroughly grasped the political relations between British Burma and Upper Burma. He always appeared to be looking at Burma through Punjabi spectacles; to be of opinion that the present King of Burma was a strong potentate like Runjeet Sing. Indeed, in my humble opinion, the province of British Burma, prior to the advent

---

delay, as pony and bullock carriage, porters and guides, had apparently all been prepared beforehand in readiness for the expedition. By pushing on, too, the expedition would probably have anticipated the assembly of the large rabble of young men and boys who fired over the heads of the expedition, and caused its return (see Anderson's "Mandalay to Momein," pp. 430–433). This attack was evidently *well understood by the Burmese escort*, and could only have been intended as a sham one to induce the return of the Mission; for, after all the heavy firing, said to have continued over a considerable period, the only casualties reported in Colonel Browne's numerous party were three men slightly wounded, and those non-combatants.

of Lord Mayo, had never received its full share of
attention from the Government of India, since the
days of the great Marquis of Dalhousie.

Accordingly, on Lord Mayo's arrival in India,
I attempted to enlist his sympathies in my own
province. I initiated a correspondence with this
view, and I venture to reprint it in the present
place. It will be interesting to all who are familiar
with the life and career of that lamented statesman.
It throws a favourable light upon the character of
Lord Mayo, and serves at the same time to
illustrate the then state of British Burma.

"RANGOON, *March* 10*th*, 1869.

"MY LORD,

"I had hoped to have had the pleasure of
meeting your lordship on your arrival in Calcutta,
and suggested to His Excellency Sir John Lawrence
the advisability of my proceeding there for the
purpose, but His Excellency was of opinion that
having regard to the state of the Burman Court I
had better defer my visit, until it should please your
Excellency to desire my attendance. I write now,
however, to express to your lordship my congratulations on your occupation of the office of Governor-
General and Viceroy, and to ask of you a favourable
consideration for the Administration over which I
have the honour to preside.

" There were matters connected with the present
and future condition of the province which I ventured
to think might be more satisfactorily represented to
your Excellency in person. Some of these will in
the course of official correspondence come before
your lordship, and will, I trust, go far to interest you
in this outlying province.

" The peculiar geographical position of British
Burma, the characteristics of its people, and its
political connection with the empire from which it
was obtained, all go to make the province deserving
of individual attention. Its system of taxation
differs from that of any Administration in the peninsula, and rated on population its revenue is more
than double that provided by any province or pre-
sidency. Its isolated position, and the enormous
yearly accession of a population coming from the
distracted country of the King of Ava, are conditions
which affect the consolidation of our rule here,
nowhere seen in India proper—while the rapid
strides the province has made in material progress
under British Government, have forced on us all
the anomalies to be seen in the sudden spring of a
capable country into extraordinary commercial and
producing activity.

"British Burma can neither be judged or managed
by rule of thumb. The Burmese portion of its inhabitants (who are the most numerous and important),

are prosperous; but they are a sensitive and
impulsive nationality, with quick feelings, crafty,
fickle, and with little depth of attachment. The
hitherto harassed state of their country has destroyed—if it ever in historical times existed—any
faith in the stability of existing rulers. The use of
capital is to them unknown, and in these generations,
at least, they will scarcely realise (or at least, will
not practically illustrate in this particular) the gain
to be derived from the permanency of a strong
authority. Apart from its local peculiarities and
provincial interest, British Burma has other and
strong grounds for attention. It promises to furnish
a highway to China, and to me the day does not
seem far distant when this question may force itself
on Government with extreme urgency.

"The extraordinary use of the Western States of
America, the hot haste with which the Government
are pushing on connection with the western sea-
board, and the predominance they have lately
advanced in Chinese diplomatic relations with other
Courts, all point to a determination on the part of
America to secure, if possible, the command of the
Chinese market. The present obstacles of difficult
communication they are in a fair way of solving, and
there will then remain the necessity of adapting their
exports to the Chinese requirements.

"Will this be possible without running us so close

as vitally to affect our commercial superiority? Further, will they long stand the commanding position we derive from our opium exports, and the hold we thus have on the Exchange? It is here the question touches India in a tender point. The derangement of our opium revenue means a most serious crisis in Indian finance, and were American interference to affect our sea-borne opium, the routes through this province would become of the highest Imperial importance. In the case of such a contingency, and for collateral reasons, in themselves sufficiently advantageous, I should consider it highly prudent on Imperial grounds that we should be in a position to substitute a western ingress to China, for the present seaboard approach, destined to be disproportionately shared, if not entirely absorbed, by America.

"If I am right in attributing so much importance to the western through route to China, it should strongly colour our policy towards the Court of Ava; but, to be of avail, it must be deliberately and seriously entertained and firmly carried out. We should, in my opinion, prosecute the exploration of the routes so as thoroughly to master their capabilities.

"There is at present before Government a proposition for the construction of a railway within our own territories from Rangoon to Prome. It is a self-contained scheme, of commercial and political importance, standing on its own merits irrespective of its prospective extension beyond our frontier, or of the adoption of any other through route to China.

" Trusting that sanction may be accorded to this, nothing would more happily inaugurate its commencement than the presence of your Excellency ; should you find it feasible with the many urgent demands upon your lordship's time to visit this province, I hope your Excellency would find signs of satisfactory progress.   Your arrival would afford encouragement to the official classes, and your lordship would realize the vast commercial interests which are yearly extending for the benefit of the State, as well as of those engaged in them.

" I have the honour to remain,

" Your lordship's obedient servant,

" ALBERT FYTCHE.

" The Right Hon. the EARL OF MAYO, K.T.

" &c., &c., &c."

" SIMLA, *April* 30, 1869.

" SIR,

" In answer to your letter of the 10th March I have to thank you for your congratulations upon my assuming the office of Governor-General of India.

" I can assure you that the affairs of the province

of British Burma occupy much of my attention, and that I look on the position of that province with the greatest interest.

" I consider that the rapid advance which the country has made under our government is one of the most satisfactory evidences of the success of British rule in India.

" I have already sanctioned with much pleasure your proposal for placing an Agent at Bhamo, and I shall look with much anxiety to the result of his residence at that place. I shall always be glad to hear from you upon the subject of the communication with Western China, but it will be necessary to proceed with great care in that matter, lest any precipitancy should destroy or indefinitely delay attempts made in that direction at their outset.

" I have not yet received Captain Sladen's report, and regret to hear that the delay has been occasioned by that officer's ill health.

" The project of a line of railway from Rangoon to Prome has already engaged my attention, and I consider that as British Burma is so far removed from India, uniformity of gauge is not necessary, and that therefore the construction of lines of a lighter and cheaper kind, and of a narrower gauge might with advantage be considered.

" I have also, after much consideration, approved

of the plan for encouraging primary education through the medium of the Buddhist monasteries of Burma. I hope that that experiment will be carried out with prudence and vigour, and I shall look with the greatest interest to the result.

"I hope I may be able, consistently with the discharge of my other duties, to visit Burma at no very distant date, and I can assure you I look forward to the possibility of such an event with great pleasure.

"I am, yours faithfully,
"MAYO.

"General A. FYTCHE, C.S.I.
      "&c., &c., &c."

"SIMLA, *June* 11, 1869.

"MY DEAR GENERAL,

"From certain expressions I have observed in some of your letters, and in those of Major Sladen, it occurs to me that it is possible that the views of the officers of your Commission as regards British policy in Burma, do not altogether agree with those entertained by the Government of India. Lest, therefore, there should be the slightest misapprehension on this most important subject, I think it my duty to inform you that I am wholly opposed to any interference in the affairs of foreign states, that can be by honourable means avoided. The future annexation of Burma, or any of its adjacent states, is not an event which I either contemplate or desire ; on the contrary, I should view with extreme regret and disapproval any course of action that would impose on the British Government the necessity of occupation, or of assuming, even in a temporary manner, the government of any of the states lying adjacent to the province now in your charge. While firmly but prudently insisting on the maintenance of all treaty obligations, and on the protection of our trade, and avoiding any act that would lower British influence, or compromise British interests, you will understand that it is the desire of the Government of India that the *status quo* as regards the relations between it and the kingdom of Burma should be strictly maintained.

"I am glad to hear that Major Sladen is so much better. I fully recognize the difficult position in which he is placed, and the uncertain character of the people with whom he has to deal. But you must never cease to impress on him the necessity of caution in all his proceedings, especially in the delicate matter of the establishment of his new court of extra-territorial jurisdiction.

"Though I am anxious that the Agency at Bhamo should be opened at a suitable time, and without any unnecessary delay, I am of opinion that, while any unusual excitement prevails among the Burmese population, it is not desirable that Captain

Strover should proceed to that place, and you should be perfectly satisfied that he can do so without danger, before you authorize his departure for Mandalay.

" I am, yours faithfully,

" MAYO.

"General A. FYTCHE, C.S.I.
    " &c., &c.,&c."

" RANGOON, *June* 29, 1869.

" MY LORD,

"I beg to acknowledge the receipt of your letter of 11th inst., containing your Excellency's views and wishes on the course to be pursued towards the Court of Ava, and the states lying adjacent to British Burma.

"Your Excellency may confidently depend on my carrying out the policy prescribed ; in fact, it is the policy that I have pursued from the commencement of my taking charge of this province, and which the whole tenor of my correspondence with the Government of India and Lord Lawrence shows.

"Burmese character, and the underhand and crooked policy of the Court of Ava is such, that it is best moulded and worked upon by the unmistakeable assumption of firmness, and use of straightforward language on the part of those who wish to influence them, and we must—as your Lordship remarks—firmly but prudently insist upon the maintenance of all treaty obligations. The King and his Court are apt to judge us, not so much by our real power, as by our concessions and endurance of wrongs, and our yielding, even in the most trivial matters, is at once looked upon as a sign of weakness.

"The pressure from the mercantile community at home, as well as in this country, will continue unceasingly until we have free and unrestricted trade, not only with Upper Burma, but what is still of much greater importance, with China, and both of these can be obtained without the danger of annexation being thrust upon us, if the terms of the treaty I concluded with the Court of Ava in October, 1867, are carried out in their integrity.

"My belief still continues that there need be no fear of collision with the Court of Ava during the present King's lifetime, such as should require us to act hostilely towards him—but a change in the occupant of the throne is a contingency that may not be overlooked. At such a time the amount and duration of the anarchy, and disorganization and stoppage of all trades that will occur in Upper Burma, will depend greatly on the promptitude with which we might use our preponderating influence, and the weight of that influence would tell in a ratio corresponding with the extent to which it had

previously been acknowledged. The customs collection on the trade of the port of Rangoon increased during the *past year more than fifty per
cent.*, and the one per cent. duty leviable under
the treaty on all goods declared for *export to
Upper Burma and overland to China, upwards of
1,000 per cent. over the preceding one*, every preparation should therefore be made and precaution used,
that such a valuable and marvellously increasing
trade receives no sudden check. Individually, I
would assure your lordship of the certain absence
of any desire on my part to push matters to ex-
tremities ; on the contrary, my natural inclination
would be to preserve Upper Burma intact, and on
friendly terms as long as possible. I have spent
many years of my life amongst the Burmese, and
whilst aware of the many defects in their character,
I am not blind to many good qualities they possess,
and I should be sorry indeed to see their nationality
extinguished, although the force of circumstances
require them, in their own interests, to yield to our
more advanced civilization.

"I shall not fail to again press upon Major Sladen
the views expressed by your Excellency, and that
His Majesty, the King of Burma should be assured
of our good faith, and of the friendly disposition of
the British Government towards him.

"Captain Strover is still at Rangoon, of which he

is Town Magistrate, and he will not proceed to
Bhamo until I am assured that no danger will
result from his doing so.

       " I am your lordship's obedient servant,

               " ALBERT FYTCHE.

" The Right Hon. the Earl of MAYO, K.T.,
      " &c.. &c., &c."

In the latter part of 1869 I had the opportunity
long desired of discussing the affairs of Burma
personally with Lord Mayo. His Royal Highness
the Duke of Edinburgh was paying a visit to
India ; and the heads of the several local governments were entertained for some weeks at the
Government House at Calcutta. Under these
circumstances I had many conversations with Lord
Mayo, sufficient to impress me deeply with his
powers as a statesman, and his capacity as a
Viceroy. I recall with much pleasure the thought-
ful interest he took in all matters connected with
Burma ; and his great social qualities and urbanity
as a host. Death allows a survivor to pay a
tribute to departed greatness, without the risk of
a charge of adulation.

On one occasion I had the honour of presenting
an address to his lordship from the European
community in Burma. I append his Excellency's
reply :—

" GENTLEMEN,

" I have received with great satisfaction your address of the 11th December, which was presented to me by General Fytche, the Chief Commissioner of British Burma, on his arrival in Calcutta.

" The growing prosperity of British Burma is to me an object of special interest. There is no portion of Her Majesty's Indian dominions where the fruits of good government, and the results of British energy and industry, have been so rapidly developed.

" I thank you most sincerely for the expression of the desire that I should visit British Burma, and can assure you that on the earliest occasion that public duty will permit, I shall not fail to comply with the wish that is conveyed to me in your address.

" MAYO."

A melancholy interest appertains to this document. It was the first announcement of a visit, which was delayed until after my departure from Burma, and had such a melancholy ending. I need say no more. The sad death of Lord Mayo at the Andamans will never be forgotten by the present generation.

Besides the treaty concluded with the King of

Burma, and the despatch of the Mission to Western China, there were other important measures carried out during my Administration. A mixed Court of Civil Justice was established at Mandalay, for the trial of cases in which British and Burmese subjects were both concerned.

A railway was proposed and planned between Rangoon and Prome. The country was surveyed, but the rails were not laid down until after I had left the province. Embankments were constructed, and large tracts of swamp and marsh were thereby converted into culturable territory which brings forth teeming harvests. Three new light-houses were also constructed under the able superintendence of Colonel Alexander Fraser, C.B., of the Royal Engineers. Jails and Civil Courts were constructed at every important station in British Burma, in lieu of the miserable huts which had been previously used for such purposes.

The trade and revenues of the province largely increased. One of the subjects which I was much interested in was the education of the rising genera tion of native Burmese. The measures carried out in this direction are closely associated with the Buddhist religion. I will therefore deal with it in the next chapter.

I might dwell upon many other matters; but as an official memorandum on my Administration of

British Burma is entered in the Appendix * for the perusal of those who may feel interested in this matter, I will avoid laying myself open to a possible charge of egotism by pursuing the subject further. I trust I may be pardoned, however, for quoting here some extracts from a speech delivered by me just before leaving Rangoon, in which I endeavoured to sum up the work accomplished during my administration :—

"It will perhaps be expected from me on the present occasion, to glance very briefly at the chief measures of my administration throughout the last four years, during which I have been Chief Commissioner.

"When I first took charge of this province in the early part of 1867, British Burma had made great progress under my predecessor Sir A. Phayre. Pegu had enormously increased in wealth and population under British rule, and Rangoon had been converted from a swampy village into a large commercial city. But still much remained to be done then, and I am sorry to say that there is still much to be done now. The King of Burma had just refused to conclude a treaty. No steamers had reached Bhamo, and only four merchant steamers had visited Mandalay. Our trade beyond the

* Appendix G.

frontier was almost nil. The province was without roads, and the idea of a railway had scarcely been ventilated. The officers of the commission were worse paid than in any province of India, although expense of living here was far higher.

"The police were also ill paid, and were consequently untrustworthy and inefficient. The gaols and civil courts were mere huts, whilst the public offices at Rangoon were in embryo.

"If I now venture to notice the progress which has been made during the last four years, I must, in the first instance, express my best thanks to the officers of the Commission, by whom I have been most ably served, and without whose cordial assistance I could have achieved but little. I beg specially to notice the services of the Commissioners of Divisions, Colonels Ardagh, Brown, Stevenson and Ryan, those of my late and present secretaries, and the officers of the Commission and Police generally ; of the latter I must not omit to mention the names of Majors Duncan and Hamilton, and Mr. Doyle.

"In the first year of my administration I concluded a treaty with the King of Burma which has led to a large increase of trade, and established our relations with the Court of Ava on a friendly footing. An expedition has been sent under Major Sladen, which has penetrated far beyond Bhamo to the borders of China ; and a new trade is springing up, which, I trust, in the course of a few years, will carry British manufactures to Yunan, whilst bringing down the commodities of Western China to Rangoon. We are now in weekly steam communication with Mandalay, monthly communication with Bhamo, and the voyage to Bhamo is no longer an expedition of danger, but a pleasant holiday trip.

"A complete system of imperial roads has been planned, and are in course of construction, and a line of railway has been surveyed between Rangoon and Prome. On my recommendation the pay of the officers of the Commission has been raised to the rates which prevail in other provinces. Our police have received higher salaries in the lower grades, and I am happy to say that during the last year there has been a decrease throughout the province of 27 per cent. in violent crime. New gaols and civil courts have been constructed at every important station, and the public offices on the Strand are an ornament to Rangoon.

"Three more new light-houses have been constructed under the able superintendence of Colonel Fraser at the Krishna Shoal, China Bukheer, and Eastern-grove; and in mentioning Colonel Fraser's name, I have to thank him for the great support and zealous assistance he has rendered me on every occasion, and to congratulate him on the completion of that magnificent series of light-houses which protect the commerce of our coasts, as well as the other works which he has either completed or are already in progress.

"A scheme for the general education of native school-masters and school-mistresses, is in course of establishment at Rangoon.

"There are, however, two objects to which I have specially given my attention, and which I trust will ever be borne in mind by my successors. I allude to the encouragement of immigration, and the reclamation of culturable land. The crying want of British Burma is population, and I have lost no opportunity to encourage immigration. At the same time large tracts of culturable land have been re-claimed from encroachment of rivers by a system of embankments, which I am glad to say have effected the object in view.

"But I need not weary you, gentlemen, with further details. I cannot, however, avoid thanking the important and growing non-official community of this province for the cordial support I have received on all occasions, and for the enlightened public opinion with which I have been favoured. If I have failed in any respect, it may be remembered that all of us are fallible, but I hope and trust that I have always endeavoured to do my duty to the best of my power. In conclusion, I beg to thank you, one and all, for the honour you have done me on the present occasion. Whether I return to Burma or otherwise, I shall always rejoice to hear of its prosperity, and treasure up pleasant memories of the country and its people, and of the many friends who honour me on this present occasion, as well as of those who may be absent from a variety of causes, and I would fain express the hope that long after I am personally forgotten, the memory of my administration may not have wholly passed away.'

CHAPTER IV.

BUDDHISM AND EDUCATION IN BURMA.

Shamanism the ancient religion of Burma.—Adoration of nats and other spirits.—Three religions preceded Buddhism in India.—Buddhism a widespread religion.—Propagated by persuasion alone.—The Buddhas previous to Gautama.—The Jātaka fables.—Birth and parentage of Gautama.—His miraculous conception.—Education of Gautama.—Gautama's four visions.—He deserts his palace and assumes the garb of an ascetic.—His trials and temptations in the wilderness.—He becomes a Buddha.—The sacred Bo-tree.—Gautama proceeds towards Benares to preach his doctrine.—He visits his father.—Attempts on his life.—Punishment of Dèwadat.—Gautama's death.—His funeral.—Gautama's relics.—The Shwé-dagon pagoda at Rangoon.—The three Synods.—The Pitakatayan or Buddhist scriptures.—Powers of memory of Buddhist priests.—Two Buddhist missionaries arrive at Thatún.—Buddhagosa.—Talaings received their religion and alphabet from Ceylon.—The Burmese from the Talaings.—Karma and Nirvāna described.—Buddhism and Brahmanism compared.—Dāna or alms-giving.—Purity of Buddhist ethics.—Singular analogy of Buddhistic rites and observances to those of Romish Christianity.—Early Roman Catholic missionaries in the East.—Their opinions regarding Buddhism.—Buddhism existent in the western world previous to the birth of our Saviour.—Gautama a saint in the Roman calendar.—Phongyees.—Rules of the Order.—The Novitiate.—Ordination.—Celibacy.—Diet.—The Habit.—The Order of Nuns.—Funerals.—Monasteries.—Education in Burma.—Monastic and lay schools.—System of education lately adopted by the British Government.—Difficulties regarding it.—How overcome.—Success of the system.

DURING the progress of this work, I have attempted to give brief accounts of the politics, literature, art, and customs, and habits of the people of Burma. Properly to appreciate and understand a people, however, it is necessary to have, at least, some

knowledge of the religion they profess.   I purpose,
therefore, if it be but for ready reference, to give
here a short description of Buddhism *—the old
moral ,and humanizing doctrine of the Ascetic of
Kapilavastu.   In ancient times, the religion of the
people of Burma was Shamanism ; in common with
the great Nomadic races of High Asia, of which
they are an offset.   This debased system of spirit
worship has been superseded by Buddhism ; but it
still lingers in the land, in the form of adoration and
dread of nats† or déwas, which order of beings

* In the brief sketch of Buddhism given in this chapter, I have selected
many of my arguments and leading points from Bigandet's "Legends of
Gautama ; " Hardy's " Eastern Monachism," and " Legends and Theories of
the Buddhists ; " " Buddhism " by Rhys Davids ; Wassilief's " Der Buddhismus ; " Max Müller's "Chips ; " " Journal Asiatique," Mohl, 1856 ; and
other eminent authorities on the subject.

† The term *nat* is no doubt synonymous with Marco Polo's *Natigay*.   In
speaking of the religion of the Tatars he says :—" This is the fashion of their
religion.   They say there is a Most High God of Heaven, whom they worship
daily with thurible and incense, but they pray to Him only for health of mind
or body.   But they have a certain other god of theirs called Natigay, and
they say he is the god of the earth, who watches over their children, cattle,
and crops.   They show him great worship and honour, and every man hath a
figure of him in his house, made of felt and cloth; and they make, also, in the
same manner images of his wife and children."   This account agrees generally
with what we are told, too, of the original Shamanism of the Tunguses, which
recognizes a Supreme Power over all, and a small number of potent spirits
called Ongot.—Yule's "Marco Polo," v. ii., pp. 224-25.

The figures of Natigay, as illustrated in Yule's work, resemble in a remarkable degree the nats which are to be seen in Burma, carved in wood.

Sir Arthur Phayre, who is intimately acquainted with all that relates to
Buddhism, remarks in a note on nats as follows :— "The modern Burmese
acknowledge the existence of certain beings, which, for want of a better term,
we call 'almost spiritual beings.'   They apply to them the term nat.   Now
according to Burmese notions, there are two distinct bodies or systems of these
creatures.   The one is a regularly constituted company, if I may say so, of
which Thagya-Meng is the chief.   Most undoubtedly that body of nat was

have been adopted into the Buddhist system, and play a conspicuous part in the affairs of this world. This worship, though in opposition with the more exalted and purer doctrines of primitive Buddhism, is nevertheless, countenanced by the Buddhist priesthood, and a large portion of the worship of the Burmese, from the highest to the lowest ranks, consists in the performance of superstitious ceremonies, and offerings made for propitiating evil nats, and obtaining favours and temporal advantages from good ones.

The habitations of these nats are situated in the

unknown to the Burmese until they become Buddhists. Those are the real *dêwa* or *dêwata*.

"But the other set of nats are the creatures of the indigenous system, existing among all the wild tribes bordering Burma. The acknowledgment of those beings constitutes *their only worship.* On these grounds, I consider that the Burmese acknowledged and worshipped such beings, before they were converted to Buddhism.

"Now if they acknowledged such beings, they, no doubt, had a name for them, similar in general import to the 'fairy,' 'elf,' and so on, among the inhabitants of Britain, for beings of a quasi-spiritual nature. I may observe there is a complete analogy in the state of Burmese belief in the existence of such beings, and that which prevailed formerly in Europe, and some remnants of which may be found even now existing among the uneducated. I mean that before the Anglo-Saxon tribes were converted to Christianity, the belief in fairies and elves was universal. With Christianity came a belief in a different order of spiritual beings, and with that a new name, derived from the Latin—angel. This is somewhat analogous to the state of things among the Burmese before and after their conversion to Buddhism.

"But to return to the Burmese. They, when they received Buddhism, appear to have generally retained their vernacular name for the beings called in Pali, *dêwa.* Why this should be done is certainly not apparent. Why have the English and all the Teutonic nations retained the ancient names Evil and Spirits, though they adopted with Christianity a new term for good spirits generally? I allude to the term *devil*, which, there is no doubt, is philologically connected with that Pali word *dêwa* or *dêva.*"

six lower heavens beyond the moon, rising in succession one above the other, and which, together
with the abode of man, and the four states of
punishment, form the eleven seats of the passions.*

Nats are endowed with forms of such ethereal
nature, as to be able to transport themselves with
the utmost rapidity to our sublunary world ; and
every mountain, tree, town, village, or other object
of importance, is supposed to be under the protection
of, and presided over by one of them. The Burmese
also believe that there are spirits peculiar to our

* "In the Buddhist system there are thirty-one seats or abodes assigned to
all beings, which are disposed on an immense scale, extending from the bottom
of the earth to an incommensurable height above it. At the foot we find the
four states of punishment. Next comes the abode of man ; above it are the
six seats of nats. These eleven seats are called the seats of passion, or concupiscence, because the beings residing therein are still subject to the influence
of passion, though not to an equal degree.

"Above the abodes of nats are sixteen seats, called Rupa, disposed perpendicularly one above the other to an incalculable height. The inhabitants of
those regions are called Brahmas, or perfect. They have freed themselves
from concupiscence, and almost all other passions, but still retain some
affection for matter and material things. Hence the denomination of Rupa,
or matter, given to these seats. The remaining portion of the scale is occupied
by the four seats called Arupa, or immaterials, for the beings inhabiting them
are entirely delivered from all passions. They have, as it were, broken
asunder even the smallest ties that would attach them to this material world.
They have reached the summit of perfection ; one step farther, and they enter
into the state of Niebban or Nirvâna, the consummation, according to
Buddhists, of all perfection. To sum up all the above in a few words,—there
are four states of punishment. The seat of man is a place of probation and
trial ; the six abodes of nats are places of sensual pleasures and enjoyments.
In the sixteen seats of Rupa are to be met those beings whose delights are of a
more refined and almost purely spiritual nature, though retaining as yet some
slight affection for matter. In the four seats of Arupa are located those
beings who are wholly disentangled from material affections, who delight but
in the sublimest contemplation, soaring, as it were, in the boundless regions
of pure spiritualism."—Bigandet, p. 5.

earth, such as beloos, witches, with powers similar
to those of mediæval Europe, and priethas. The
beloo is an ogre who haunts forests and solitary
places, and feeds on human flesh. It has the face
of a man with eyes of a deep red hue, and body of
so subtle a nature as not to project a shadow. The
prietha is a being in a state of punishment on
account of sins committed in former existences, and
is doomed to live in the recesses of uninhabited
mountains, smarting under the pangs of unsatiated
hunger. Its body, and particularly its stomach, is
of gigantic dimensions, whilst its mouth is so small,
that the point of a needle can scarcely enter it. A
remnant of tree worship exists in the veneration
bestowed on the Bó-tree (*ficus religiosa*), which will
be remarked upon hereafter.

We know that at least three religions preceded
Buddhism in India : the wild devil-worship of the
Aborigines, the religion of the Aryan invaders as
represented in the Vedic hymns, and Brahminism,
with its distinctive features of priestly mediation,
caste, and pantheism.* In fact, Buddhism has been
described " as little more than a revival of the
coarser descriptions of the aboriginal races, purified
and refined by the application of Aryan morality,
and elevated by doctrines borrowed from the intel-
lectual superiority of the Aryan races." " As a part

* "Fairburn's Studies," p. 130.

of the reform which Gautama introduced, ancestral worship was abolished, and the sepulchral tumulus became the depository of relics of saints. Serpent worship was repressed, and its sister faith of tree worship elevated to the first rank." *

Buddhism is the most wide-spread religion now existing on the earth, and one which in its various branches, according to statistical tables lately published by Mr. Rhys Davids, holds beneath its sway the minds of 500,000,000 of human beings, or forty per cent. of the estimated population of the world. "The yellow robe has never been covered by a coat of mail, nor the voice of Sramana been heard amongst the din of battle." During an existence of nearly 2500 years, the doctrines of Gautama have been propagated by persuasion alone, and "though Buddhists themselves have been frequently persecuted even to destruction, no instance is on record of a religious war having been waged by them, or an attempt made to spread their faith by force in any part of the world." †

Previous to the time of Gautama, the founder of the present Buddhist system, twenty-four Buddhas are said to have appeared, twenty of whom made their appearance in different previous successive worlds,‡ and four during the present world; of

---

* Fergusson's "Tree and Serpent Worship," p. 62.   † *Ibid.*, p. 63.

‡ The duration of a revolution of nature, or the time required for the formation of a world, its existence and destruction, is divided into four periods. The

these latter Gautama was the last Buddha. There is still one more Buddha to appear, Aramāitrīya, the Buddha of kindness, who will again " open the door of Niebban to man," and he closes the present dispensation.

Gautama is thus represented to be only one of a long series of Buddhas that have appeared at intervals on the earth. Such Buddhas, indeed, may be said to have been known from the very beginning of things, only, in the Buddhist imagination, there is no beginning and no ending. The details of their teaching and lives strongly resemble those of the last Buddha, and as Orientals are great adepts at dovetailing the past with repetitions of the present —mapping out its eternity, as it were, into vast cycles, strongly resembling the present one—the tradition of their former legendary Buddhas may possibly have been invented since Gautama's time, with the intention of giving more extension

---

fourth period, or that which begins with the apparition of man on the earth, until its destruction, is divided into sixty-four parts, called Antrakaps. During one Antrakap, the life of man increases gradually from ten years to an almost innumerable number of years ; having reached its maximum of duration, it decreases slowly to its former short duration of ten years. We live at present in that second part of an Antrakap when the life of man is on the decline and decrease.

Matter is eternal ; but its organization, and all the changes attending it, are caused and regulated by certain laws co-eternal with it. Both matter and the laws that act upon it are self-existing, independent from the action and control of any being. As soon as a system of worlds is constituted, Buddhists boldly assert and perseveringly maintain that the laws of *Karma*, or those of merits and demerits, are the sole agents that regulate and control both the physical and moral world.—See Bigandet, p. 22.

and solidity to the basis whereupon his system is founded.

The religion of Gautama is to last 5000 years, of which 2420 have now elapsed. Buddhas appear after long intervals of time. Gautama, before attaining to the state of a Buddha, passed through 550 * different phases of existence, at one time re-

---

* The history of these 550 separate existences (called by the Burmese *dzats*) is contained in the Jātaka, the tenth division of the Sutta Pitaka, or second book of the sacred canon of the Buddhists. They form a valuable *corpus fabularum*, or compilation of folk-lore current in the East in ancient times. Many of the stories are substantially the same as those to be found in Æsop and Phædrus, whose fables strongly resemble Oriental rather than original Greek compositions. Their tales, too, are imbued with Asiatic manners and customs, and the animals mentioned in them, such as monkeys and peacocks, &c., are only found in Eastern countries. We may therefore infer that the fables found under their names, if not taken from the Jātaka, have at least an Eastern origin, and found their way to Europe, first amongst the Greeks, and next reached the Western nations through La Fontaine and others.

The Jātaka stories, however, were not retailed at convivial parties, as is said by Aristophanes to have been customary with the "drolleries of Æsop" (Αἰσωπικὰ γελοῖα); but are supposed to have been narrated by Gautama himself to his disciples, and others, in order to make them acquainted with the events that happened to him when he was passing through the different phases of metempsychosis. Almost all of them end in showing that the personage who played the most important and praiseworthy *rôle* was Gautama himself, and those who befriended or assisted him were now his most favourite disciples and hearers, whilst those who had opposed him were the heretics and unbelievers of that day, particularly the wicked Déwadat.

My readers will recognise the following story taken from the Jātaka. On one occasion, when Gautama was speaking to his disciples regarding the conduct of Déwadat, he said, "Once when I was a stork, he was a lion. In his haste to eat, a bone stuck in his throat. He implored my assistance, and, with my long neck and beak, I took the bone from his throat. When I asked him for the reward he had promised me for the service, he answered it was quite enough that he had allowed me to withdraw my head safe from his gullet."

The "Thousand And One Nights," commonly called "The Arabian Nights' Entertainments," which are such favourite stories in Europe, are also of Indian origin, written in Sanskrit, and afterwards translated into Persian and then into Arabic. They are called in Sanskrit, *Vrihatkathá*.

ceiving birth as a nat, at others, that of a bird or other animal,* gradually accumulating at each birth a greater degree of merit, and gravitating towards the centre of matchless perfection. In the birth in which they become Buddha, they are always of woman born, and pass through infancy and youth like ordinary beings, until at a prescribed age they abandon the world and retire to the wilderness, where, after a course of ascetic observance, at the foot of a tree they receive the supernatural powers with which the office is endowed. But their greatest distinction and highest glory is, that they receive the wisdom by which they can direct sentient beings to the path that leads to Niebban or Nirwâna, the cessation of existence.†

Gautama ‡ is said to have been born on a Tuesday, the day of the full moon of the month of May, in the year answering to 623 B.C.,§ and was the

---

* According to Buddhistic notions, animals are beings in a state of punishment, differing from man, not in nature, but in merits. They are supposed to possess reason to a certain extent.

† "Monachism," p. v.

‡ Gautama is the name by which the last Buddha is usually known to southern Buddhists, and that of Sakya-Muni, the Sakya Sage, to northern Buddhists. He has other names, but they are, properly speaking, titles, such as Siddârtha, said to have been given to him five days after his birth, and meaning he whose objects have been accomplished ; Sâkya-Singha, the lion of the Sâkya tribe ; Loka-nâtha, the Lord of the world ; Dharma-raja, the King of righteousness ; Jina, the conqueror ; Suttha, the teacher, &c.

The southern Buddhists are inhabitants of Burma, Ceylon, Siam, and Anam ; and the northern of China, Japan, Tibet, and Nepaul. The sacred books of the former are written in Pali, and the latter in Sanskrit. The works in Pali are considered the most reliable and complete.

§ The Chinese give the year 1029 B.C. as the date of the birth of Gautama, son of Saddhódana, chief of the tribe of Sákyas, and King of Kapilavastu,* or Kapilawot, a small principality situated on the banks of the river Rohini, the modern Kohāna, about a hundred miles north-east of Benares.   His mother was Máiya, daugher of Suprabuddha, chief of the neighbouring and kindred tribe of Kolyans.   Both tribes were of pure Aryan race, and branches of the Suryavansi, or line of the Sun.

Many stories are told of the miraculous and mystical conception and birth of Gautama, and also of his precocious wisdom.   His mother, who had lived to the age of 57 years without bearing a child, after seven days of fasting, dreams† she is conveyed

---

and the year 951 B.C. for that of his death ; but they admit that the religion was not introduced into China until 1000 years later.   De Guignes, Klaproth, and Sir William Jones adopt from the Chinese nearly similar dates for these events.   A comparison of many epochs, however, has established in India the date 628 B.C. for the year of the birth of Gautama ; and 543 B.C. for that of his decease.   This difference of some 400 years has led some to believe the Chinese era refers to an anterior Buddha.   Correct dates are so far important, as the extraordinary similitude in many parts of the Buddhist doctrine, and of the books, and rituals, and forms, and institutions of this religion, with those of Romish Christianity, which was remarked by the Jesuits who visited Tibet in the seventeeth century, and even by Father Rubruquis in the thirteenth, might lead to the belief that they had been borrowed entirely from this latter, if the chain of evidence that established their greater antiquity were less complete.—Princep's " Tibet, Tatary, and Mongolia," p. 145.

* The village of Nagara has been identified by General Cunningham with Kapilavastu, and Gautama is still the name of the Rajput Chief.—Cunningham's " Ancient Geography of India," vol. i., p. 417.

† In the East, miracles are generally made to precede the birth of remarkable men.   The life of Daghda, the mother of Zoroaster, the founder of the religion of the Parsees, is said to have been so spotless as to attract the favour of the Deity, who foretold to her the greatness of Zoroaster while yet in the womb, through the medium of dreams ; and the birth was attended with many miracu-

on her couch by four nat princes to their heavenly abode, and placed in a grotto on a mountain slope. While there she sees the future Buddha in the form of a beautiful white elephant* descending from the side of an opposite hill, who enters the cave, and after walking three times round her couch, opens her right side, and conceals himself in her womb. On her relating this dream to her husband, sixty-four learned Brahmans are sent for to expound it.

lous circumstances, calculated to make the persons who saw it adopt and spread the belief in the divine mission of the new-born infant. Many of these miracles have found their way into classical writings, and Pliny mentions that Zoroaster laughed on the day on which he was born, and that his brain palpitated so violently as to repel the hand when placed upon it. The life of the Persian prophet was nearly co-etaneous with that of Gautama. He was born 589 B.C., and died 513 B.C.—See " Hist. Nat." vii. c. xvi. ; H. Lord's " Account of the Parsees in India," c. iii.

Grote, in his " History of Greece," vol. iii., p. 85, says "that the century between 620 and 500 B.C. appears to have been remarkable for the first diffusion and potent influence of distinct religious brotherhoods, mystic rites, and expiatory ceremonies, none of which find any recognition in the Homeric epic." This was the age of Gautama and Zoroaster. The Greeks were generally free from the ascetic element, with one exception. It is said that Lycurgus in his wanderings, penetrated as far as India ; and there are many points of resemblance between the precepts promulgated by Gautama and the laws of the Spartans. " The submission of the young was strictly enforced in the code of the Spartan legislator, and great respect was paid to the aged ; there was a community of property ; nearly all distinctions of rank were abolished ; the education, dress, and food of all classes were the same ; the diet was of the simplest kind ; the use of gold and silver was forbidden ; and all were taught to endure the greatest hardships unmoved. The young were set free from the restrictions under which they had previously laboured when twenty years of age, the same age at which the Sramana novice was admitted to ordination. But the Spartan annihilated self that he might become a patriot ; the Buddhist ascetic, that he might become non-existent."—" The Voice of the Past," R. S. Hardy, p. 353.

* This form is said to have been deliberately chosen by the future Buddha, because it was the form indicated by an angel who had in a previous birth been one of the Rishis, the mythical poets of the Rig Veda !—Foucaux, p. 52.

Their interpretation is, that the Queen will bear a
son who will live among men, and become a Cha-
kawati, or mighty ruler, whose sway all the human
race will acknowledge ; or, withdrawing from the
world, he will become a recluse, and in that condition, after disentangling himself from the miseries
of existence, will become a Buddha, and remove
the veils of ignorance and sin from the world.   A
holy man, like Simeon, also bears witness to the
child's divine mission, and laments that age will
prevent his hearing his doctrine.

At the conception, or the moment Gautama, or
the Phura-loung, entered Mâiya's womb, a great
commotion is said to have been felt throughout
the four elements—the blind recover their sight,
the dumb speak, the lame walk, springs of cool
water burst out in many places, rivers suspend
their course, all nature rejoices, and even the fires
of hell are temporarily extinguished.   During her
nine months of pregnancy, Mâiya enjoyed a perfect
calm and sweetest happiness ; fatigue and weariness
never affected her ; and the child was distinctly
visible " sitting cross-legged, unsoiled, and dignified," in her womb, which resembled an elegant *tsé-
dee* or *dágoba* (pagoda).*

---

* Our term pagoda is a corruption of the word *dágoba*, which is derived
from *dá, dátu,* or *dhátu,* an osseous relic, and *gebi,* or *garbha,* the womb.
The word tope, a corruption of *thúpa,* a relic, is not unfrequently used in the
same sense.--" Monachism," p. 217.

"As a dagoba holding sacred relics cannot be used to guard any less sacred object, so his mother can bear no other child, and on the seventh day after his birth she dies."* When the child is born, he steps forward seven paces on the ground, and facing the east, after looking around towards the four quarters of the globe, exclaims with a loud voice : " I am the most exalted in the world ; I am Chief of the World ; I am the most excellent in the world ; this is my last birth ; hereafter there is to me no other existence."†

Gautama was brought up in unrestrained luxury, after the manner of Oriental princes, and everything was done by his father to amuse him ; as he was anxious that the first prediction of the Brahmans should come true, and the heir to his throne become

* " Buddhism," Rhys Davids, p. 185.

† " This myth of the conception of Mâiya and the white elephant is probably in some way connected with the older superstition of sun-worship, the white elephant, like the white horse, being an emblem of the sun, the universal monarch of the sky. M. Senart, in his learned work, 'La Légende du Buddha,' has attempted to trace many of these coincidences, and has certainly established enough to show that in this direction an explanation may be found of much that appears at first sight bizarre and unnecessary in our legend of the Buddha. The idea that a man should enter his mother's womb in the form of a white elephant seems a most grotesque folly, until the origin of the poetical figure has been thus ascertained."—See Rhys Davids' " Buddhism," p. 184.

It bears a curious resemblance to the myth of Vitzliputzli, the god of mercy, in the religious system of the Mexicans, whose name refers to the sun, and the renovation of the world is ascribed to him. He is said to have been the off-spring of a virgin, who was impregnated by a plume of feathers invested with all the colours of the rainbow, which descended from heaven into her bosom. The rainbow in ancient mysteries is a celebrated symbol, typifying the re-appearance of the sun.

a great monarch, rather than a recluse. Gautama, however, was naturally of a serious turn of mind, and never so happy as when sitting alone wrapt up in meditation in some retired spot. It was on one of these occasions, in about his sixteenth year, that his father discovered him when he had thought him lost ; and in order to divert him from such melancholy moods, he hastened on his marriage with his first cousin, the beautiful Yasodhará.

The marriage is said to have proved a happy one —notwithstanding that his old habits continued ascendant in his mind, and he, often as before, remained absorbed in meditation on the problems of life and death. " Nothing is stable on earth," he used to say ; " nothing is real. Life is like the spark produced by the friction of wood. It is lighted and is extinguished—we know not where it comes or whither it goes. It is like the sound of a lyre, and the wise man asks in vain from whence it comes and whither it goes. There must be some supreme intelligence where we can find rest. If I attained it, I could bring light to man ; if I were free myself, I could deliver the world."

He continued thus, we are told, until his twenty-ninth year, when the nats, who knew the time was approaching when the Prince would become a Buddha, placed before him four successive visions, namely, that of an old, broken, decrepit man leaning on a staff; a man suffering from a loathsome disease, frightened at the sight of himself, and the approach of death; a corpse green with putridity and the prey of creeping worms; and lastly that of a recluse or religious mendicant, gentle and meek in manner, wearing his religious vestment with dignity, his face glowing with perfect contentment, and outwardly showing he cared for none of the things of this world. These visions appeared only to the Prince, and his attendant charioteer, Tsanda, who appears to have been specially inspired to explain them. The first three are allegorically a compound of the miseries of human existence; and the last the pattern the Prince was to follow to attain to that state of perfection, regarding which he felt a strong but confused desire of possessing.

Gautama, who was surfeited with pleasure and worldly enjoyments, and pining for seclusion and peace of mind, was mightily struck with the appearance of the recluse. His determination to follow his example was made at once, and at midnight of the day he had seen the hermit, when all his guards were asleep, he sent his faithful attendant Tsanda for his horse; and accompanied by him rode out from his palace into the forest to become a homeless wanderer. To increase the estimate of his self-denial, it is recorded that just before his departure, he took the first look at his first-born son lying in the arms of its sleeping mother, and which had only been born that day. This passage in the life of Gautama is called by Buddhists the Great Renunciation.

Gautama rode a long distance that night, and did not stop until he had passed the river Anauma, the bordering stream of his father-in-law's territory, where he divested himself of his royal ornaments, and directed Tsanda to return with them and his horse to Kapilavastu. He then cut off his long hair* with his sword, and exchanging clothes with a passer-by, hurried on alone towards Rajagriha the capital of Magadha. In a cave, in the vicinity of that city, he placed himself under the tuition of two Brahman ascetics, named Alāra and Udraca, and having learnt all they could teach, but not sufficient to enable him to obtain the dignity of Buddha-hood, he resolved to devote himself to a life of penance and meditation. For this purpose he

---

* Gautama is described as cutting off his long hair with his sword, leaving what remained about one and a half inches in length, and which is said never to have grown longer than that during the remainder of his life. All statues of Gautama are represented with short points of hair on the top of the head, in some of which the hair bears a curled or woolly appearance. This, combined with other circumstances, led Sir William Jones to form an opinion that the inhabitants of India, previous to its invasion by the Aryan tribes from the north, were of African descent, and that in the sculptured representations of their Sage this characteristic of the Negro race had been preserved. — "Asiatic Researches," vol. i. p. 427.

The custom of thus representing the hair, however, may be considered satisfactorily accounted for by the above passage in Gautama's life, and was doubtless designed to remind all Buddhists of the ever continued miracle of the stationary growth of Gautama's hair.—See Bigandet, p. 60.

retired to the solitudes of the wilderness near the present Buddha Gayá, where he was joined by five other ascetics.

He remained here for some six years practising excessive austerities,* adding vigil to vigil, and penance to penance, till his "fame spread abroad like the sound of a great bell hung in the canopy of the skies." At last one day after a more than usual long fast, while walking up and down lost in meditation, he fainted and fell to the ground. His fellow ascetics thought he was dying, but he slowly recovered. During his illness he arrived at the conviction that extreme penance, "far from giving peace of mind, and preparing the way to salvation, was a snare and stumbling-block in the way of truth,"† and, when able to walk again, despairing of further profit from fasting and self-mortification, he took his alms-bowl ‡ and went to the neighbouring

---

* Fastings, and other works of mortification, have always been much practised by the Indian philosophers of past ages, who thereby attracted the notice, respect, and veneration of the world. Such rigorous exercises, too, were deemed of great help in enabling the mind to have a more perfect control over the senses, and subjecting them to the empire of reason. The fast of Gautama, preparatory to his obtaining the Buddhahood, recalls to the mind that which Our Lord underwent, "ere He began His divine mission."—See Bishop Bigandet, p. 68.

† Max Muller, "Chips," p. 214.

‡ Gautama's alms-bowl, *pátra,* or *thabeit,* as it is called by the Burmese, is believed to have been the same one as was used by the three former Buddhas of the present Búddagábbá, or mundane universe, and is destined to serve also the fifth and last Buddha of this dispensation. "It is said to have been sent by King Asoka to Ceylon, and is still shown there in the Malagawa Vihara at Kandy. As usual in such cases, there are several rival relics, for Fa Hian

village for food. On seeing this, his companions at once deserted him as an apostate, and he was left to bear the burthen of his wavering faith alone.

Left alone, he wandered out into the forest and seated himself under a Bó-tree, where, after having fed upon some miraculous food, he remained wrapped up in profound meditation (*dhyana*) for forty-nine days without any further nourishment. During this period he was assaulted by numerous

found the alms-bowl preserved at Pesháwur.   Hwen Thsang says in his time it was no longer there, but in Persia."

" Fa Hian writes of the alms-bowl at Pesháwur, that poor people could fill it with a few flowers, whilst a rich man could not do so with 100, nay, with 1000 or 10,000 bushels of rice ; a parable doubtless originally carrying a lesson like Our Lord's remark on the widow's mite.

" This alms-bowl is the Holy Grail of Buddhism.   Mystical powers of nourishment are ascribed also to the Grail in the European legends.   German scholars have traced in the romances of the Grail remarkable indications of Oriental origin.   It is not impossible that the alms-bowl of Buddha was the prime source of them.   Read the prophetic history of the alms-bowl as Fa Hian heard it in India ; its mysterious wanderings over Asia till it is taken up into the abode of the nats, where Aramâitriya, the future Buddha, dwells. When it has disappeared from earth the Law gradually perishes, and violence and wickedness more and more prevail."—Colonel Yule's " Marco Polo," ch. xv. p. 264.5.

> " A gentle sound, an awful light !
> Three angels bear the Holy Grail :
> With folded feet, in stoles of white,
> On sweeping wings they sail.
> . . . .—What is it ?
> The phantom of a cup that comes and goes ?
> The cup, the cup itself, from which our Lord
> Drank at the last sad supper with His own.
> . . . . If a man
> Could touch or see it, he was healed at once
> By faith of all his ills.   But then the times
> Grew to such evil, that the holy cup
> Was caught away to heaven and disappeared."
>
> Tennyson's " Holy Grail."

demons, led by the evil nat Mára or Manh,* the arch enemy of mankind; and subjected, also, to the allurements of beauty, and all the forms of temptation that licentiousness could devise. But he conquers and rejects them, and comes out triumphant out of all his numerous trials. On the morning of the fiftieth day, sitting cross-legged †

* This contest between Gautama and Manh is an allegory exemplifying the triumph of truth over error. Manh is the personification of evil and the implacable enemy of mankind, or, in Christian terminology, the devil. Amongst the plans adopted by Manh to oppose the benevolent designs of Gautama to teach men the way of deliverance from all miseries, was that of flattering his ambition, and promising him, as the Brahmans foretold at his birth, "All the kingdoms of this world and their glory." At other times, to distract his attention when wrapt up in meditation, he causes whirlwinds, earthquakes, and storms of rain. His last attempt was to awaken the fire of lust by the aid of his three daughters, who, severally, assumed the appearances of a pretty girl, a blooming virgin, and a middle-aged beauty; but these, and all other attempts, proved powerless against a man who had conquered himself.

The conflict between Gautama with Mára and his demons, Paulinus imagines to be the same with the doctrine of the Magi, concerning Ormuzed and Arimanius. — "Compendium legis Barmanorum," Museo Borgia, p. 51.

† Most of the statues of Gautama represent him sitting cross-legged, the left hand open on the lap, and the other hanging over the right knee; the expression of the face attempted by the sculptor being that of sublime abstraction. In one of these statues of Gautama in my possession, he is represented in this position with a serpent coiled round the pedestal, on which he sits enthroned, in seven folds, with its hood extended over his head. This is the Nága, or nat snake, who presided over a large pool near the Bó-tree, and who, as a means of obtaining great merit, acted thus to protect Gautama during one of the great storms of rain raised by Manh. The pedestal, or throne, on which these statues rest, is in shape that of two triangles joined at the apices, typifying fire and water, the two elements mainly instrumental in the destruction and reproduction of the world.

Statues of Gautama, recumbent on the right side, with the left leg placed directly over the right one, the head resting on the palm of the right hand supported by the elbow, and the left arm extended at length over the left leg, are, too, not uncommon. This is the position he is described to have assumed when he died, or entered Niebban.

These two positions of his statues are intended to force upon the attention

under the Bó-tree, with his face turned towards
the east,* his meditations are rewarded by an
inspiration of the divine spirit, the light of truth,
in all its effulgent beauty, bursts upon him, en-
compassing his mind with its pure rays, and he
became Buddha, that is, Enlightened,† "wiser than
the wisest, and higher than the highest."

The Bó-tree (*ficus religiosa*), under whose shade
Gautama attained perfect knowledge, is dedicated
to him, as the *ficus indica* was to the predecessor;
and every preceding Buddha had also an appro-
priate tree. The next and last Buddha will obtain
supreme intelligence under the *Mesua ferrea*.

Gautama's Bó-tree is said to have sprung miraculously from the earth at the moment of his birth,
and is supposed to have stood in the centre of the
world. The word *bó*, or *bódi*, as it is called by

and memory of his followers the two great stages of his last existence, namely,
that of his obtaining Buddhahood, and that of his entering the state of Niebban
or Nirvâna.

* Turning to the east is an ancient Buddhist practice. When Gautama was
born, he glanced towards the east; and at the supreme moment when he
attained the acme of knowledge, the science of the past, present, and future—
the state of a perfect Buddha—his face was turned in the direction of the east.
Bishop Bigandet, remarking on the preference shown by Gautama to the east
over the other three points of the compass, thinks it might, possibly, have
reference to the tradition universally prevailing throughout the whole east
previous to the coming of Our Lord, that from the east there was to come an
extraordinary personage, who would confer the greatest benefits upon the
human race, and have induced him to look in that direction.

† Buddha means the Enlightened, and is often used as a proper name,
instead of an appellative, in a similar manner to Christos the Anointed, or
Mohamed the Expected.— See "Das Leben des Mohammed," Sprenger, vol. i.
p. 155.

the Burmese, means wisdom, knowledge, and Bishop
Bigandet thinks, "it may not be quite out of the
limits of probability to suppose that it is a remnant
of the tradition of the tree of knowledge, that
occupied the centre of the garden of Eden." The
Bó-tree is worshipped* by Buddhists, and its similarity to the aspen-tree of Syria (the *Khashafa*,
meaning to be agitated) has been remarked, with
regard to the constant quivering of its leaves. The
Buddhists say that out of the respect to their great
sage, the leaves of the Bó-tree "have always an
apparent motion, whether there be any wind stirring
or not ;" and the Syrians "aver that the wood of
Our Saviour's cross† was made of aspen, and that

---

* Few species of idolatry have been more common than arbor-olatry.
Among the Greeks and Romans nearly every deity had some particular tree,
and nearly every tree was dedicated to some particular god. It was under the
oak that the Druids performed their most sacred rites, and the principal tree
of the grove was consecrated with ceremonies of a description peculiarly
solemn. The ancient inhabitants of Canaan appear to have been greatly
attached to the sacred groves in which they were accustomed to worship ; and
the Israelites were especially commanded to destroy them.—"Monachism,"
p. 216. A sacred bough or plant is introduced into all the ancient mysteries :
such as the Indian lotus, the rose-tree of Isis, the fig-tree of Atys, the myrtle
of Venus, the mistletoe of the Druids, and the acacia of free masonry.

† In a note at p. 397 of Colonel Yule's "Marco Polo," an extract is given
from an interesting paper by Signor Adolfo Mussafia, "On the Legend of the
Wood of the Cross" (*Sulla Legenda del Legno della Croce*, Vienna, 1870),
bearing on the curious myth of the Arbre Sec or Arbre Sol, of which there are
numerous versions. It is as follows :—"Adam, drawing near his end, sends
Seth to the Gate of Paradise to seek the Oil of Mercy which had been promised to his penitence. Seth is allowed to put in his head at the gate. 'In
the midst of Paradise he beheld a glorious fountain, from which flowed four
rivers. . . . And over the fountain rose a Great Tree, with vast roots, but
bare of bark and leaves.' A great Serpent is coiled about the denuded stem ;
the upper branches reach to Heaven, and bear at the top a new-born wailing

the leaves of the aspen have trembled ever since in commemoration of the event."

A cutting of the original Bó-tree is said to have been taken to Ceylon 245 years before Christ, and planted at Anurādhapura, near the Ruwanwali Dagoba. The tree was then growing on the site of the present temple at Buddha Gayā, and the cutting was brought by Sanghamittā, the daughter of King Asoka, who followed her brother Mahinda to Ceylon, where he had preceded her a few years as the first Buddhist missionary to that island. The tree which sprang from this cutting still exists in a flourishing state at the place where it was planted, and is the oldest known tree in the world, its age being now 2,123 years. Sir Emerson Tennant says of it : " The estimates of the ages of other old

infant swathed in linen ; whilst (as the legend proceeds in a poetical French version, from a MS. in the Vienna library, given by Mussafia) :—

' Les larmes qui de lui issoient
   Contreval l'Arbre en avaloient.
   Adonc regarda l'enfant Seth
   Tout contreval de L'Arbre Secq ;
   Les rachines qui le tenoient
   Jusques en Enfer s'en aloient,
   Les larmes qui de lui issirent
   Jusques dedens Enfer cheirent.'

The Angel of the Gate gives Seth three seeds from the fruit of the Tree. Seth returns in time to see his father die. He buries him in the *Valley of Hebron*, and places the three grains under his tongue. A triple shoot springs up, of cedar, cypress, and pine, symbolizing the three persons of the Trinity. The three eventually unite into one stem, and this tree survives in various forms, and through various adventures in connection with the Scripture history, till it is found at the bottom of the Pool of Bethesda (to which it had communicated the healing virtue), and is taken to form the cross on which Our Lord suffered."

trees in the world are matters of conjecture ; and such calculations, however ingenious, must be purely inferential : whereas the age of this Bó-tree is matter *of record*, its conservancy has been an object of solicitude to successive dynasties, and the story of its vicissitudes has been preserved in a series of continuous chronicles, among the most authentic that have been handed down by mankind. Its green old age would almost seem to verify the prophecy pronounced when it was planted that it would ' flourish, and be green for ever.' " *

Gautama hesitated for some time, whether he should not keep the divine knowledge he had attained to himself. He revolved in his mind the unprofitable weariness that would be caused in trying to persuade men to believe in his simple doctrine of salvation—" salvation merely by self-control and love, without any of the rites, any of the ceremonies, any of the charms, any of the priestly powers, any of the gods, in which men love to trust."† But compassion for the sufferings of humanity finally prevailed, and he resolved to preach his doctrines to the world.

He accordingly proceeded towards Benares, and in the Mrigadāwa wood,‡ in the vicinity of that city,

* See "Ceylon," vol. ii., p. 613 ; "Buddhism," Rhys Davids, p. 232.
† "Buddhism," Rhys Davids, p. 41.
‡ Now called Dhamek, and is still a fine wood. In the third century before Christ, King Asoka built a tower there to commemorate the place where

he met again the five recluses who had deserted him
in the wilderness, when he threw off the yoke of
asceticism ; and they, after hearing him preach his
new doctrines, were amongst the first to acknowledge him as Buddha, and accept in entirety his
plan of salvation.

During the rest of his long life, some forty-one
years, he spent nine months of the year in travelling
through India, teaching and preaching to the people.
The remaining three—the rainy season commencing
about the middle of July, and ending in the middle
of October*—he lived in one of the numerous
monasteries built for his accommodation by his many
wealthy supporters, where he devoted himself to
teaching his doctrine to his disciples, and the
crowds of hearers that daily resorted thither to
listen to his preaching.

Gautama first publicly preached his doctrine.   The remains of this tower still
exist, and have been described by General Cunningham in his "Archæological
Reports," 1862, vol. i., pp. 103-20.

 * This period is called the religious season, or Buddhist Lent.   In Burma, on
the days of the new and full moons of these months, crowds of people resort to
the pagodas with offerings of flowers and small wax candles.   Alms, too, are
abundantly bestowed on the Phongyees or priests.

Many people on these occasions remain all night in open sheds, called *dzeats*,
erected for the purpose near the pagodas, conversing on religious subjects, or
wrapt up in contemplation telling their beads, and repeating certain devotional
formulas, the most common of which is "aneitsa, duka, anatta," meaning
that everything in this world is subject to the law of change and mutability, to
that of pain and suffering, and to that of entire and uninterrupted illusion.
These rosaries are often made of amber beads ; but more commonly of seeds,
especially those of *canna indica*, or "Indian shot."   This plant is considered
to be peculiarly sacred, as it is supposed to have sprung from Gautama's blood,
when once on a time he had cut his foot by striking it against a stone.

About twelve years after Gautama had attained
Buddhahood be was invited by his father, King
Suddódhana, to visit Kapilavastu.   On his first
arrival there, some of his kinsmen, actuated by
jealousy, did not pay him proper respect ; but
ultimately, after the performance by him of several
miracles, the whole tribe of Sákyas were converted
to his faith, including his father, his cousin Ananda,
who became from that time his personal attendant,
his own son Rahula, and his brother-in-law
Déwadat.   His wife Yasodharā, and his foster-
mother, Prajapûti, also followed the same course ;
and when, sometime afterwards, Gautama formed
the order of female mendicants, they became the
first two of the Buddhist nuns.

The position of Gautama was, however, not without its difficulties and trials.   A serious schism in
his Order was not long after this caused by
Déwadat, whose sectarists, at his instigation, made
three separate attempts on Gautama's life.   On
these all failing, Déwadat proceeded himself in
person with a large retinue to the monastery where
Gautama was then residing, in order to enforce
upon him the reforms he advocated.   But on his
reaching its vicinity an awful fate awaited him—the
earth burst open under his feet, and, surrounded
by devouring flames, he fell down to the lowest
hell, where three red-hot irons transfixed him

perpendicularly, whilst three others pierced his shoulders in a transverse direction.*

On another occasion an attempt was made by Gautama's enemies to destroy his reputation by suborning a woman to accuse him of breaking the law of continence ; but both she, and all concerned in instigating the slander, met with terrible deaths. Gautama, in speaking to his disciples regarding the troubles caused him by this charge, said that " it was but a just retribution for his having in a former existence been drunk, and, when in that state, abused and slandered a holy personage."

Gautama was thirty-five years of age when he attained Buddhahood, and lived to the age of eighty. The accounts extant of the last twenty-five years of his ministry are more imperfect and fragmentary than those of the preceding ones ; but it is to be presumed that he was employed in a similar manner, namely, visiting distant places and preaching † *bána* to men and gods : ‡ or, as described

---

* This story respecting Déwadat, according to Bishop Bigandet, has given rise in Burma to a very strange misconception. The Burmese, with their usual thoughtlessness, on being told of the particulars respecting the sufferings and mode of death of our Saviour, concluded that he must have been no other personage than Déwadat himself, and for holding opinions opposite to those of Gautama Buddha he suffered on the cross. A somewhat similar opinion appears to exist in Siam, namely, that Déwadat is the god of Europe, and that he, by opposing the good intentions of Gautama, produces all the evil in the world.

† Bána, or the Word. The term is generally accepted now as meaning the exposition of the doctrines of Gautama, whether orally delivered or written in books.

‡ The preachings of Gautama were not confined to the narrow limits of

in his own words, "teaching all sentient beings the way to salvation by providing them with a ferry-boat over this vain sea of passions, and guiding them into the path leading to the eternal city" (Neibban or Nirvâna).

He died at the age of eighty in a grove of sâl (*Shorea robusta*) trees, near the town of Kusinâra, of diarrhœa produced by a meal of rice and young pork, prepared for him by a goldsmith named Tsanda. When dying, he said to his favourite disciple, Ananda, "You may perhaps begin to think the Word is ended, now our Teacher is gone; but you must not think so. After I am dead let the Law (*dhâmma*) and the rules of the Order (*sangha*), that I have taught, be a teacher to you." And his last words to his assembled disciples, which are very remarkable and are well authenticated, were, "Mendicants! I now impress upon you the parts and powers of man must be dissolved; the principle of existence and mutability carries along with it the germ of destruction;"—

man's abode. All beings inhabiting the mansions of the gods or nats benefited by the publication of his doctrines, and he occasionally visited the celestial regions where they reside. On one occasion he proceeded there for the purpose of specially announcing the perfect law to his mother.

The condition of nats is that of a state of pleasure and enjoyment allotted them for meritorious works performed in former existences. Their condition is not a permanent one. They are far from the perfect state of Niebhan. When their sum of merits is exhausted, they return to the abode of man, commence a new existence, and endeavour to advance themselves on the road to perfection.

after saying this, while the dawn was just breaking,
he became unconscious, and in that state passed
away.*

At the moment of his death a violent earthquake
is said to have happened, and at the cremation of
his body many miraculous incidents are stated to
have occurred. The body refused to be moved
until the wish of the gods was obtained as to the
direction in which it was to be borne. The funeral
pile would not burn until the head of the Order, the
venerable Maha Káthaba arrived, embraced the feet
of the corpse, and walked three times round the pile,
when it took fire spontaneously. When all the
parts of the body were consumed, except the seven
bones,† which it was ordained should be preserved
as relics, showers of rain fell and extinguished the
flames.

The relics were eagerly sought for by seven
princes, and tsé-dees,‡ or pagodas, built over them.

* See " Buddhism," Rhys Davids, p. 83 ; Bigaudet, p. 318.

† These were the four canine teeth, the two collar bones, and the frontal
bone. They form the seven great relics, and are called *Athambinana*.

‡ During the reign of King Asoka, who was remarkable for his religious
zeal, the erection of these edifices was greatly multiplied throughout India, as
visible mementos of Gautama. As such, they continue to be built at the present
day throughout Burma, and are to be seen, embosomed in groves of trees, on all
rising grounds in the neighbourhood of towns and villages. The form of the
most ancient pagodas in India, or topes, as they are often called there, appears
to have been hemispherical, an expanded umbrella wrought in stone being
placed at the summit ; and those of Burma, square three-storeyed ones with
external flights of steps, one on each face, leading up to shrines or sanc-
tuaries ; as are still to be seen at Thatún and Pugan. But the normal shape
the modern *tsé-dee* takes in Burma is that of a cone or circular pyramid of

The ashes of the funeral pile were also carefully gathered, and distributed amongst the most distinguished believers.

solid brick-work, supported on a square base, and crowned by a tapering spire of gilt iron-work, formed in three crowns, called a *hter*, bearing a strong resemblance in its shape to the Pope's tiara, and typical of the Buddhist triad. On each side of the quadrangular base are four niches, in direction of the four cardinal points, in which are placed statues of Gautama. These monuments are of all sizes, varying in their ornamentation, and ranging from those of a few feet in elevation, to that of the colossal dimensions of the Shwé-dagon pagoda at Rangoon, which rises majestically to the height of 320 feet.

The Shwé-dagon is the most celebrated object of worship in all the Indo-Chinese countries, deriving its peculiar sanctity from the belief of its having enclosed in its interior shrine, below the surface of the ground on which it stands, relics of the four Buddhas who have appeared during the present Buddhagàbbà, the staff of Kōkoothánda; the water-dipper of Kōnaggammá; the bathing-garment of Káthàbà, and eight hairs from the head of Gautama.

Tsé-dees in Burma may be arranged into four classes, the last two of which are by far the most numerous, viz.:—1st. *Dat-dau-tsé-dee*, or those containing supposed relics of a Buddha or Rahanda. 2nd.—*Paree-bau-ga tsé-dee*, or those containing supposed implements or garments which have belonged to Buddhas, or sacred personages. 3rd.—*Dhámma tsé-dee*, or those containing books or texts. 4th.—*Oo-deit-tsa tsé-dee*, or those built from motives of piety, and containing statues of Buddha or models of sacred buildings, generally in precious metal.

Hence in Burma a pagoda is worshipped as being the depository of a relic; a monument to Buddha; or as representing Dhámma, that is Divine Law. —See Sir Arthur Phayre's article on the Shwé-dagon pagoda, A. S.'s J. 1859, p. 479.

The adoration paid to the statues of Gautama, to his relics, and the monuments called *tsé-dees*, is difficult to understand. The Buddhist knows that Gautama is no more, and therefore can afford him no assistance whatever, that there is no virtue inherent in his relics or statues—in fact, there is no Providence. This moral phenomenon is accounted for, however, from Gautama having, it is said, shortly previous to his decease, declared to his favourite disciple, Ananda, that when he was not present to his believers in a visible manner, the objects proper to be worshipped, and which he wished the same honours paid as were offered to his living person, were of three kinds:—Serírika, uddésika, and paribhógika. The first includes the relics of his body, which were to be collected after his cremation; the second those things that were hereafter erected on his account, or for his sake, which, the commentators say, mean statues of his person, and tsé-dees; and the third the Bó-tree under which he attained Buddhahood, and the articles personally used by him, such as his leathern girdle, his alms bowl, the robe he put on when he bathed, the

With a view of preserving intact the doctrines
and institutions of his beloved teacher in their
original purity, the venerable Maha Káthaba—
whom Gautama shortly before his decease had
vested with his own robe *—determined to hold
a council; and for this purpose, he selected five
hundred of the most distinguished members of
the Order, from the large number of his brethren
whom the ceremony of the cremation of the body
of Gautama had brought together. The council
was held accordingly sixty-one days after Gautama's
death in the Sattapani cave situated in the Vaihara
hill, near the city of Rājagriha, and which had been

---

vessel from which he drank water, and his *palleng*, seat or throne, on which he
used to sit. Hence, in obedience to his commands, these devotional practices
have intrinsic worth, and are believed to add to the law of merits, or the
good influence which will procure the worshipper abundant rewards in future
existences, and help him on the road to the harbour of deliverance, from
successive existences.

The offerings made to the statues of Gautama and his shrines are very simple.
They consist of flowers, rice, small flags made of cloth or paper, wax candles,
earthen oil lamps, and sometimes incense and scented wood, which are placed
on altars, or pedestals of masonry, erected for the purpose in their vicinity.
When the offerings are presented, the worshippers prostrate themselves and
bow their heads three times, the palms of the hands being placed together,
and the thumbs touching the forehead : after which they rise to a sitting
posture, resting on their heels, with the body slightly bent forward, and mutter
the three-fold formulary of protection, called *tun-surâna*, stating that they seek
refuge in Buddha, Dhamma, and Sangha ; or they take upon themselves a
certain number of the ten obligations, the words being often first chanted in Pali
by a Buddhist priest. There are four Oo-bö or worship days in a month,
namely, the eight of the waning of the moon, the full, the eight of the waxing,
and the change.—See " Monachism," pp. 206-15. " Bigandet," pp. 306-7.

* Gautama's conferring his robe upon Káthaba—his long-tried and faithful
disciple—calls to mind the passages in 2 Kings ii. 9-15, regarding the spirit and
mantle of Elijah falling upon Elisha, and Elisha's succession to his ministry.

prepared for the purpose by Ajātosatra, King of Magadha.

At this Synod, and at each of the two subsequent ones ; the second being held at Vésali, one hundred years after the first, and the third at Pátaliputrá, near the modern Patna, in the eighteenth year of the reign of King Asoka, or 308 B.C. ; although the whole text of the Pitakattayan* is stated to have been rehearsed, an authentic version established, and the *ipsissima verba* of Gautama repeated with the utmost precision, they do not appear to have been committed to writing until some 458 years after the great Teacher's death, or about 85 B.C.† During this long period the doctrines are asserted to have been handed down by oral tradition ; and though it is almost incredible that they could be retained in the memory for so long a space, yet the documents themselves are an evidence that some considerable period must have elapsed between the death of Gautama, and the compilation of the Pitakas in their present form. Like the Koran, they may have been compiled, not from the memory of one man, but from the remembrance and imagination of numerous different persons.

---

* From *pituka*, a basket, and *tayo*, three. The text containing the three grand divisions of the Buddhist scriptures, called by the Burmese *Bedigat-thoon-bon*.

† The Pitakas are believed to have been reduced to writing in Ceylon during the reign of Watta Gámini, who was then king of that island.

Many of the monks in Burma, in the present day, devote a large portion of their lives to learning portions of their scriptures by heart. They may frequently be heard repeating for hours together, without reference to books, long discourses from the Pitakas to attentive audiences, and the retentiveness of their memory appears very extraordinary. Their method of delivering being recitative, half chanting half speaking, tends to give them confidence, by affording them, in case of their memory failing, the opportunity of dwelling by a shake or quaver on the last syllable, instead of coming to an abrupt stop.[*]

During the third convocation it was determined by the President, that missionaries should be sent into all lands to preach the doctrines of Buddhism, and two missionaries, named Oo-tara and Thau-na,

---

[*] As regards the enormous powers of memory of Indian and other priests, the Vedas are supposed to have been handed down by Brahmins from memory for many centuries. The Vedas are believed by the Hindus to be contemporary with the creation. Uyâsa, who is said to have lived about 1580 B.C., which, according to Hebrew chronology, carries us back to about the time of Moses, formed with great judgment a complete compendium of them, adjusting the texts which appeared to contradict each other. He called the work Vedantá, a name formed from two Sanskrit words, meaning the explanation or completion of the whole Vedas.

The Druids are said by Cæsar to have been able to repeat a great number of verses by heart, some remaining in the course of training for twenty years, as they considered it unlawful to commit their statutes to writing. The Egyptian priests, too, are stated by Herodotus to have had great powers of memory. And the poems of Homer and of Hesiod are supposed to have been preserved in the memory of rhapsodists, by whom they were recited, for the space of 500 years.—See on this subject, "Monachism," pp. 173-85 ; "Buddhism," Rhys Davids, p. 9.

were despatched in a south-eastern direction to Suvana Bhumi, the country of the Mōn or Talaing race, whose chief city was then at Thatún. They appear to have gone there by sea, as the Maha-radza-weng relates that on their landing in their yellow robes, on the sea-shore at Thatún, they created great consternation, and were at first taken for beloos. By their preaching, however, they seem to have rapidly gained the confidence of the people of the country, many of whom shortly entered the priesthood; and even the King himself was ulti-mately converted, and became a zealous adherent and supporter of the new religion.

The Buddhist doctrines were propagated here, as elsewhere, orally, and the Talaings did not possess the Buddhist scriptures in a written form until they were conveyed to them from Ceylon by Buddhagosa in 450 A.D. The Talaings claim this celebrated monk as a countryman of their own, and their history states that he went from Thatún to Ceylon, where he stayed three years, and then returned with a copy of the scriptures. This is, however, a fallacy, for he was a native of Mâgadha, and born near the Bó-tree, at Buddha Gāyā. He went to Ceylon in about 430 A.D., and there compiled " his great work, the *Visuddhi Magga*, or *Path of Holiness*, a cyclopædia of Buddhist doctrine; and from the great knowledge he displayed, was

employed by the rulers of his Order in Ceylon
to rewrite, in Pali, the commentaries which had, 'till
then, been handed down in Singalese."* Buddhagosa was a convert from Brahmanism, and owing to
his great eloquence, the appellation of Buddhagosa
(the voice of Buddha) was conferred upon him.

In 1080 A.D. the Talaings were conquered by
Anaurata, the Burmese King of Pagan, who burnt
and sacked Thatún, and took away with him to
Pagan the Buddhist scriptures brought by Buddhagosa, as also the most learned of the priesthood.
During this King's reign, and up to the time of
King Nara-thee-ha-pa-dé in 1284 A.D., when Burma
was invaded by the forces of Kublai Khan, and
Pagan itself destroyed, a great revival of Buddhism
took place at Pagan, and the numerous square and
other shaped Buddhist temples † were built, the
remains of which excite the admiration of travellers.

From Buddhist writings preserved at Ceylon and
elsewhere, there can be no doubt that the Talaings
first obtained their knowledge of the Buddhist
religion through the two missionaries, as above
described ; and owing to their being on the sea-
board, received it at a much earlier period than the

---

* "Buddhism," Rhys Davids, p. 236.

† Besides the damage done by the invaders, the Burmese King Nara-thee-
ha-pa-dé caused "1000 large arched temples and 4000 square temples to be
destroyed," for the purpose of obtaining materials for enlarging the fortifications
of the city.— See p. 71, vol. i.

Burmese. But as to when, and by what means, the Burmese first obtained their knowledge of it, no authentic record exists. Sir Arthur Phayre is of opinion that they were converted by Buddhist missionaries from Gangetic India, who reached Upper Burma through Bengal and Munipúr. Others, amongst whom is Rhys Davids, suppose that Buddhism was introduced from China. It is not unlikely, however, that the Burmese obtained both their religion and their alphabet through the Talaings. The Burmese alphabet is almost the same as the Talaings, and the circular form of both strongly indicate the influence of the Singalese, or the Tamulic type of letter.

According to the doctrines propounded by Gautama, nothing is eternal, but the law of cause and effect and change. There is no creator, no being that is self-existent and eternal. There is a Supreme Power, but not a supreme being. "All sentient things are homogeneous: The difference between one being and another is only temporary,* and results from their degrees of merit."†

The supreme power that controls the universe is *karma*,‡ literally action; consisting of *kusala* and

* An old Burmese friend of mine, whom I visited in his last moments, said to me that his great aspiration was that he might wake up in the next world as an *Engli bô*, or English officer. It was not said out of compliment, for he knew that he was dying.

† "Eastern Monachism," p. 5.

‡ The doctrine of merits and demerits, and of their concomitant influences,

akusala, or the merit and demerit of intelligent existence. There is no such thing as an immortal soul. At the death of any being, the aggregate of his merit and demerit is transferred to some other being ; which new being is caused by the *karma* of the previous being, and inherits from that *karma* all the consequences, whether good or evil, that have been accumulated during an unknown period by an almost endless succession of similar beings, all bound by this singular law of production to every individual in the preceding link of the chain, so as to be liable to suffer for their crimes or be rewarded for their virtues.

Thus, like the revolutions of a wheel, there is a regular succession of death and birth, the moral cause of which is the cleaving to existing objects, whilst the instrumental cause is *karma*. This state of things goes on for myriads of existences until the influence of *upádána*, or attachment to sensual objects is broken, and the consequences of all past demerits exhausted. Then, and not till then, the being obtains *nirvána*,* and ceases to be, " as the

are fully illustrated in the person of Gautama himself during his former 550 existences, as given in the Játakas. He said of himself to his disciples that he had passed, with various fortune, through the range of the animal kingdom, from the dove to the elephant ; that being man, he had been often in hell, and in various positions of riches and poverty, until by his mighty efforts he had at last freed himself from all evil influences, and reached the state of highest perfection.—See Bigandet, p. 130.

* Nirvána is a passive participle of the Sanskrit root *vá*, "to blow," with the preposition *nir*, "out," "away from," prefixed to it : the word is also

light of a lamp when its flame is extinguished."
There is no appeal by the Buddhist to a supreme
being or any exterior power to assist him in the
attainment of this, to him, grand consummation.
He joins no one else in seeking assistance by
prayer, though from the teachings of another he
may receive aid, to do in a better manner what,
after all, must be entirely his own work.

To escape from this whirlpool of countless existences was the great principle of salvation that
Gautama proclaimed. Existence in the eye of
Buddhism is nothing but misery. It involves
disease, decay, and death. " It is subject to grief,
pain, and despair. It resembles a blazing fire which
dazzles the eye, but torments us by its effects.
There is nothing permanent or real in the whole
universe." To get rid of decay and its accompanying misery we must get rid of life. Whatever is
material is subject to change and dissolution, and
there is no life which is not material. As long as
man *is*, he must be miserable. His only salvation
is *not to be.* The only deliverance from evil is by
the destruction of existence and attainment of
nirvâna, the characteristics of which are—that which
is void, that has no existence, no continuance,
neither birth nor death, that is subject to neither

used with *nir* as a negative prefix, and then implies "what is no more
agitated," "what is in a perfect calm."

cause nor effect, and that possesses none of the essentialities of being ;* in a word, perfect annihilation.

" No person who reads with attention the metaphysical speculations on the *nirvâna* contained in the Buddhist canon, can arrive at any other conviction than that expressed by Burnouf, namely, that *nirvâna,*† the highest aim, the *summum bonum* of Buddhism, is the absolute nothing."‡

Gautama's first teachers were Brahmins, and the doctrines of Buddhism and Brahmanism so far agree, that " a man is born into the world he has made ; " that by some operation of nature, too subtle to be defined or explained, he passes through countless

---

* "Legends of the Buddhists," p. 174, *et seq.* ; Alwis's "Lecture on Buddhism;" "Mahomed, Buddha, and Christ," p. 154 ; Wassilief, "Der Buddhismus," p. 101 ; Mohl, "Journal Asiatique," 1856, p. 94.

† Dr. Marcus Dods, in his learned lecture on Buddhism (p. 168), says of *nirvâna :* "*Nirvâna*, then, is the moral condition which accompanies the eradication of self-will, self-assertion, self-seeking, self-pleasing. And had this been the ultimate aim of Buddhism, nothing could have been worthier of human effort. But this moral self-renunciation is only a means to the great end of annihilation, extinction of self in every sense. Self is to be renounced, not that man may come into a loving concord with the will of God, and with every living creature, but that he may himself escape the misery which inevitably accompanies all existence. The moral condition of *nirvâna* is attained in order that at death there may be no re-birth. The oil is withdrawn and the flame dies out, so that no other wick can be lit from it. Unconsciously it would, no doubt, be the moral attainment which satisfied high-minded Buddhists ; but theoretically the moral attainment is not the ultimate end in view, but only the means by which the man attains to non-existence. He reaches the highest development, not to become serviceable to the world at large, but to pass away into nothingness. 'He that hateth his life in this world shall keep it unto life eternal,'—that is the well-balanced, far-seeing, quiet enunciation of the real law of existence ; but the Buddhist *nirvâna* is a travesty of this, and magnificent as is the conception of man's moral state, it is stultified by the end for which it is to be attained."

‡ "Buddhist Nihilism," Max Müller, p. 11.

existences, during which he can become slowly
purified of his imperfections, and advance to perfection; but they differ as to the end to be
arrived at.

The Buddhists are atheists, and the Hindus
pantheists. They both deny the existence of a
separate *ego*, or self; but "the Hindu idea is that *I*
is Brahma; the Buddhist, that *I* is a nonentity."[*]
The Buddhist, ignoring a creator, conducts a being
that has become emancipated from the thraldom of
passions to the state of *nirvâna*. The Hindu, on
the other hand, believing in Brahma, or a supreme
being, from whom all things have emanated, and to
whom all things must return, leads the perfected
being after he has passed through a purgatory
proportioned to his guilt, to be absorbed into the
divine essence, in which he loses all personality,
and forms a whole with the divine substance, "as
a lump of salt thrown into the sea becomes dissolved
into the water from which it was produced, and is
not to be taken out again."

Gautama holds the first place in the Buddhist
triad,[†] and is worshipped by Buddhists, as one who

---

[*] "Eastern Monachism," p. 307.

[†] On some Buddhist coins in my possession the emblem of the Buddhist
triad is represented by three parallel horizontal lines, and also in three perpendicular lines joined together at the bottom in the shape of a trident. The
former symbols, I believe, express the three members of the triad separately,
and the latter the three in unity (Thärāna-gon). In ancient times three scores,
or marks, appear to have been emblematic of the Deity, either as among the

has attained the highest possible point of perfection, and the first and greatest of all beings. The protection derived from the triad, *tun-surana*, or three most precious gems, Buddha, the sacred books, and the priesthood—the latter by the wonderful gift for personification, imbuing the Oriental mind, being elevated into a quasi-divine rank, is said "to destroy the dread of reproduction, or successive existence, and to take away the fear of the mind, the pain to which the body is subject, and the misery of the four hells. The protection of Buddha may be obtained by keeping his precepts ; and by this aid the evil consequences of demerit are overcome. The protection of the sacred books is likened to a steed to one who is travelling a long journey. The protection of the priesthood is ensured by alms or offerings.

Hebrews by the three *yods*, 777, or by the high priest distending the thumb and two forefingers as he stretched his right hand over the assembled multitudes, when bestowing his yearly benediction :—which practice has evidently relation to the ancient cult of Priapus, and is followed, also, by the Pope at the present day.

Whilst on the subject of symbols, I may allude to a remark made by an educated Chinaman when visiting the cathedral at Hong Kong, and mentioned by Mr. F. H. Balfour in "Waifs and Strays," p. 222. "After noticing the stained-glass windows, the altar, the organ, and the font, the Chinaman took up his position in front of the pulpit, from the cushion of which hung a silken fall, inscribed with the sacred monogram I. H. S. arranged in cipher. His attention was immediately aroused, and calling the Englishman who had accompanied him to his side, he asked him how it was that a Buddhist symbol was permitted in a Christian church? His companion was somewhat perplexed, and requested an explanation. 'There,' said the Chinaman, pointing to the letters, 'that is what I mean. That is the sacred symbol of Buddha, and has been so from time immemorial. In China it is written thus 卍 .'"

"One of the chief modes of acquiring merit is said to be that of *dāna,* or almsgiving, and it is placed first on the list of the four cardinal virtues, which are almsgiving, affability, promoting the prosperity of others, and loving others as ourselves. The reward for the giving of alms, is not merely a benefit that is to be received at some future period; it promotes length of days, personal beauty, agreeable sensations, strength, and knowledge. There is no reward in this world or the next, that may not be received through almsgiving." *

The social and moral precepts of Buddhism apart from its metaphysical theories are remarkable. In no religion except Christianity is such stress laid upon the grace of universal charity, and love for all

---

* "Eastern Monachism," pp. 81—82. A great inducement truly for the bestowal of alms! The noble principle of charity implanted in the human heart by God, has been seized upon by priestcraft in all ages. How similar to Buddhist precepts, and how mournful such passages as the following are from St. Chrysostom (χρυσοστομος, the "golden-mouthed")! "Alms are the redemption of the soul. Almsgiving, which is able to break the chain of thy sins. Almsgiving, the queen of virtues, and the readiest way of getting into heaven, and the best advocate there. Hast thou a penny, purchase heaven. Heaven is on sale, and in the market, and yet ye mind it not! Give a crust and take back Paradise; give the least and receive the greatest; give the perishable, and receive the imperishable; give the corruptible and receive the incorruptible."—Taylor's "Ancient Christianity."

St. Eligius, or Eloi, in the seventh century, exhorts people to make oblations to the Church, and when our Lord comes to judgment they may be able to say, "Da, Domine, quia dedimus."—Mosheim's "Ecclesiastical History."

By the exercise of charity the sick were taught to expect cures. The rich as well as the poor were accustomed to put a written schedule of their sins under the cloth which covered the altar of a favourite saint, accompanied by a donation; and a day or two afterwards, when they re-examined the schedule, the virtues of the saint had converted it into a blank.—Fosbroke's "British Monachism."

living beings. Gautama himself said, "A man who foolishly does me wrong, I will return to him the protection of my ungrudging love; the more evil comes from him the more good shall go from me." As a mother, even at the risk of her own life, protects her son, her only son, so let there be good-will without measure among all beings. Let good-will without measure—unhindered love and friendliness—prevail in the whole world, above, below, around.*

The five great commandments† are the essence of morality. They contain almost word for word the same commands as those of the decalogue,‡ and are enforced by a singular variety of separate rules and precepts. The object being to guard man against every temptation to commit sin; to warn him at the very threshold of danger; to induce him to keep a constant watch upon his thoughts, words, and actions. For instance, to guard against the sin of murder, there are precepts against anger, malice,

---

* Beal's "Buddhist Scriptures," pp. 193-4; Dr. Dodd's "Lecture on Buddhism," p. 173.

† They are: 1. Kill not. 2. Steal not. 3. Commit not adultery. 4. Lie not. 5. Take nothing that intoxicates.

‡ The fifth Commandment may be excepted. Though we are enjoined to "be temperate in all things," we are taught at the same time that it is not the use of intoxicating liquors, but the abuse of them, which is an evil.

In Plato's "Laws," Book II., Education, it is laid down: "No young person is to taste wine before eighteen years of age; he is to be very moderate till thirty, and never to be drunk. After forty more wine may be taken. It makes us, in opinion, renew our youth; it is the remedy against the austerity of old age, and is a temporary suspension of all our miseries."

revengeful thoughts, and threatening language.   In
like manner, the precept not to covet is associated
with the commandment not to steal.

All authorities who have written on Buddhism
praise its moral code and acknowledge the purity of
its ethics.   Bishop Bigandet in his valuable work
on the life of Gautama (pp. 494–95) says : "The
Christian system and the Buddhistic one, though
differing from each other in their respective objects
and ends, as much as truth from error, have, it
must be confessed, many striking features of an
astonishing resemblance.   There are ·many moral
precepts equally commanded and enforced in common by both creeds.   It will not be deemed rash to
assert that most of the moral truths prescribed by
the Gospel, are to be met with in the Buddhist
scriptures ; and in reading the particulars of the
life of Gautama, it is impossible not to feel reminded
of many circumstances relating to our Saviour's life
sketched out by the Evangelists."

Again in the preface (p. viii) of his work, he adds :
"It may be said in favour of Buddhism, that no
philosophico-religious system has ever upheld, to
an equal degree, the notions of a saviour and
deliverer, and the necessity of his mission for
procuring the salvation of man in a Buddhist sense.
The *rôle* of Gautama, from beginning to end, is
that of a deliverer, who preaches a law designed to

N 2

secure man the deliverance from all the miseries he
is labouring under.   But, by an inexplicable and
deplorable eccentricity, the pretended saviour, after
having taught man the way to deliver himself from
the tyranny of his passions, leads him, after all, into
the bottomless gulf of a total annihilation."

Doubtless, many of the precepts of the gospel are
to be found in Buddhism,* but they are merely moral
ones and nothing more.   The most invincible objec-
tion to Buddhism, like some more modern speculations which could be mentioned, is, the absence of
all belief in an Almighty God, or indeed in a First
Cause † of any description.   Matter is looked upon
as eternal.   The existence of the world, its destruction and reproduction, all the different combinations
to which matter is subject, are the immediate results
of the action of eternal laws.‡   Gautama has ceased

* Hodgson describes Buddhism as monastic asceticism in morals, and
philosophical scepticism in religion.   Trans. R. A. S., vol. i., p. 413.

† Most of the Grecian philosophers agreed in acknowledging that one
Supreme Being (to whom, however, they apply different designations) presided
in the Universe, every part of which was animated by his influence.   To this
Being they gave the appellation fate, destiny, necessity, in order to evince the
truth of their great tenet, that all things originated in him.   Thus Chrysippus,
according to Cicero, denominated God the necessity of future events (Chrysippus Deum dicit esse—fatalem umbram, et *necessitatem* rerum futurarem.   De
Natur. Deon. Lib. i. c. 15) : and Seneca applies to him the term fate, as
being expressive of the great cause or principle to which all events are suspended.   (Vis illum *fatum* vocare ?   Non errabis.   *Hic* est exquo suspensi
sunt omnia.   Natur. Quest. Lib. ii. c. 45.)   *Fate*, in the judgment of the
former philosopher, is the epithet whereby we express an eternal succession
and revolution of things involving each other in an uninterrupted series, somewhat similar to the Buddhistic dogma.   To this series the Parcæ or destinies,
the daughters, as Plato calls them, of necessity belonged.

‡ See, " Waifs and Strays," p. 138.

to be, and there can be no intelligent prayer in Buddhism, as there is no one to listen to its voice.

Can anything be more dark and cheerless than the belief that a man has no soul; * that in the myriads of existences he has to pass through, he must expect much pain and sorrow, but no real happiness; and that the noblest reward to be reaped at last is a state of blank unconsciousness? Its

* It is a very curious fact, attested by such eminent theologians as Warburton and Chalmers, that Moses does not mention or allude to the immortality of the soul, or a future life in any part of the Pentateuch. See also Le Clerc (Prolegomena ad Hist. Ecclesiast. Sec. i. c. 8), who has written a learned commentary on the books of the Old Testament. Plato, in his tenth book of laws, defines the soul to be *the self-moving substance*. Hence he infers that the soul is the origin and first mover in all things that have been, are, or shall be. He observes also, that atheists use the word *Nature*, improperly; for if mind is older than air and fire, *mind is the cause of all*. The whole strain of his arguments is to that purpose: *Mind is older than matter, because the mover is superior to that which is moved*. Pythagoras supposed the soul to be a divine emanation, a vital spark of heavenly flame, the principle of reason and perception, doomed from unknown causes to remain during certain periods imprisoned in matter, and that all its impulses, not immediately derived from the material organs, were impulses of the Deity.

Cicero in his admirable treatise on Old Age, and in his Tusculan Questions, rehearses all the remarkable dicta of the Greek and Roman philosophers respecting the immortality of the soul. He notices that many of these sages perceived that the material properties of man had nothing in common with the properties of thought, memory, imagination, and judgment, and that these faculties must, therefore, belong to something distinct from the body, in its nature immaterial, indestructible, spiritual, and immortal.

From these specious and noble principles these ancient sages not only deduced the future immortality of the soul; but likewise inferred, in common somewhat with the Brahminic doctrine, the false conclusion of its pre-eternal existence, and of its being an emanation of the infinite eternal Spirit that pervades and sustains the universe, proceeding from it as the rays do from the sun, without diminishing or impairing the intrinsic light, power, and warmth of that celestial body.

This latter philosophical and speculative view annihilates what is dearest to man—the hope of individual existence after death, a hope which, founded on the rock of revealed religion, is of more value to us Christians, than all that the depths of metaphysics can offer.

much vaunted code of morality, also, with its selfish and venal process of traffic in merit, is deficient in many of the most essential social qualities, such as spontaneous goodness; the doing what is right, apart from hope of reward or fear of punishment; and indeed in most of the promptings of genuine sympathy and real benevolence. In all radical doctrines Christianity and Buddhism are diametrically opposed. The fundamental idea of Buddhism is deliverance from a vortex of endless existences. The basis of Christianity is the atonement—the sufferings of our Saviour on the cross as an atonement for the sins of all mankind. The Buddhist seeks for eternal death; the Christian for eternal life.

The singular analogies that exist between the rituals, institutions, and outward observances of Romish Christianity and Buddhism is very startling; and was accounted for by some of the early Roman Catholic missionaries who visited the East, with the supposition that Satan had travestied the true religion. "Diabolo ecclesiam Christi imitante!" exclaimed St. Xavier in his perplexed annoyance at observing the practices of the Buddhists in Japan;* and the whole ritual of the Buddhist

* Sir Rutherford Alcock, in his "Narrative of Three Years' Residence in Japan," in describing the funeral of one of the Japanese members of the British Legation, says that "It was impossible for a Protestant not to be struck with the outward similarity between the ceremonial of this Buddhist burial with

religion is so tinged with Romanism that it might
well justify such a remark.

Father Rubrugius, who travelled in Tibet in
the thirteenth century, and Fathers Dorville and
Grueber about the middle of the seventeenth, were
much surprised at finding a pontifical court there,
and much struck with the extraordinary similitude
to be found, as well in the doctrines, as in the
rituals of the Buddhists of Lassa to those of the
Romish faith. The latter missionary, in the published account of his travels, notices : " 1st, that the
dress of the lamas corresponded with that handed
down to us in ancient paintings, as the dress of the
Apostles ; 2nd, that the discipline of the monasteries, and of the different orders of lamas and
priests, bore the same resemblance to that of the
Roman Church ; 3rd, that the notion of incarna-

those of the Greek and Roman Churches. The altar, the taper, the incense,
the very costume and gesture of the priests, were in many striking particulars
alike—a resemblance too close to have been fortuitous ; but whence the
seeming identity is yet a question, and one which I do not pretend to discuss."
The Japanese are not such sincere and true believers in Buddhism as the
Burmese, for he goes on to say, "As regards any faith the Japanese generally
may have, the more immediate end which they propose to themselves is a
state of happiness in this world. They have indeed some, but very obscure
and imperfect, notions of the immortality of the soul, and a future state of bliss
or misery. But, so far as I have seen, the educated classes scoff at all such
doctrines, as fit only for the vulgar and the ignorant ; and believe, with the
ancient poets and philosophers, that after death there is no future, or as Catullus
expresses it in his Epistle to Lesbia ;—

" ' Vivamus mea Lesbia, atque amemus,
Nobis, cum semel occidit brevis lux,
Nox est perpetua una dormienda.' "

tion was common to both, so also the belief in
paradise and purgatory ; 4th, he remarked that
they made suffrages, alms, prayers, and sacrifice for
the dead, like the Roman Catholics ; 5th, that they
had convents, filled with monks and friars, who all
made the three vows of poverty, obedience, and
chastity, like Roman monks, besides other vows ;
and 6th, that they had confessors, licensed by the
superior lamas or bishops ; and so empowered to
receive confessions, to impose penances, and give
absolution.   Besides these, there was found the
practice of using holy water, of singing service in
alternation of praying for the dead, and a perfect
similarity in the costumes of the great and superior
lamas to those of the different orders of the Roman
hierarchy."*

The Father might have added to the above,
worship of a Queen of Heaven and Child,† tonsure,
repetition of prayers with the rosary, use of bells
and incense,‡ works of merit and supererogation,

* Prinsep's "Tibet, Tatary, and Mongolia," p. 13.

† "On the altar of a Chinese temple, behind a screen, is frequently a
representation which might answer for that of the Virgin Mary, in the person
of *Shin-moo*, or the sacred mother, sitting in an alcove with a child in her
arms, and rays proceeding from a circle, which are called a glory, round her
head, with tapers burning constantly before her."—Lord Macartney's
"Embassy to China," vol. ii., p. 100.

See, also, the mention made of the worship of the Queen of Heaven by the
Buddhists of China, in Davis's "Chinese."

The monasteries of Tibet possess also similar representations to that described
by Lord Macartney.

‡ As incense is now burnt in some of our high ritualistic churches, it is well

fast days and feast days, images and pictures and fabulous legends,* bowings, prostrations, and turnings to the east, councils or synods to settle schisms or points of faith, the worship of relics and working of miracles through them. I may state, too, that the tiara or triple crown of the Pope bears a very strong resemblance to the *htees* which crown the spires of Burmese Buddhist temples ; and to the crown worn by the King of Burma on great state occasions.

Within the last few years, even, Abbé Huc wrote in a very similar strain as Father Grueber ; and he pointed out the resemblance between the Buddhist and Roman Catholic ceremonials with such *naïveté*, that, to his surprise, he found his delightful " Travels in Tibet" placed on the " Index Expurgatorius." " On ne peut s'empêcher d'être frappé," he writes, " de leur rapport avec le Catholicisme. La crosse, la mitre, la dalmatique, la chape ou pluvial, que les grands lamas portent en voyage, ou lorsqu'ils font quelque cérémonie hors du temple ; l'office à deux

---

that it should be known what its real origin is. Incense was burnt in ancient heathen temples with the object of neutralizing the offensive colour arising from the burning of animal sacrifice, and by the primitive fathers of the Christian Church was looked upon as a Pagan abomination.

* Notably so in the legend of St. Veronica and the Sudarium, and of Gautama's footprints in the instances of Rome and Poitiers, and on the sacred summit of Olivet. There is a legend also, that when St. Augustine landed at Thanet, he left perfect marks of his feet in the rock as if it had been wax : "And the Romanists will cry shame on our hard hearts," says Fuller, " if our obstinate unbelief, more stubborn than stone, will not as pliably receive the impression of this miracle."

chœurs, la psalmodie, les exorcismes, l'encensoir
soutenu par cinq chaines, et pouvant s'ouvrir et se
fermer à volonté ; les bénédictiones données par les
lamas en étendant la main droite sur la tête des
fidèles ; le chapelet, le célibat, ecclésiastique, les
retraites spirituelles, le culte des saints, les jeûnes,
les processions, les litanies, l'eau bénite ; voilà
autant de rapports que les Bouddhistes ont avec
nous."[*]

It is impossible, however, that there can be any
real analogy between the higher and better moral
precepts of our Gospel, and its doctrine of the
separate immortal existence of the soul, its hopes in
futurity, and promises of salvation, with the wretched
materialism of Buddhism. The resemblance is
superficial, but not accidental. It has been accounted for by the fact that, under the name
Mythraic,[†] the belief in the doctrines of the
Buddhist faith at the time of our Lord's appearance were widely spread over the western[‡] as well
as the eastern world. The general expectation of
the birth[§] of a great prophet, redeemer, or saviour,
which is alluded to even by Tacitus, as prevailing
at the period when Our Lord appeared, was not

---

[*] Quoted from Max Müller's "Chips," p. 189.

[†] "Tibet, Tatary, and Mongolia," p. 171.

[‡] An Indian philosopher, Ζάρμανος (Sramana, or Buddhist priest), came to
Europe with an embassy to Augustus from King Porus, and voluntarily burnt
himself at Athens.—Strabo, XV. ch. i. pp. 719, 720.

[§] See note * at foot of page 156.

confined to the prophecies of the Old Testament,
but had also a Buddhistic origin.* To minds
already imbued with Buddhistic doctrines, the birth
of a saviour, therefore, for the western world
recognized at the same time by "wise men from the
East," that is magi,† sramanas, or lamas, was
readily believed in when announced: and after the
acceptance of Christianity, many of the rites and
observances of Buddhism, which had been current
in the East for many previous centuries, gradually
crept in and were adopted by one community after
another until they became universal.‡

Gautama was at one time identified with Christ.
The Manichæans were actually forced to abjure
their belief that Christ and Gautama were one and
the same person;§ and some of the ancient Catholic

---

* St. Augustine says: "Res ipsa, quæ nunc religio Christiana nuncupatur,
erat apud antiquos, nec defuit ab initio generis humani, quousque Christus
veniret in carnem, unde vero religio, quæ jam erat, cœpit appellari Christiana."
—"August. Retr." i. 13; Max Müller, "Chips," p. 11.

† Paulinus supposes the religion of the magi to have been the same with that
of the Buddhists; it was introduced into Persia from India during the reign
of Cyrus, about 560 years before the birth of Christ, and from Persia was afterwards dispersed over the western nations —"Compendium legis Barmanorum,"
Museo Borgia, p. 141, *et seq.*

This opinion of Paulinus is supported by Pliny (lib. 30, ch. i.), who thought
that magic was first introduced into Europe by the army of Xerxes.

‡ The primitive Christians perpetually trod on mystic ground. The
Samancæans in Aram adopted many of the principles of Buddhism, and the
Gnostics, though Christians, partially followed this doctrine. Johannes von
Müller ("Allgemeine Weltgeschichte," book ix.) even affirms that Clement, a
disciple of St. Paul's, participated in Buddhist views, and that Simon Magus
was not only a Christian Gnostic, but a Buddhist.

§ Neander, "History of the Church," vol. i., p. 817: Τὸν Ζαραδὰν καὶ Βουδὰν

writers report that his mother's name was Maha
Maria (Malya)—the Great Mary—and there were
sramanas who represented him as a brother of
Christ.* One of the most curious circumstances,
however, connected with the legend of Gautama,
is that of his being entered as a saint in the Roman
calendar, and ordered to be worshipped as a saint
on every 27th November, under the title of St.
Josaphat. How this came about has been told by
Professor Max Müller in his paper on the migration
of fables in the " Contemporary Review " for July,
1870.

" A certain St. John of Damascus, who wrote in
the eighth century, was the son of Sergius, minister
at the Court of Khalif Almansūr. St. John became
a monk, and wrote many books. Amongst other
works ascribed to him is a religious romance called
the " Life of Barlaam and Jōasaph," which has been
distinctly proved † to be derived, as to the narrative
part of it, from the story of Gautama, as told in the
Játaka commentary, or the *Lalita Vistara*. The
Greek text of St. John's romance will be found in

καὶ τὸν Χριστὸν καὶ τὸν Μανιχαιὸν ἵνα καὶ τὸν αὐτὸν εἶναι—Max Müller,
" Chips," p. 222.

* Loubère, " Journal du Voyage de Siam," p. 90. Loubère was sent by
Louis XIV., as ambassador to the King of Siam in the year 1687.

† See especially Liebrecht, " Jahrbuch der Romanischen und Englishen
Literatur," vol. i. 1. He compares the Catholic romance with the " *Lalita
Vistara*," and the likeness to the Játaka is still closer.—" Buddhism," Rhys
Davids, p. 196.

Migne's Patrology, with a Latin translation. The bulk of the work consists of long theological and moral instructions to the Prince Jōasaph by his teacher, Barlaam, in the course of which some Buddhist Játaka stories are inserted. As the moral tone of the book, which here and there seems to betray Buddhist influence, was so popular in the Middle Ages that the romance was translated into several European languages, we need not wonder that the hero was subsequently canonized.*

" To have been made a Christian saint, is not the only curious fate which has befallen the great teacher. He takes his place also in the ' Dictionnaire Infernel,' of M. Collin de Plancy,† a quaintly illustrated dictionary of all matters relating to devils, fairies, magic, astrology, and so on. There he appears in a curious woodcut as 'Sakimuni, génie ou dieu,' in the character of the Man in the Moon." ‡

In Burma, the Sramana,§ or Buddhist monks, are called Phongyees, literally great glory, or Rahans, which means perfect. The life of a phongyee is still a popular one in British Burma, and must have

---

* Antiquity had made Priapus a god, the middle ages raised him into a saint, and that under several names. In the south of France he was worshipped under the title of St. Foutin, of St. Regnaud in Burgundy, and St. Cosmo in the south of Italy.

† Paris, 1863 (sixth edition).

‡ Quoted from Rhys Davids' '' Buddhism," pp. 196-7.

§ From *Srama*, '' the performance of ascetism."

had still greater charms in the troublous times
which preceded British rule. In the quiet and
solitude of his monastery, the monk was safe from
all the care and turmoil of the outer world, he could
not be pressed to serve as a soldier, was free from
all taxation and forced labour, and no robber was
sacrilegious enough to attack a monastery.

For admission to the Order, only a few necessary
conditions are required, and the rules to be observed
convey more an obligation to refrain from certain
usages, rather than as imposing a class of duties that
he has to perform. "On the part of the candidate, it
is an acknowledgment of the excellence of asceticism,
with an implied declaration that its obligations
should be observed ; and on the part of the priests
by whom the ceremony is conducted, it is an admission that the candidate is eligible to the reception
of the office, and that so long as he fulfils its duties,
he will be received as a member of the ascetic
community, and be entitled to all its rights and
privileges." *

The Buddhist *kyoung*, or monastery, plays an
important part in the life of every Burman. It is
almost the universal custom for Burmese parents in
every class of life, to cause their sons to enter the
monasteries as novices, for the purpose of learning
to read and write. Then, again, Gautama preached

* "Eastern Monachism," p. 44.

that every man should become a monk ; and in
theory, if not in practice, every man does become a
monk, at least once in his life. It may be only for
a few days or a few weeks ; or it may be for months
or years. All this while he is subject to monastic
discipline, even if he is a member of the royal
family.

As soon as boys are able to read and write,
religious books are put into their hands, from which
they imbibe religious notions, and become acquainted
with at least some portions of their creed. The
consequence is, that when they grow up to manhood,
a large proportion of them possess a respect for their
religion, and a kindly regard for monks and monasteries ; and there is none of the fear or dislike with
which the Brahmins are often regarded by the
lower castes of Hindus in India.

Before a lad can obtain the novitiate, he must be
at least eight years of age, and his entrance into a
monastery is a marked event in his life. He proceeds through the streets to the monastery, dressed
in the richest apparel his parents can afford, riding
on a horse gaily caparisoned, or sitting in a handsome
litter borne on the shoulders of four or more men,
with gold umbrellas held over his head, and accompanied by music, and a large procession of kinsfolk
and acquaintances. On reaching the threshold of
the monastery, the postulant is delivered by his

parents over to the Superior or Tsaya-dau, after whom he repeats the two Buddhist formularies of the "Three Refugees" (*tun-surana*) * and the ten obligations (*dasa-sil*).† His head is then shaved, and his fine secular dress is changed for the yellow robe. From that time his identity is lost, he is subjected to monastic discipline, the monastery becomes his home, and he must go round every morning with his alms-bowl, and subsist on the daily food that is given him.

The above display is an honour paid to the postulant on his giving up the pomps and vanities of the world, and symbolical of a somewhat similar event in the life of Gautama, who went to his palace in great pomp the day before he threw off his rich attire and assumed the garb of the ascetic. Novices do not generally remain in the monasteries beyond a few years, and then they return to secular life ; but in the event of their remaining until they are twenty years of age, they can then, if they wish it, receive full ordination, and became *patsengs*, or professed members of the Order.

* "I take refuge in Buddha ; I take refuge in the Law ; I take refuge in the associated Priesthood."

† The ten precepts are : 1. I take the vow not to destroy life ; 2. I take the vow not to steal ; 3. I take the vow to abstain from impurity ; 4. I take the vow not to lie ; 5. I take the vow to abstain from intoxicating drinks ; 6. I take the vow not to eat at forbidden times ; 7. I take the vow to abstain from dancing, singing, and music ; 8. I take the vow not to use scents or ornaments ; 9. I take the vow not to use high or honourable seats or couches ; 10. I take the vow not to receive gold or silver.

The obligations prescribed for patsengs* are contained in a manual called Pátimokkhan, which is ordered to be studied and learnt by heart. Every member of the Order must renounce his own will, and no room is left for the independent exertions of the mind. Every action of the day, the manner of performing it, the time it should last, the circumstances that must attend it, have all been minutely regulated.

From the moment a rahan rises in the morning, to the moment he goes to his natural rest in the evening, his only duty is to obey and follow the will and commands of the founder of the society. He advances in perfection proportionately to his fervent compliance with the injunctions, and to his conscientiously avoiding all that has been forbidden. But at the same time he must conquer self by himself. Γνῶθι σεαυτὸν is one of the chief of Buddhist maxims, and "the observance of no ceremony, the belief in no creed, will avail him who fails in obtaining a complete mastery over himself." †

The various sins a rahan is liable to commit, are comprised under seven principal heads, which are again subdivided and multiplied into the number of 227. The *Paradzeka*, or four unpardonable sins,

---

* From *patsnya*, five, and *enga*, a part—that is, proficient in the five obligations.

† " Buddhism," Rhys Davids, p. 168.

are fornication, theft, murder, and a false profession of the attainment of the Order. If any one of these sins is committed, it involves permanent exclusion from the priesthood. But all the others are subject to the law of confession, and can be expiated by virtue of the penances imposed upon the delinquent, after he has made an avowal of his sins.

The phongyees in Burma take precedence according to the number of Lents, or annual fasts of three months, which they have to keep. Those who continue phongyees for life are regarded with peculiar sanctity. Every monastery has a *tsaya-dau*, or abbot, who regulates its affairs and attends to the religious and moral training of its members. All towns and large villages contain a number of these religious houses, and the country, at least in Upper Burma, is portioned off into ecclesiastical divisions or dioceses subject to the authority of a *gŏn-ŏk*, or bishop. The religious communities residing in these divisions form, under the authority of the gŏn-ŏk, a province of the Order, similar to that of several Romanist Orders in Europe. The gŏn-ŏk is much respected, and his monastery outshines all others in the division in the splendour of its carving and decorations.

At Mandalay is stationed the *thā-thănā-boing*, or patriarch. He is supreme in all matters connected with religion, and, next to the King, is the person to whom the greatest external homage is paid. He is generally made patriarch from having been the King's instructor during youth. Hence, it generally happens that each King, on his accession, appoints his own patriarch, and the one in possession of the office has to retire. Great respect is paid by the King to this high dignitary of the Church. When he goes to visit His Majesty, or visits other monasteries, he is carried on a gilt litter in great state. He lives in a magnificent monastery, highly decorated with carving, and richly gilt; and from the centre of which rises a lofty *shwé-pyathat,** a dignity which even is not allowed an heir apparent to the throne. Spiritual commissioners are sent by him from time to time on tours of inspection in the provinces, to investigate and report as to whether the rules of the Order are duly observed, and if the professed members of the religious fraternity are really qualified for their holy calling.†

By an express ordinance of Gautama, a priest is

---

* For a description of this, see page 252, vol. i.

† With the exception of those of the tsaya-daus, or Abbots, the description given above of the powers of gŏn-ŏks and of the thǎ-thǎnǎ-boing, refer only to that portion of Burma still remaining under native rule, and where civil and religious institutions form component parts of the national life.

In British Burma, no such high dignitaries are acknowledged, and the old ecclesiastical organization is deteriorating in consequence. The English Government, while tolerating every form of religion, will not appoint spiritual heads, or enforce the canons of any religious sect by the secular arm, and schisms have crept in since the establishment of our rule, which threaten to disorganise the ecclesiastical structure.

allowed to retire from the Order and return to the
ordinary vocations of life; or, as the Burmese express
it, "throw off the robe and become a man." The
circumstances under which this can be done, are
"inability to remain continent; impatience of restraint; a wish to enter upon worldly engagements;
the love of parents and friends; or doubts as to the
truth of the system propounded by Gautama." But
to prevent abuses, no priest, after having been once
ordained, can throw off the robe without express
permission being first obtained from a legal Chapter.

This ordinance acts no doubt as a great safety-
valve to the Order, and resembles the usage of the
Church when celibacy was first enjoined among
Christians. "The custom was then, that as long
as a spirit of penitence and a desire of Christian
perfection animated the conduct of a priest, he was
exercised in the several duties of the monastic profession; if he repented of his choice, the road was
open, and he was at liberty to depart." Even
Cyprian (Epist. 62), after extolling the merit of the
virgins who had taken the vows, says, "but if they
are unwilling to persevere, it is better that they
should marry." It was by Benedict (Reg. C. 58)
that the law was first peremptorily made that all
who entered a convent should remain for life. This
system was soon adopted in other convents besides
the *monasterium Cassinense* in which he resided; and

these several convents " becoming united under one form of discipline, gave rise to the first monastic Order." *

Poverty is strictly enjoined upon priests, as the possession of temporal goods is supposed to offer a barrier to the perfect abnegation of self, and contempt for material things. The disciples of Gautama possess no common treasure, and a priest in his individual right is only allowed to possess the following eight articles, called *ata-pirikara*—namely, the theng-gan, composed of three robes (theng-boing, kō-wōt, and dō-gōt); a girdle for the loins; a thabeit, or alms-bowl; a razor, to shave his head and beard ; a needle to stitch his clothes ; and a perahankadar, or water-strainer. The latter is a necessary article, not for rendering the water more pure by straining, but to prevent the accidental destruction of life. The rule in the Pátimokkhan referring to this is, "if any priest shall knowingly drink water containing insects, it is a fault that requires confession and

* Lingard's " History of the Anglo-Saxon Church," ch. i. v. ; Giesler's " Text-Book of Ecclesiastical Literature," ch. xxxiv. ; " Eastern Monachism," p. 56.

The chaste severity of Benedict and other fathers of his type extended to whatever related to the commerce of the two sexes. One of their favourite theories was, that if Adam had preserved his obedience to the Creator, he would have lived for ever in a state of virgin purity, and that some harmless mode of vegetation might have peopled Paradise with a race of innocent and immortal beings. The use of marriage was permitted only to his fallen posterity, as a necessary expedient to continue the human species, and as a restraint, however imperfect, on the natural licentiousness of desire. See Gibbon's " Decline and Fall of the Roman Empire," ch. xv., p. 323.

absolution." The strainer is to be a cubit square, without a single broken thread.

According to an injunction of Gautama's, the monk's habit was to be composed of cast-off rags picked up in the streets, or among tombs ; and to observe this law as closely as possible, when new clothes are presented to the priests, they tear them into shreds, so as to deprive them of all commercial value, and then sew them together again. Hence, a priest has very little that he can call his own. The monastery in which he lives, his food and raiment, are all supplied to him by the neverfailing pious liberality and ever-watchful attention of his supporters. He never concerns himself about political matters, or takes part in worldly affairs of any description, He has "no care for the morrow," and his whole attention can be concentrated on the performance of the duties of his calling.

In the early morning in all the towns and villages of Burma are to be seen long files of phongyees perambulating the streets at a measured pace, with their alms-bowl slung round their necks, into which people pour food as they pass. They are barefooted and have no covering for the head. In the right hand they carry a large palm-leaf fan, which they hold before their face in the presence of women, so that no evil thought may enter the mind. They are forbidden to ask for food, to look to the right or to the left ; and they may not enter or loiter about the doors of houses. Gautama said : " The wise priest never asks for anything ; it is a proper object for which he carries the alms-bowl ; and this is his only mode of solicitation." When anything is poured into their bowls, they do not return thanks, but content themselves by saying " *thado, thado,*" that is, well, well ; and when suffi- cient has been obtained to appease their hunger they return to the monasteries to eat it.

Many Burmese consider it a great act of merit to make a vow never to partake of a meal without reserving a portion of it for the phongyees. Nothing whatever is cooked in the monasteries. The hours during which food can only be eaten is between sunrise and noon ; for after that time it is con- sidered liable to cloud the intellect, and unfit a priest for devoting himself to meditation, and the right performance of religious exercises.

In the early days of Buddhism there was an Order of female rahans, or nuns. The Order was established by Gautama himself, and amongst its first members were his wife Yasōdhara, and his foster-mother Prajapûti; but from the system having been found to be connected with so many evils, it has fallen into disrepute, and the Order is now represented by only a few old women dressed in white, who reside near the monasteries, sweep about pagodas, and attend funerals.

The state of a priest when alive is regarded as one of great sanctity, and their very persons thereby rendered holy. Great honours are therefore in consequence paid to their mortal remains. As soon as a priest has expired, his body is opened, the viscera extracted, and the body embalmed ; after which the corpse is closely swathed with bandages of linen, and covered over with a thick coat of varnish. It is then placed between two solid pieces of wood hollowed out for the purpose, and boiling resin poured into the interstices until every crevice is filled. When this is completed, the coffin is gilded, and placed on a platform under a handsomely decorated canopy, in one of the rooms of the monastery ; or in a separate building erected for the purpose in its vicinity, and there lies in state until preparations are completed for the cremation, which often extend over some months.

If the monastery where the priest died is situated in the neighbourhood of a large town, sixteen or twenty of the most comely damsels are chosen from some of the best families of each division of the place, and taught to perform in honour of the funeral a slow, graceful dance, accompanied with a song. The dancers are arranged in parties of

FUNERAL PROCESSION OF A BUDDHIST PRIEST.

four ; each of which performs separately at intervals, and has its own music and song. An equal number of young men are similarly selected, and go through their performances in like manner. The day before the ceremony, when all are supposed to be thoroughly proficient, they proceed in procession through the town, dressed in their gayest attire, to the houses of the different heads of the community, and rehearse their performances for the following day.

On the morning of the funeral the coffin is taken from its platform and deposited inside a lofty catafalque,* placed upon a large car with four or more wheels, and drawn out by bullocks to the cemetery. Arriving there, the bullocks are taken out, and ropes fixed to the front and back of the car, which are quickly seized by a number of men, one party of them pulling the car in the direction of the monastery where the deceased lived, and the other towards the centre of the cemetery. To the uninitiated this scene is anything but a mournful one. The car, creaking and shaking, moves slowly backwards and forwards, until at last, with shouts of delight, the strongest party carries it off with a

---

* The illustration shows the catafalque on the car, and the coffin borne on the shoulders of eight men. This is sometimes done, as a matter of precaution, where no road exists, and the procession has to travel over rough ground. The coffin in such case is not then placed within the catafalque until the arrival of the car at the entrance of the cemetery.

run along the grass ; more men then join and assist the beaten party, and after a little coquetting away goes the car back again.

At last the car is allowed to reach the centre of the cemetery, where heaps of inflammable matter are piled up in and about it ; after which the people go to refresh themselves at the numerous extempore booths, see the dancing, which is going on all the time, and place the *doons*, or rockets, in position that are to fire the pyre.

These rockets are made out of the stem of a tree, hollowed out and filled with gunpowder, and other compound combustibles rammed down with great force, and are often fifteen feet long, with a diameter of bore of nine inches. They are firmly fixed to small cars on four wheels, and each division of the town has several of them, in which they take great pride. The rockets are planted about 150 yards from the pyre, and discharged in succession according to a plan previously agreed upon.

They are fired by means of a match applied to a small vent at the breach, and the matter with which they are charged burning gradually, propels the car they are fastened to with considerable force and speed. Many of them, however, are discharged before the pyre is struck ; a slight inequality in the ground being liable to divert the car from its direct course. Some even curve back and burst among the crowd, when severe accidents not unfrequently happen.

At last one strikes the pyre, scattering around its contents and igniting the combustibles about the car, and amidst the shouts of triumph of those to whom the rocket belongs, and renewed dance and song, the bright flame shoots up, embracing each gay pinnacle and flag, till the whole catafalque comes down with a crash, and all is soon reduced to ashes.

In the towns of Burma, a particular spot is generally allotted for the construction of monasteries, and, for the sake of quietude, is isolated from the buildings of the laity. The general form of the building is oblong. The floor or platform is raised on piles about eight feet from the ground. The framework of the edifice is all of wood, supported by five posts often sixty to eighty feet long, and the walls are made of planks. Above the first roof rises a second of smaller dimensions, and beyond that again a third one, smaller than the second. This style of roof is only allowed to royal palaces, and buildings devoted to religion ; and the eaves, gables, fineals, and ridge ornaments of all the roofs, are often elaborately and beautifully carved.

On the front face there are frequently three flights of steps, and the building is generally

arranged as follows. A large open gallery runs
on all four sides of the building, within which is
a second one protected by the roof, and forming
what may be called a *vestibulum*, as all the rooms
in the monastery are connected with and open upon
it. Large shutters, working on hinges, which can
be raised up and supported on poles, or closed at
pleasure, separate the inner from the outer gallery.
The central portion is taken up by a large hall with
a handsomely carved ceiling, and the floor of which
is raised about a foot higher than any other part of
the building. In it are arranged the images of
Gautama, and often, also, those of his favourite
disciples ; and the book-cases containing the library
of the monastery. The state-room of the abbot
is separated from the hall by a richly panelled
wall, and the inner gallery partitioned off for the
accommodation of the priests and novices—the
western side being generally reserved for the
monastery school.

Some travellers in Burma have supposed that
Buddhism is rapidly declining, because they see
many religious buildings neglected and going to
decay. This is not a correct inference. A large
amount of both honour and merit attaches to the
founders of new pagodas and monasteries. The
honorary title of " Phura Taga," and of " Kyoung
Taga," meaning the builder or supporter of a

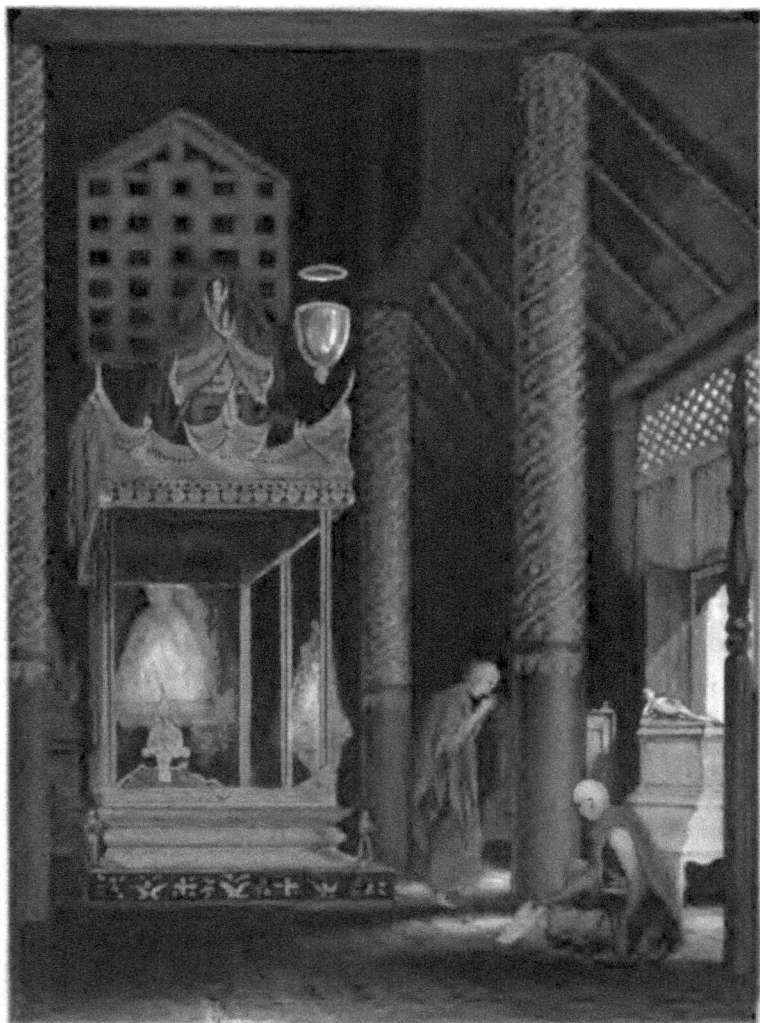

INTERIOR OF A BUDDHIST MONASTERY

pagoda or monastery, is assumed by them, of which they are very proud, and always append to their signature. The religious merit which is supposed to attach to mere repairs of such edifices is of a very much smaller value in the scale of good works; and the consequence is that many of these buildings are allowed to go to ruin, whilst new ones are founded for the sake of gaining merit and fame.

The monastic system in Burma has a practical interest from its being connected with national education. Every monastery has its school, where in harmony with the national religion are learnt the same lessons which have been taught from generation to generation for a couple of thousand years. On arriving at some obscure spot in the interior of the country, the first sign of life that often strikes the ear, is the murmuring sounds proceeding from the monastery school; and there is not a town or village, scarcely even a hamlet, I think, that has not at least one of such schools.

The instruction of the young is one of the several means by which merit in a Buddhistic sense is obtained, and has given rise to lay schools, also, or, as they are called, "house schools." These, though comparatively few in number as compared with monastic schools, are of great importance, as they are free from some of the disabilities that are attached to the religious seminaries—notably so in

the absence of the rule precluding the attendance
of female scholars.* Owing to these two classes
of indigenous schools, there is scarcely a man in
Burma who cannot read, write, and cipher. Statistics show that there are few convicts in our
gaols, natives of Burma, who are not so far grounded
in the rudiments of education.

The masters of the lay schools are men who have
retired from active life, and whose piety gives confidence to their neighbours. The schools are conducted in their private houses, a large portion of
which is given up for that purpose, and the system
of teaching and the text-books are the same as those
used in the monasteries. The school hours, lay and
monastic alike, extend over the whole day, with
fixed intervals. The discipline is strict, and there
is no sparing of the rod when such is necessary.

From an early period of our occupation of the
country, in addition to this two-fold system of indigenous education, the British Government established
denominational schools at the four chief towns for
teaching the English language and literature ; and
several smaller schools connected with Christian missionaries were also opened out in different parts in
the interior of the province. These latter being
under European or American supervision and con-

* The last education report of British Burma goes so far even to state " that
the lay schools, where girls are taught with the boys, are almost invariably found
in better order than the monastic ones, where boys are exclusively educated."

trol, and furnishing a higher order of education than
the indigenous ones, were supported by grants of
yearly allowances from Government, under the provision of certain rules known as the grants-in-aid
system.

This plan was followed until 1866, when my predecessor, Sir Arthur Phayre, drew the attention of
the Government of India to the large number of
monastic schools in the province, and suggested
that they might be made the basis of a national
system of education. The idea was one which
recommended itself in every way, and the scheme
was adopted. A Director of Public Instruction was
appointed, together with a small staff of inspectors
and circuit teachers, to be increased if the plan was
found to work successfully, and a few manuals of
geography and arithmetic, after the European
system, were printed in the Burmese language for
gratuitous distribution in the monasteries. I need
hardly say that, on my assuming charge of the
province in the following year, every encouragement
and assistance for the development of the scheme
was afforded.

The literature studied and taught by the Buddhist
priests is entirely religious. Here and there a
hierophant may be found, like the priests during
the revival of letters in the Middle Ages, who is
anxious to acquire some knowledge of European

literature and science. But there the analogy ends. The ambition of a Buddhist priest is confined to his own monastery, or, at any rate, to the attainment of ecclesiastical rank only. He cannot aspire to political power like the ecclesiastical statesmen who took the lead for centuries in many European cabinet councils, the fundamental rule of his Order being that he must abandon all concern with the outer world, and never receive money on any pretence whatever.

For the harmonious and successful working of the new scheme, the great difficulty, therefore, as regarded the monastery schools, for none were apprehended or have been found connected with the lay ones, which had to be solved was, how the co-operation of the phongyees could be obtained, and a stimulus introduced into the monasteries.

This has been surmounted to some considerable extent in several ways : by multiplying the instruments of teaching, in the increase of inspectors and circuit teachers, and translations of English books of literature and science ; and also by publishing in a printed form the Pali text in most common use in the monasteries. " Fixed standards have been laid down for the examination of pupils in the three subjects most commonly taught, the Burmese language, the Pali language, and arithmetic ; and money prizes, varying in value with the standard passed, are awarded at periodical examinations to both teachers and pupils. The difficulty of making such offerings to the monk bound to poverty is overcome either by handing over the amount to the lay patron of the monastery, or by substituting for money a gift of books.

" A certificate is granted with each prize, and a keen competition has by this means been called forth among rival scholars, and between rival schools.

" A still more useful measure, and one accepted with a no less surprising readiness, even by the monks, has been the attachment to selected schools of masters (natives of the country) trained in a Government school, appointed and salaried by the Government, and accustomed to European methods of teaching and school arrangement. Special grants of public money are also made under stated conditions for school buildings, and for books or school apparatus, and the English school-slate and printed text-book are already widely supplanting the palm-leaf manuscript and black board which have been in the hands of preceding generations." *

Shortly previous to my leaving Rangoon a Government normal school was established for the training of both male and female teachers, which now furnishes an annual supply of both ; and it may, I think, be fairly considered that the leaven introduced

* " Buddhist Schools in Burma," Fraser's Magazine, November, 1877.

into the national system by all the above measures, and now working under the able superintendence of Mr. Peter Hordern, the present director of Public Instruction, whom I especially selected for the post from the officers of the Educational Department in Bengal, is full of promise for the future of the rising province of British Burma.

With these remarks this work is closed. Its progress has awakened many pleasant memories, and it is with a feeling of regret, heightened by a consciousness of short-comings, that the book is brought to a conclusion, and laid before the public.

APPENDICES.

APPENDICES.

APPENDIX A.

OFFICIAL REPORTS

REGARDING AN

EXPEDITION AGAINST AN ARAKAN HILL TRIBE.

Extract of Station Orders by Major F. V. MacGrath, Commanding at Akyab, dated Akyab, 8th January, 1842.

A FEW words are due from the Commanding Officer on the return of the Detachment Arakan Light Infantry, commanded by Lieutenant Fytche, ordered against a clan of Walleng Hill Tribes, as the duty has been performed in a highly creditable and efficient manner, and which the Civil Officer has reported will facilitate his intercourse with the Hill Tribes, and be a check to these independent races of Wallengs in future attacking, or otherwise molesting, the mountain clans under British rule and protection.

2. The conduct of the detachment, composed of 1 lieutenant, 1 subadar, 1 jemadar, 3 havildars, 3 naicks, 2 buglers, and 80 privates, in the attack of from 200 to 300 men posted greatly to advantage on precipitous mountain cliffs, forming strong natural fortifications, renders great credit to all employed ; nor is it less to their credit the cheerfulness with which they undertook the extreme fatigue and exposure, without tents, they were subject to.

3. To Lieutenant Fytche, for his personal exertion and gallantry in leading so spirited a dash, to the native commissioned and non-commissioned officers, buglers, and soldiers under his command, in whose praise he speaks so highly, Major MacGrath feels much pleasure in offering the assurance of his acknowledgments and thanks, which he will not fail to report with a detail of their proceedings to higher authority.

Extract of District Orders by Lieutenant-Colonel Pogson, Commanding in Arakan, Head Quarters, Kyouk Phyoo, dated 11th January, 1842.

Lieutenant-Colonel Pogson, Commanding in Arakan, has received from Major MacGrath, Commanding Arakan Light Infantry, a report detailing the arduous exertions and gallantry of the detachment of that corps, under the command of Lieutenant Fytche, in attacking the Wallengs, taking their stockade by storm, and expelling them from a position which, on account of its great strength and inaccessibility, had been occupied by them for the last five-and-thirty years, enabling them to commit depredations on the territories under British rule and protection, and to carry their inhabitants into slavery.

2. To the judicious arrangements of Lieutenant Fytche, accompanied by Lieutenant Phayre, the Senior Assistant Commissioner at Akyab, difficulties were overcome insurmountable to everything but their judgment and gallantry, and the devotion and bravery displayed by those under their command.

3. The lieutenant-colonel therefore feels it incumbent on him to record the high sense he entertains of the talent, zeal, and intelligence so conspicuous on the parts of Lieutenants Fytche and Phayre on this occasion, and to add that it will be a gratifying part of his duty to report their gallant and meritorious exertions, and those of the detachment, to His Excellency the Commander-in-Chief.

From Lieutenant-Colonel Pogson, Commanding in Arakan, to Major-General Lumley, Adjutant-General of the Army, No. 13, dated Kyouk Phyoo, 11th January, 1842.

I have the honour to forward a letter from Major MacGrath, dated 8th instant, containing a detailed report of the gallantry of Lieutenant Fytche, and the Detachment Arakan Light Infantry recently employed against the Walleng Hill Tribe, and the entire success of his operations, also copy of a District order, which the occasion seems to demand.

2. Lieutenant Fytche having been a passenger to Arakan in the same vessel with myself, I am enabled to add my testimony in his favour to that of Major MacGrath, as he possessed the characteristics of a well-informed, intelligent, and promising officer. I therefore feel much pleasure in recommending him to the favourable consideration of His Excellency the Commander-in-Chief.

Despatch from Lieutenant, now Major-General, Sir Arthur Phayre, to Captain Bogle, the Commisssioner of Arakan, dated 17th January, 1842.

I have the honour to report to you that on the 10th December last I left Akyab in company with a party of the Arakan local battalion of the strength stated in the margin, and under the command of Lieutenant Fytche, 7th Regiment N.I., for the purpose of proceeding

1 Subadar.
1 Jemadar.
3 Havildars.
3 Naicks.
70 Sepoys.
2 Buglers.

against the Koomee clan called Wulleng, which had been guilty of making several attacks on tribes within the British frontier, as detailed in my letter to your address of the 23rd July.

2. The detachment proceeded by water to the Koladyne Thannah, which is about 100 miles north from Akyab. We reached it by the night of the 12th, and then went without delay as far up the Mee Khyoung as the boats could proceed. Early on the 13th the detachment continued up the Mee Khyoung in canoes; a drizzling rain had commenced falling before daylight,

and continued throughout the day.   At 5 p.m. we reached the
halting-place.   It rained very hard all night.   The next morning,
the 14th, the stream was so much swollen, and the rain still
falling so heavily that it was evident we could not now continue
our march, which from this point lay up the beds of mountain
streams, generally dry, or nearly so, at this season.   As this spot
was not a fit one for a halt of some days (for it was now evident
that several days' detention was inevitable), it was judged expedient to return to the Thannah, which we reached at 5 p.m.
The rain was heavy and incessant throughout the day.   During
the 15th and 16th it rained at intervals, and we could not with any
chance of finding open paths proceed on until the evening of the
20th, when we advanced up the Mee Khyoung as far as our
boats could go.   This unavoidable detention necessarily gave the
Wullengs notice of our approach, and though I had not from the
first deemed it practicable for us to surprise them, yet we should
have been able to inflict considerable injury upon them by the
seizure and destruction of their property.   As the capture of any
of their persons was scarcely to be expected, this was the only
means we had of making any impression on them, and of securing
the object in view, namely, by retaliation convincing them of
their insecurity in their much-vaunted position, and thereby
working on their fears and preventing their making attacks upon
their neighbours, or those at least within the British frontier.

On the 21st we again proceeded on in the canoes, and reached
the mouth of the Sumeng Khyoung by 5 p.m.

4. On the 22nd, finding still too much water on the bed of the
Sumeng to allow of marching through it, we had to take a more
difficult route across the hills, until we joined the Sumeng higher
in its course, and halted for the day at 4 p.m.

5. On the 23rd, leaving the Sumeng, the route lay up a small
mountain torrent, and we crossed some steep hills into the
Sumeng once more, where we halted for the night.   Early on the
24th we were afoot, having a stiff march before us to the village
of attack, it being at an elevation of about 4,000 feet above the
Sumeng.   It stands near the summit where the face of the moun-

tain is nearly perpendicular. About 10 a.m. we were sufficiently near to hear yells and shouts from the village, or rather from men stationed above it, but not a man could we catch a glimpse of; numerous masses of rock, trunks of trees, and other missiles were hurled down by them from above, with the object apparently of intimidating us, for we had not yet advanced sufficiently near for these to take effect. Lieutenant Fytche now judiciously ordered the detachment to make a detour from the regular path, and we advanced by the left flank of the village, having Koomees ahead with dhás, to cut a path through the thick stunted bamboo jungle. A few shots were fired at us, but the Wullengs concealed themselves so effectually, that not one of them could be seen, though their position was disclosed by the smoke of their muskets. When we were within about 100 yards, Lieutenant Fytche directed a few shots to be fired at the particular rocks and bushes where parties of the enemy were known or suspected to be ensconced, which had the effect of dislodging them; some were wounded by our fire while springing from their hiding-places. The detachment now advanced, or climbed, as quickly as the steep, indeed almost perpendicular, nature of the ground would admit of, until they reached the village. The houses were all empty, as was to have been expected. So steep was the spot where the village stood, that the inhabitants, I found, could only leave their houses and go down the face of the hill, or communicate with each other by means of ladders; they had now removed all these and retired to the summit of the hill, pulling their ladders after them. A pursuit of them would have been useless. The precipitous nature of the ground, which rendered an ascent, save by ladders, next to impossible, and the fatiguing march the men had already performed, rendered it extremely improbable that we should be able to overtake any of the fugitives. Provisions also would not have been procurable, and it was advisable not to exhaust our supplies by delay in chasing an enemy, whom there was little or no chance of ever overtaking, and in a country where we could expect to find nothing. The village consisted as reported of about eighty houses. We set it on fire, and after halting here about two hours and a half, we descended the hill, and returned to the place we started from in the Sumeng, having had a very hard day's work. None of our men were wounded save in the feet, by the sharp bamboo spikes with which the hill-side was studded in grassy spots where they could be concealed.

6. From the Sumeng we returned by a different route to that we had travelled in our advance, through a difficult mountainous country, never before travelled by an European. The fact of a military detachment having marched by these paths will, I am convinced, have a great moral effect on the whole of the surrounding tribes. For a detail of each day's march I beg to refer you to a copy of a private Journal I kept, which is herewith annexed. We arrived in Akyab on the 30th ultimo.

7. In conclusion, I beg to state that although none of the people of this clan have been captured, yet I feel assured that the fact of a military detachment having reached and taken possession of the village of a people so feared by the adjoining tribes as the Wullengs were, will have a great effect on the Koomees generally. It will give confidence to those subject to our rule, and I have hopes that it will be the means of deterring other tribes beyond our frontier from attacking those within it.

From Lieutenant Phayre, Senior Assistant Commissioner, Akyab, to Major MacGrath, Commanding Arakan Light Infantry, dated Akyab, 3rd January, 1842.

Having applied to you for a party of the Arakan Light Infantry, to proceed against a Clan of Koomees, termed Wallengs, who had made some attacks on tribes residing within the British frontier, and the party having returned to cantonments, I beg herewith to express through you my thanks to Lieutenant Fytche, commanding the detachment sent on service, for the efficient assistance he gave me in every way, to secure the objects I had in view.

2. The very strong position occupied by the Walleng Clan having been reached after a toilsome march through a moun-

tainous country, I feel assured that the Wallengs have received a check which will give confidence and security to the neighbouring clans. I cannot conclude this letter without expressing my admiration of the spirited style in which the men of the detachment scaled the steep and almost inaccessible rock upon which the village of attack was situated, and which, even if undefended, would have proved a serious obstacle to any advancing party.

3. Lieutenant Fytche having returned by difficult mountain paths which no European had hitherto traversed, will have the effect of showing many of these tribes that they are much more within our power than they had hitherto supposed, and my intercourse with them will be much facilitated thereby.

APPENDIX B.

―•―

OFFICIAL DOCUMENTS

CONNECTED WITH

SERVICES IN THE BASSEIN DISTRICT.

―――――

From Major Phayre, Commissioner and Governor-General's Agent in Pegu, to C. Allen, Esquire, Secretary to the Government of India, dated Rangoon, 10th March, 1853.

I BEG to submit for the information of the Most Noble the Governor-General of India in Council, copies of the accompanying Reports from Lieut. Fytche, Deputy Commissioner of Bassein, reporting an expedition in company with Captain Rennie, I.N., and the boats of the steam frigate *Zenobia*, also of H.M.'s steamer *Nemesis*, against the late Burmese Governor of the Bassein district.

2. The operations have been gallantly and successfully conducted. The force of the late Governor was mainly composed of up-country Burmese soldiers, numbering more than three thousand men ; these were, from the excellent arrangements of Lieut. Fytche, cordially and ably supported by Captain Rennie, met and routed by a very inferior force. I beg respectfully to bring the affair prominently to the notice of the Most Noble the Governor-General of India in Council, as it appears to me exceedingly creditable to the above-mentioned officers, and all concerned therein. I now have strong hopes that the Bassein district will ere long be quieted.

From Lieutenant A. Fytche, Deputy Commissioner, Bassein, to Capt.
A. P. Phayre, Commissioner and Governor-General's Agent
in Pegu, Rangoon, No. 13, dated Bassein, 14th January, 1853.

Having received information that a Burmese chief of marauders named Nga-tee-lwot was ravaging the country to the S.E. of this city, I proceeded on the morning of the 5th instant, in H.M.'s steamer *Nemesis*, to attack and disperse his band.

2. On our passage down the river we were informed by some villagers near Na-poo-tau that a large detachment from this band had passed a few hours before us to attack the village of Houng-gyee-kywon. We immediately proceeded on to that island, and were in time to save the village; but the marauders escaped through a small creek, where our boats after a fruitless pursuit were obliged to return on account of the shallowness of the water. On the following morning we proceeded up the Pamawadie Creek in progress to Woing-ka-na, stated to be Nga-tee-lwot's head-quarters, and anchored in the evening off Myoung-mya-myo, which was as far as the steamer could advance in that direction.

3. At daybreak next morning I left the steamer with two paddle-box boats and a cutter, each boat mounting a 3-pounder gun and manned by Europeans, accompanied also by a considerable force of Karens in their own boats, and about midday came upon a large detachment of the marauders at Tsago-mya village, who fired upon our boats, but were dispersed after a few discharges of grape, leaving several muskets and a number of spears and other arms behind them in their flight. After taking possession of these and destroying a quantity of their boats and stores of rice, &c., we proceeded on our journey, and anchored that evening at Pegon, which place we left at 2 a.m. on the following morning, and about 8 a.m. came upon the outpost guard of the marauders at Kya-gyan, who commenced a sharp fire of musketry upon us from behind a breastwork that they had erected; but our boats, dashing forward and opening their fire, soon silenced that of the marauders, and drove them from behind their works. Three large war boats, and the standard of the officer commanding the

detachment, were captured here.   After a short halt we then proceeded on to Woing-ka-na, which consisted of three large villages,
one of which was strengthened in the same way as their outpost
with strong breastworks. The marauders, however, would not await
our arrival, but fled, some to the jungle and others in their boats;
the latter we pursued, but could not come up with.   The Karens
in their boats might have overtaken them, but they hold these
marauders in the greatest dread, and I failed in my endeavours to
urge them in their pursuit.   The marauders were completely
surprised, and in their flight left almost everything behind them,
which, together with their houses, stores of rice, &c., I ordered to
be destroyed. We remained at Woing-ka-na that evening, and
left next morning for the steamer, which we reached on the
evening of the following day, and next morning, the 12th instant,
returned to Bassein, off which we anchored the same evening.

4. Myoung-mya-myo has been a very large place, and consisted,
I should imagine from the ruins, of upwards of 1,500 houses, but
the whole place has been completely destroyed by Nga-tee-lwot.
It is situated in a fine country, with very extensive plains all
around it, admirably adapted for the growth of rice.   All the
villages on our route had been destroyed in the same manner,
and not a single house was left standing except in the villages
where the dacoits had taken up their quarters.   None of the
plains, with the exception of small patches about Woing-ka-na,
appeared to have been cultivated this last season.   I appointed a
head man at Woing-ka-na, one at Kya-gyan, and another at Myoung-
mya-myo, with directions to call the people in from the jungle and
settle them down on the old sites of their villages.   They each had
one or two hundred followers with them, and spoke confidently of
success now that the robber bands had been dispersed ; but I much
doubt whether they will be able to hold their ground, unless
detachments of police are stationed at different commanding
points to overawe these robber bands and give confidence to the
people.

5. During the expedition I received the greatest attention from
Captain Goodwin, commanding H.M.'s steamer *Nemesis*, who

showed himself most anxious to meet my wishes in every respect, and nothing could have exceeded the gallantry and endurance of Mr. Baker, 1st officer of the *Nemesis*, and his noble boat's crew, in the arduous duties which they had to perform.

From Lieutenant A. Fytche, Deputy Commissioner, Bassein, to Captain A. P. Phayre, Commissioner and Governor-General's Agent, Pegu, No 27, dated Bassein, the 3rd February, 1853.

Having found that every effort of mine to settle this district would be fruitless until the Meng-gyee, or old Burmese governor, and other Burmese chiefs acting or professing to act under his orders, were driven out or destroyed, they having complete possession of the whole of the upper portion of the district above Bassein, I applied on the 19th ultimo to the naval officer commanding in the Bassein river to furnish, in conjunction with the officer commanding this garrison, such force as they might consider necessary for the purpose; supplying them at the same time with an account of the positions and strength of the enemy as my means of information concerning them admitted of. The officer commanding the garrison refused to furnish any assistance whatever, stating his force far to weak to detach, and that he had stringent orders not to move out from the vicinity of his post. But the senior naval officer entered most cordially into my views and promised me every aid in his power.

2. It being an object of the greatest importance that the Burmese troops should be attacked without delay, I determined in consultation with Captain Rennie (the senior naval officer here) not to wait the result of any application of troops from Rangoon, where it was improbable, we believed, they could be spared, but to proceed at once against the enemy with the naval force here and about 1,500 armed Karens and Burmese, whom I had collected for the purpose.

3. We accordingly left this on the morning of the 21st ult. in H.M. steamer *Nemesis* with boats of the H.C.S.F. *Zenobia* in tow, and proceeded up the Dugga creek (which enters the Bassein

river, about ten miles above the town of Bassein), and anchored
that afternoon off the Karen village of Kyan-gyee-doung, which
was as far as the steamer could proceed in that direction.   The
stronghold of the Burmese chiefs, which was the first object of
our attack, was situated about thirty miles further up this creek,
and we left the steamer the same evening in boats, accompanied
with our native force, and arrived off their outpost about 2 p.m. on
the following day.   The outpost was situated on the bank of the
creek, strongly entrenched, and the river staked across with the
rows of stakes, and was as strong a military position as could well
have been taken up.   Immediately we arrived within range of
their guns they fired upon us ; but our guns opening their fire,
soon silenced that of the enemy ; and the sailors rushing into the
water, stormed the place with the bayonet, and drove them from
behind their works.   After destroying the place we proceeded
up the stream to Kon-ghoung, the head-quarter of the Burmese
chief Nga-thein, which, however, he deserted on our approach,
and retreated to a place called Eng-ma, situated about sixteen
miles inland, where two other chiefs, Nga-tha-bon and Mow-oo,
had also their head-quarters.   We remained that night in our
boats at Kon-ghoung, and on the following morning landed four
guns, which, with eighty sailors and a native force of about 1,500
men, we marched on to Eng-ma, and within five miles on this
side of it came upon the enemy, who were drawn up in the jungle
and across the road to oppose our passage.   Our advanced guard,
consisting of about 600 natives, were at first driven back, but
were soon rallied, and the flanking parties being reinforced, the
enemy were driven through the jungle into an open plain, where
they attempted to make a stand, under their chief Nga-tha-bon,
who boldly advanced in front of his men, cheering them on ; a
fortunate shot from my rifle, however, disabled him, when the
whole of his force broke and dispersed.   The other two chiefs
escaped with difficulty, one of them, Nga-thein, almost naked ;
he throwing off his gilt hat and gold-embroidered robes of office
in his flight.

4. Eng-ma we found abandoned ; but towards evening a

number of the inhabitants came in from neighbouring jungles and informed us that the enemy had retreated up the country, and, they supposed, had gone to join the Meng-gyee ; but they begged us to burn the place down to prevent the chance of their collecting there again, and that they themselves would return to their old places of abode, from which they had been driven. Eng-ma was formerly an insignificant village, but when we found it, it contained upwards of 3,000 houses, nearly the whole of which had evidently been run up in the last few months, the people having been driven to it from Pantanau and Donabew and the neighbouring villages. The chief Nga-tha-bon, mentioned above as disabled, was Myo-thoo-gyee of Pantanau, and died the day after the receipt of his wound. We bivouacked that night in the open plain opposite Eng-ma, marched back to our boats the following morning, and the evening after that, the 25th ult., reached the steamer at Kyan-gya-doung.

5. On the 26th we started up the river, anchored for the night at Phura-gyee, left that on the following morning, and reached Nga-thaing-ghyoung (within a few miles of Kyouk-khyoung-ko-lay, where the Meng-gyee was said to be encamped) about 1 p.m., where we anchored, that being the extreme point to which the *Nemesis* could ascend the Bassein river. There learnt that the Meng-gyee had been joined by the troops that we had dispersed at Eng-ma and Khyoung-gon, and had marched out from his position towards Lemena. We determined on pursuing him, and pushed on in the morning in the boats to Lemena, a distance of about thirty miles by water, where we arrived about 5 p.m. The inhabitants of the village, which is a very extensive one, appeared at first, if not absolutely hostile, to be very lukewarm in our cause, and it was not until late at night that I could extract from them the exact position of the Meng-gyee, which turned out only to be eight miles distant. On my gaining this information I formed a resolution to cut off his retreat by sending a select party of our native auxiliaries round his right flanks to march that night and attack him in the rear, while we marched down upon his front in the morning. Mr. Baker, first officer of the *Nemesis*, very gal-

lantly volunteered to lead the native party, which started at 3 a.m.
Our main body left at 7 a.m. and marched on until 1 p.m., when
we came up with our advanced party, who it appeared had succeeded in getting in front of the Meng-gyee, but at the sight of his
overwhelming force, after firing a few shots, retreated into the
jungle.   After coming up with our advanced party we halted, and
I sent forward scouts to bring intelligence of the Meng-gyee's
movements, who shortly returned and reported that he had halted
five miles in our front, and imagined that he had only been encountered by a band of marauders, and had no idea that we were
so close to him.   I immediately determined, in consultation with
Captain Rennie, to halt where we then were, and to make a night
march round his right flank with the whole of our force, and get
in his front by daylight if possible.   Everything succeeded as we
wished, and we arrived in front of his encampment about half-an-
hour before daylight, and drew up our forces across the road,
masking the guns in some low jungle.   A little after daylight the
enemy's camp began to break up, and their advanced guard,
consisting of about 800 Ava soldiers, marched down upon us,
followed close by the main body, composed of about 2,500 fighting
men under the Meng-gyee.   They had heard that some body of
men were in their front, but merely thought it was the same party
that had fired on them the day before.   They therefore advanced
boldly, and seeing only our native force (all the Europeans were
lying down in a line behind the guns) opened a smart fire ; they
were allowed to advance within 150 yards, when our guns opened
upon them with grape, which tore through their masses, throwing
them into complete disorder, and they broke and fled in all
directions.   Forty-eight bodies were found in front of our guns,
and a great number were killed in the pursuit.   Fifty prisoners
were taken, two of whom are the Meng-gyee's adopted sons.   Seven
guns were also brought in, together with a number of muskets,
spears, and dahs, and a quantity of ammunition.

6. The loss in the European portion of our forces was trifling ;
during the whole expedition only one officer and three seamen
were wounded.   The exact loss of our native auxiliaries I have not

yet been able to ascertain, but it was of small extent. After pursuing the Meng-gyee's forces for some distance we marched back to our boats, where we arrived the same evening, and returned the following day to the steamer at Nga-thaing-ghyoung, at which place I remained one day, making arrangements for the settlement of the country from whence we had driven the Burmese troops, and on the morning of the 2nd returned to Bassein, where we arrived this day, the 3rd instant.

7. Immediately the Burmese forces were dispersed, the whole country turned out against them. I offered a reward of one viss of silver for the capture of the Meng-gyee, and think it not improbable that he will be brought in, as his horse was shot, and he escaped on foot to the jungle. At any rate, his power in this district is completely destroyed, and if not captured he will not remain here, but endeavour to effect his escape to Upper Ava, by jungle road, which leads under the Yoma-doung range.

8. The results of my first expedition, reported to you in my letter to your address, dated the fourteenth ultimo, have turned out everything that could be wished. The men whom I appointed there have been able to hold their ground, and the people are coming in from the jungles and quietly settling down on the old sites of the villages. I have no doubt that the effect of the present expedition, which has completely destroyed Burmese influence in this district, will be equally favourable. Many men of influence are now coming forward for appointment in the upper portion of the district, which before we started I could get no one to accept. I have also seen a large portion of my district during the late expeditions, and become to a certain extent acquainted with the feelings of the inhabitants, and I shall not now be working entirely in the dark in making arrangements for the settlement of the country.

9. Nothing could have exceeded the admirable arrangements made by Captain Rennie, commanding H.C.S.F. *Zenobia* throughout the whole expedition, who was most ably seconded by Captain Goodwin, of H.M.'s steamer *Nemesis*, 2nd Lieutenant Aylesbury, of the *Zenobia*, Mr. Baker, 1st officer of the *Nemesis*, and Lieu-

tenant Manderson, of the Bengal Artillery, who acted as a volunteer with the force, and commanded the guns. The endurance of the boats' crews was most surprising, and the cheerfulness with which they performed forced marches and other duties they were unaccustomed to, call for the highest praise, and I hope you will not fail to bring the conduct of all concerned before the notice of Government.

From C. Allen, Esquire, Secretary to the Government of India, to Major Phayre, Commissioner and Governor-General's Agent in Pegu, dated Fort William, the 19th March, 1853.

I have the honour to acknowledge the receipt of your two despatches, dated respectively the 19th ultimo, No. 18, and 10th instant, No. 24, enclosing Captain Fytche's reports of a successful attack upon bands of marauders, and of an expedition against the late Burmese Governor of the Bassein District.

2. In reply, I am directed by the Most Noble the Governor-General of India in Council to observe that the services reported in these two despatches, especially against the Meng-gyee, near Bassein, reflect the greatest credit on all concerned. The enterprise, judgment, and gallantry conspicuous in the conduct of Captain Fytche, the Deputy Commissioner, are highly honourable to him, while the excellent spirit with which all who were engaged carried on the joint duties of the expedition are worthy of all praise.

3. On a report from His Excellency Commodore Lambert, the Government has already conveyed its acknowledgments to Commander Rennie, and those who served with him, and it has now, I am desired to state, to offer to Captain Fytche the special thanks of the Governor-General of India in Council for his conduct as reported on the present occasion, and to express his warm approbation of that officer's proceedings, as well as of the conduct of Captain Goodwin (of the *Nemesis*), Mr. Baker, and Mr. Manderson, who accompanied him. His Lordship in Council, I am desired to state, anticipates the best consequences from these spirited and skilful proceedings.

From Major Phayre, Commissioner and Governor-General's Agent in Pegu, to C. Allen, Esquire, Secretary to the Government of India, dated Prome, 19th April, 1853.

I have the honour to forward for the information of the Most Noble the Governor-General of India in Council, copy of a despatch, No. 43, dated 26th March, 1853, to my address from Captain Fytche, Deputy Commissioner of Bassein, reporting the proceedings of the force of seamen and marines, under Commander Rennie, I.N., and of the native levies under himself, in co-operation with the attacks made by the detachment under Sir John Cheape, K.C.B., during last March, upon the bandit chief Myat-htoon, in the neighbourhood of Donabew. The force under Captain Fytche was employed in a very arduous service, and I feel assured rendered essential aid to the general operations under Sir John Cheape. I trust that the people sent in pursuit of the bandit chief by Captain Fytche may yet capture him.

From Lieutenant A. Fytche, Deputy Commissioner, Bassein, to Captain A. P. Phayre, Commissioner and Governor-General's Agent, Pegu, No. 43, dated Bassein, the 26th March, 1853.

I have the honour to inform you that about midday of the 25th ultimo I received a communication from the Goung-gyok of Lemena that a large British force had arrived at Heng-tha-da from Prome to attack the Talaing chief Myat-htoon in his stronghold at Kywn-ka-dzeng, and commenced their march for that place on the evening of the 22nd ultimo. Although I had received no intimation, official or otherwise, from any British officer that a force was being moved against Myat-htoon, the information coming from a Burmese chief in whom considerable reliance could be placed, and knowing Heng-tha-da to be only three days' march from the enemy's position, I determined to act at once upon it and proceed myself, in company with such force as the naval officer commanding in the Bassein river could furnish (any aid from the military garrison at Bassein being hopeless, as I had been officially informed that not a single man should be detached from that post without an order from General Godwin), and raise the country in Myat-htoon's rear, to cut off his retreat when attacked, or co-operate with Sir J. Cheape's force, as circumstances might point out as most fit.

2. I accordingly placed myself in communication with Captain Rennie, the senior naval officer here, who entered most cordially into my views, and at 2 P.M. of the 26th ultimo we proceeded up the Bassein river in H.M.'s steamer *Nemesis*, with the boats of H.C.'s steamer *Zenobia* in tow, and anchored at 8 A.M. at Kang-gyee-doung in the Dugga creek, which was as far as the steamer could proceed in that direction. We left the *Nemesis* here, and advanced in the boats up the Dugga creek, and arrived at Kyoung-gon at 8 a.m. of the following morning, where we found a note from Captain Smith, the Deputy Commissioner of Tharawah and Political Officer with Sir J. Cheape, dated the 25th ultimo, informing us of the arrival of the force at Khai-boung, within one day's march of Kywn-ka-dzeng. I hastened forward my arrangements for a native force which I had ordered to be collected here, to close the Wet-Khyoung road, leading from this on the enemy's position, and pushed on in the evening to Eng-ye', at which place and at Tounglo the main body of our Burmese and Karen auxiliaries had been directed to assemble. On the morning of the 28th ultimo a note arrived from Captain Smith, dated 27th ultimo, stating that Sir J. Cheape "had made a flank movement to the westward," which might delay his advance. Knowing, from the direction in which Sir J. Cheape marched, that he could not be more at any time than one day or two easy day's march from the enemy, I informed him in reply that we would advance on Myat-htoon's position by three roads on the 2nd instant (this letter, however, does not appear to have reached him). All our preparations being completed by the evening of the 1st instant, we advanced on the morning of the 2nd instant, the Europeans consisting of 90 seamen and marines, with four small field-pieces,

and a native force of 1,200 men, marching on the centre road, and two detachments under the command of the Goung-gyokes of Lemena and Kyoung-kon, the former with 500 men and the latter with 300, marching by the roads on our right and left flanks (*vide sketch annexed*), our base of operations extending about 12 miles. We only marched four miles that day, driving in *en route* an outpost of Myat-htoon's consisting of about 100 men, and bivouacked in the large plain of Tho-gyo-pyeet, hoping to receive further information of Sir John Cheape's movements, or to hear the welcome sound of his guns. Having received no information whatever of Sir John Cheape's force, but imagining that he must be in our immediate vicinity, and that his attack could not possibly be delayed beyond the 3rd, we determined on advancing. Little or no resistance was met with on our march, the enemy retreating from their breastworks as we advanced, until our arrival at his strongly-entrenched position on the left bank of the Dunan lake, which was occupied in great force, and from which a very heavy fire was opened upon us. Having got our guns into position, however, and lined the banks with musketry, we kept down their fire somewhat, and parties being pushed across the lake to the right and left, turned the flanks of the enemy's entrenchments, when they fled in the greatest confusion, leaving behind them a nine-pounder carronade, 3 brass jingals of large calibre, and 32 muskets. We came to a determination to halt in the enemy's works that day, and push on to Myat-htoon's position, from which we were only 2 miles distant, the next morning. Myat-htoon himself, however, with the whole of his forces, came down to attack us at half-past 4 P.M. ; and our native force having fired away the whole of their ammunition by daybreak (the attack extending to that period), and hearing nothing of Sir John Cheape's force, we thought it advisable to make a retrograde movement to our boats. The enemy, from the severe treatment they had received, and the perfect order in which we retired, did not attempt to arrest our movement, and we reached the boats without the loss of a single European. The native auxiliaries, who behaved uncommonly well, and protected our flanks when recrossing the guns, suffered,

I am sorry to say, a loss of eleven killed and several wounded. The enemy's loss I have since ascertained to have been forty killed and a large number wounded.

3. Nothing of any consequence occurred up to the 12th instant, when we moved to A-toung, at which place the Dugga creek is fordable, and from whence a good road leads to Myat-htoon's position. We here heard from Captain Smith that Sir John Cheape had made another retrograde movement, and we were advised if we thought necessary to take up another position. On sounding the feelings of the natives, who were very much disheartened by the delay that had taken place in the attack on Myat-htoon, I found that if we retreated the whole of the people in that part of the country, as also some portion actually of my own native force, would lose all confidence in us, and for their own protection go over to Myat-htoon, and that his power and influence would be at least doubled thereby. I therefore resolved to hold our position at all hazards, informed Captain Smith of the feelings of the natives and our own resolve, and most strongly urged the *necessity of an early advance*. On the 17th instant we received information that Sir J. Cheape would decidedly break ground on that date, and march upon Myat-htoon's position the following morning. On receiving this information we determined also to advance, and marched from A-toung on the 18th and halted half way at Ain-gyee. At 8 p.m. we fired three guns as a signal, which was returned by three rockets from Sir J. Cheape's camp. On the following morning we pushed on to the enemy's position, on reaching which we found Sir J. Cheape's advanced guard had arrived about twenty minutes before us. We experienced little opposition on our route, our flanking parties turning the breastworks wherever we encountered them, when the enemy invariably retreated. The works, however, were none of them occupied in strength, the greater part of their defenders having been withdrawn to oppose Sir John Cheape's force. We remained at Kywn-ka-dzeng until half-past 1 P.M. of the 22nd, when we were abruptly turned out of it by the place accidentally taking fire. During the halt at Kywn-ka-dzeng I sent out my native forces in all directions

in pursuit of Myat-htoon. They came upon his traces on two occasions, shot down several of his followers, and recovered a number of tools that had been taken from the Engineer Park, but he himself escaped. The native force with me, who had been ordered out for only a five days' campaign, and had by this time been out nearly a month, having become, moreover, gorged with the plunder of Myat-htoon's village, were most anxious to return to their homes, and I found it hopeless to attempt to keep them out any longer. I therefore returned with them to Bassein, where my presence was much required, and ordered up the Goung-gyoks of Pan-ta-naw, Shwe-lon and Kyeng-gon, with their people, to pursue Myat-htoon, and have every hope that they will ultimately succeed to bring him in. Myat-htoon is, however, well acquainted with the deep forest country, to which he has fled, and some time will probably elapse before he is taken. My people, too, are ignorant of the jungles in which he has taken refuge ; he therefore should be pursued also from the side of Donabew, Dza-lon, Yeng-don, &c., when he must fall into our hands.

4. During our stay at Kywn-ka-dzeng about 5,000 families came in who had been driven from the surrounding country ; these returned at once to their homes, and appeared to be delighted to escape from Myat-htoon's sway. Between three and four hundred muskets were given up by them to me, one 2-pounder brass gun, and two brass jingals.

5. I cannot conclude this letter without expressing my admiration throughout the whole expedition of the conduct of Commander Rennie, I.N., 1st Lieutenant Selby of the H.C. steam frigate *Zenobia*, Mr. Baker, 1st officer of the *Nemesis ;* and indeed of every officer and man who accompanied the expedition; nothing could have exceeded the cheerfulness with which they performed long marches and other duties they were unaccustomed to, and I hope you will not fail to bring their conduct to the notice of Government.

From C. Allen, Esquire, Secretary to the Government of India, to Major Phayre, Commissioner and Governor-General's Agent in Pegu, dated Fort William, 5th May, 1853.

I have the honour to acknowledge the receipt of your despatch, No. 31, dated 19th ultimo, forwarding a report of Captain Fytche's proceedings in co-operation with the force of Brigadier-General Cheape, against Myat-htoon, in the neighbourhood of Donabew. In reply, I am directed to request that you will communicate to Captain Fytche the full approbation of the Government of India, and the satisfaction with which it has viewed the spirited and persevering conduct of himself and of those who acted with him on this occasion.   In the event of Myat-htoon being captured, I am directed to request that you will take special orders regarding him.   His Lordship in Council is aware that this man is not an officer of the Burmese Government, and consequently is no better than a robber chief.   But the magnitude of his force, his pro-tracted defence, and soldierly conduct forbid his being ranked as a mere dacoit, and require some special treatment.

From Major A. Fytche, Deputy Commissioner, Bassein, to Captain Phayre, Commissioner and Governor-General's Agent in Pegu, Rangoon, No. 29, Judicial, dated Bassein, 18th February, 1854.

In continuation of my letter No. 11, of 22nd January last, to your address, I have the honour to inform you that agreeably to my intention stated therein, I moved out against the rebels on the morning of the 23rd ultimo, leaving in boats about 2 A.M. with a force as per margin, and 400 of the inhabitants of the country who had acted with me against the Burmese troops and marauders on former occasions.

1st Madras Fusiliers.
1 Bat. Major.
1 Assistant Surgeon.
2 Sergeants.
3 Corporals.
20 Privates.

10th M.N.I.
1 Ensign.
2 Native Commissioned Officers.
6   ,,   Non-Commissioned Officers.
45 Sepoys.

2. We moved up the river all that day, anchoring for the night at Taboo village, proceeded on our journey next morning at day-

break, and arrived at Keintalee about 11 A.M. Information that I could strictly depend upon here reached me that the rebels were marching down on Bassein by both banks of the river, that a force of about 300 men were at Phura-gyee, ten miles above us on the right bank, and that Nga-tha-oo, the Pe'neng of Ye'gyee, with 800 men, and another force under the dacoit chief Hla-bau, consisting of about 300 men, a short distance in his rear, were on the left bank. I determined to attack the smaller force first, and destroy it if possible, and then move against the larger force on the opposite bank, to gain correct information in the meantime of whose movements and intended halting-place for the night, I despatched scouts.

3. I left the main road from Keintalee to Phura-gyee, and marched by a circuitous route, with which I was acquainted, in the hope of being able to surprise the rebels, requesting Major Barker to move up the river at the same time with the boats. I arrived at Phura-gyee at 5 P.M., but the rebels had obtained information of our movements, and retreated on their head-quarters at Nga-thaing-khyoung.

4. The spies whom I had despatched from Keintalee to gain information returned during the night, and stated that Nga-tha-oo had halted in a large plain called Mug-gay-la-ha, Hla-bau resting at a small village five miles in his rear. I dropped the boats down immediately to Byan-gyee village, about five miles from the rebel encampment, and half an hour before daybreak disembarked the whole of my Burmese auxiliaries, twelve men of the 1st Madras Fusiliers, and thirty-two sepoys, and marched upon Nga tha-oo's position. Arrived there I detached 100 picked Burmese with orders to watch Hla-bau's force, and when they heard us open fire, to fall upon and attack it. About 6 A.M. my advance guard came in sight of the hostile force, and drove in their pickets, on which the main body moved out and drew up in the open plain. The rebel chief, Nga-tha-oo, was most conspicuous in the centre of his men, himself and body-guard being dressed in scarlet. I formed the troops in line, European and sepoys in the centre, supported on each flank by the Burmese auxiliaries, and

marched down upon them. We had reached within half a mile
of the rebel line when they detached parties of some 200 men
each to turn our flanks. I extended the Burmese in skirmishing
order to meet them and cover our flanks as we advanced, and then
making a dash at the rebels' centre, firing a volley and charging
with the bayonet. Our fire was very feebly returned, and they
broke and fled. Nga-tha-oo, who appeared to handle his men
very ably, contrived, however, to keep a large body of them
together, and their retreat was very orderly. I despatched a note
to Major Barker informing him of our success, and requested
him to move up the river to Nga-thaing-khyoung (the head-quarters
of the rebels) with the remainder of the force, where I would
meet him the following morning about 7 A.M. I then urged on
the pursuit for thirty miles to Pandaw (a large village of 1,500
houses), on which they had retreated ; the place was evacuated
on our approach, and we occupied it for the night. During the
night the village was surrounded by Shwè-too (the person who had
proclaimed himself Viceroy in the province) with a force of 800
men, who, on hearing of our approach, had moved out from Nga-
thaing-khyoung to form a junction with Nga-tha-oo. Our pickets
kept them off during the night, and at daybreak I moved out
against them. The rebels had taken up a position at the head of
the village, and were drawn up in a plain, with their flanks resting
on groves of mango trees, and low bushes lined with skirmishers.
My Burmese auxiliaries drove the skirmishers out of their cover,
and the regular portion of the force advanced by the open plain,
where the rebels stood a few volleys, but ultimately broke and
fled before the bayonet. The struggle was a very close one, and
one of the principal rebel leaders * sought me out, engaged me
hand to hand, and perished in the struggle. After pursuing the
rebels for some distance, inflicting a considerable loss upon them,

---

* A Shan chief, and a very tall, muscular man. He was supposed to be
invulnerable, owing to certain charms which had been tattooed on his body ;
and from plates of thin gold with mystic characters on them, that had been inserted under his skin. These latter were afterwards taken from his body and
brought to me.

and taking a number of prisoners, I marched for Nga-thaing-khyoung, which I reached at 7 A.M., and there found Major Barker, according to appointment, as also the Burmese that I detached from my force to attack Hla-bau, who had been completely defeated and brought in as a prisoner.

5. At Nga-thaing-khyoung I found that the large town of Doung-gyee on the opposite bank of the river had been burnt down the day before in a fight between Kyau-dzan-hla (the person who had proclaimed himself commander-in-chief of the rebels), and my Myo-ok of Lemena. The latter had attacked the rebels with 900 men, but was totally defeated with great loss, and Kyau-dzan-hla was still in pursuit of him. It struck me that if I moved at once by the route which Kyau-dzan-hla had taken (with which I was intimately acquainted), it was possible I might take him by surprise, and I applied to Major Barker for the portion of the force that had just arrived by the boats, and started off at once, putting the men in the light riding carts of the country to keep them fresh for the attack. We covered twenty-five miles of ground before nightfall, halting at Ke-khoo village, and next morning at daylight started again in pursuit. Every village on our route had been entered and plundered by the rebels, the inhabitants deserting their houses, and concealing themselves in the neighbouring jungles. They came out on our approach, and numbers of them joined us and fell in in our rear. On the advance we met several villagers who had been carried off and made their escape from the rebels. They informed me that it was the intention of Kyau-dzan-hla to halt at Lay-dan-nay village in a grove of mango trees, where they would arrive about 1 P.M. On approaching Lay-dan-nay I halted, and sent forward scouts to reconnoitre, who returned and reported that the rebels had halted totally unconscious of our being near them.

6. Lay-dan-nay village is situated close under the Yumatoung range, from which a spur runs down to the village ; with this exception the whole country is one open plain. In order to cut off the retreat of the rebels to the jungle, I turned off the road and marched down by the spur on the village. The surprise was

complete; we fell upon them whilst eating their food; a few muskets were snatched up and fired at random, and then the whole force broke and ran, most of them leaving their arms behind them. They were hotly pursued by my Burmese auxiliaries and the exasperated villagers, who did dreadful execution amongst them. The commander-in-chief escaped on horseback, accompanied by his secretary. They were pursued for a distance of twenty-five miles to Kyouk-ywa, where they plunged into the Bassein river, and were captured while ascending the opposite bank. By this time I was thoroughly exhausted with fatigue, having had no sleep for four nights, and was unable to accompany my men in their pursuit of the rebels, who were fearfully cut up, many, I am afraid, being killed who ought to have been brought in as prisoners. But the Burmese, more especially those who had hung in my rear, were so maddened at the manner in which they had been treated, that they gave no quarter. The rebels had also a large amount of booty in silver and gold upon their persons, and cupidity as well as revenge doubtless urged on the pursuit.

7. I was joined that night at Lay-dan-nay by the Lemena Myo-ok, and marched next morning for the town of Lemena, which had been burnt to the ground by the rebels. I halted that day and the next to recall and give confidence to the people of the place, and then marched back to Nga-thaing-khyoung, and remained there until joined by my new assistant, Lieutenant Dangerfield, on the 6th instant, when I left for Bassein, which I reached on the 8th instant, and left again next morning for the lower part of the district. At Myoung-mya-myo I met the reinforcement of troops that had been sent from Rangoon. They had an engagement there with the rebels, whom they defeated, and the chief ringleader in that part of the country, Nga-tee-hlwot, had been pursued and killed by the Karens. Lieutenant Shuldham, 26th M.N.I., was in command of the detachment, and appears to have displayed great judgment and gallantry. He has, I believe, despatched a report of the affair to the general commanding the division, a copy of which you will doubtless be furnished with. No troops accompanied me to Myoung-mya-myo,

and those I found there I despatched to Bassein, with the exception of 20 sepoys whom I took on with me to Pantanau. I arrived at Pantanau on the 13th instant, and found all quiet there, and that the people had almost all returned to the place. I remained at Pantanau one day and then left for Bassein, visiting the different villages *en route*, and arrived at the station this day, the 18th instant.

8. This rebellion has been secretly brewing for the last three months. Various rumours reached me from time to time concerning the same, and during the above period I twice despatched the gunboats of the *Nemesis* through the different creeks in the upper portion of the district, on one occasion of which my assistant, Captain Grant, accompanied them, but all was reported quiet. I should have proceeded into the interior myself had I not been tied down by the heavy press of arrears in the three departments of my office at the Sudder Station, my only assistant being removed in December last.

9. The chief leaders of the rebellion are Shwè-too, Kyau-dzan-hla, Nga-tha-oo, and a Buddhist priest. The two former had lately returned from Ava, and showed "royal warrants" to the people, proclaiming that they had been appointed by the Kanoung-Meng (the heir apparent), one the Viceroy of the Province and the other Commander-in-Chief, with orders to drive the English out of the country and take possession of it. They gradually assembled a number of desperate characters about them from the borders of this district and Sarawah, and made a dash upon, and took possession of, the three principal towns in the upper portion of the district, where they were joined by large numbers. Nga-tha-oo was formerly Pe'neng of Ye-gyee under the Burmese rule. He fled to Ava on our taking possession of the country, but returned about six months ago and was at large on parole. The Buddhist priest has been an inhabitant of this district for some years. The whole conspiracy is said to have been concocted in his monastery, and he is stated to have given the "leaders of the rebellion charms," and, from his "knowledge of the stars, to have informed them of the auspicious time of the

breaking out of the rebellion." He also furnished the Commander-in-Chief with a " very sacred idol," on which to swear his followers. The priest is said (with what truth I cannot say) to be a near connection of the present King of Ava. The " royal warrants " (which I believe are forgeries, though the people say they are genuine), together with a large portion of their correspondence, have fallen into my hands.

10. The rebels have been completely over-reached in their own peculiar warfare, and the outbreak is completely crushed. Our marches, which I was able to effect with great rapidity from a knowledge of the country, gained in former expeditions, found them unprepared, and prevented them from stockading themselves, or combining to attack the small force which circumstances allowed me to bring into the field. The commander-in-chief of the rebellion, the high priest, and most of the inferior leaders have been either killed or captured. The Viceroy and Nga-tha-oo are the only persons of note at present at large, and they, too, I have reason to hope, will be apprehended in a few days. From the last accounts I received, they were surrounded in some heavy jungle, with only two or three followers, and it was supposed that they could not escape. In the defeat and pursuit of these rebels a large number of them were cut down by their own countrymen who accompanied me. But it is to be regretted that means did not exist for trying the ringleaders, and executing some of them on the spot without a day's respite. Among half-civilised men, accustomed to violence and bloodshed, a degree of severity is required far beyond what will suffice in a country where submission to law is long established and general, and is much the wisest and most merciful policy.

11. Lieutenant Dangerfield, the new assistant appointed to this district, I have left at Nga-thaing-khyoung, and would strongly recommend that he be permanently posted there. I applied to Major Barker for a detachment of troops for Nga-thaing-khyoung, and he has furnished a force as per margin. Lieutenant Dangerfield also brought over with him half a company

1 Ensign.
2 Native Commissioned Officers.
6 „ Non-Commissioned Officers.
45 Sepoys.

of the 10th B. N. I. This force should, I think, be increased to two companies. I have several times recommended one assistant being stationed at Nga-thaing-khyoung ;. one, too, should be stationed at the other extremity of the district at Shwè-long or Pantanau, also with a small detachment of troops, and this isolated district should never be left without at least one steamer. My report of the rebellion which broke out on the 14th January could not be forwarded to Rangoon from Bassein before the 7th February, and then only by a chance opportunity by sea ; our communication with Rangoon by the creeks (as I predicted it would be on an occasion of this kind) having been cut off.

12. During the Burmese Government this district was divided into eleven divisions under Pe'nengs, and three under Myo-thoo-gyees. Each of these officers had under them from three to six hundred armed retainers. A portion of these retainers have gone into the Ava territories, a few have turned cultivators of the soil and fishermen ; the remainder, by far the greater proportion, are at large, without any means of honest livelihood, and it is they who form the bands of "dacoits," and keep the country in a disturbed state. The Pe'nengs and Myo-thoo-gyees we have replaced by Goung-gyops, and given them in place of these large bands of retainers two (2) Peons (the only police in the country), and curtailed their authority to an extent which, contrasted with the power exercised by the Pe'nengs, &c., under the Burmese Government, renders them ridiculous in the eyes of the people. When the rebellion broke out, there was only one Myo-ok amongst them (the Myo-ok of Lemena) who could make any head against the insurgents ; the remainder either concealed themselves in the jungle or fled into Bassein. Could not an irregular corps for police purposes be raised to absorb these old retainers of the Pe'nengs ? If one was ordered to be raised for this district, provided that strict military discipline was not at first enforced, but introduced by degrees, I could guarantee 6 or 800 men, who would in a few months be an over-match for the "dacoits," or any troops that the Burmese Government could bring against them.

13. By accounts which have reached me on my return to
Bassein, I learned that the people are settling down again quietly
in their villages. Such disturbances were of common occurrence
during the Burmese rule, when any Pe'neng could make war on
the other. The rebellion has necessarily unsettled the minds of
the people, but from the anarchy formerly prevailing under the
Native Government, not so much as would generally be supposed.
No great loss in revenue will, I hope, be experienced. No grain
whatever has been destroyed.

---

*From J. P. Grant, Esquire, Secretary to the Government of India,
   to Major Phayre, Commissioner and Governor-General's Agent
   in Pegu, No. 41, dated Fort William, the 18th March, 1854.*

With reference to the despatch to your address from Major
Fytche, Deputy Commissioner of Bassein, No. 29, dated the 18th
ultimo, reporting the particulars of the rebellion which has taken
place in that district, I am directed by the Most Noble the
Governor-General of India in Council to communicate to you the
following sentiments of the Government thereon.

2. The outbreak it appears has been excited by two persons,
who have lately arrived from Ava, and by a Buddhist priest. The
two persons displayed commissions, which purported to appoint
them respectively Viceroy and Commander-in-Chief in Bassein.
These commissions, though regarded as genuine by the people,
are considered to be forgeries by the Deputy-Commissioner.

3. Major Fytche, with a very small force of regular troops and
a levy of Burmese, moved out against these insurgents, and after
several affairs, completely dispersed their followers, of whom very
many were destroyed by the villagers. Some of the leaders have
been taken, the rest are surrounded, and it is expected will be
captured also.

4. Much praise is due to Captain Fytche for the promptitude,
judgment, and personal gallantry with which he has met and put
down the serious outbreak which has disturbed his district. The

Governor-General of India in Council desires to offer to him this acknowledgment of the qualities he has shown, and of the service he has rendered.

5. Having performed this agreeable duty, it is necessary for the Government to consider what lessons are to be deduced from the experience gained on this occasion, and what measures are to be taken to prevent, or speedily to crush, any similar outbreaks in future. The Deputy Commissioner has especially urged—1st, that power should be given him to punish with prompt severity any persons taken in the act of insurrection : 2nd, that Bassein should never be left without a steamer and gunboats ; 3rd, that an armed police should be sanctioned.

6. The Governor-General concurs with Major Fytche in thinking that power should be given to punish with prompt severity any person taken in the act of insurrection. Power was last year given to you to execute such sentences without the delay of a reference to Government. The Honourable Court approved of these orders. The same principle would now require that a similar power should be given to the Deputy Commissioner in the case of all persons convicted of participation in open and armed insurrection ; because your necessary distance and absence will often, as in the present instance, create as much delay as a reference to Government.

7. Evils which involve plunder and bloodshed require swift and sharp remedies. The Governor-General thinks that it would be wise for the Government, and merciful in the end, to entrust the power of administering such remedies to its Deputy Commissioner in Pegu, Major Fytche, at all events for the present.

8. The recommendation of the Deputy Commissioner that Bassein should never be left without a steamer, is, in the opinion of His Lordship in Council, a very reasonable and proper one. The *Nemesis*, whose station is at Bassein, is under repair at Rangoon. The reason his Lordship in Council apprehends why no substitute in her place was sent to Bassein was the great demand for steamers in the Irawadi, by reason of the relief of troops, the loss of the *Medusa*, &c. But undoubtedly it should

be a general rule that Bassein, an isolated position, should never
be left without a steamer. Her boats will always serve as gunboats. Besides these, the boat or boats attached to the European
troops in garrison at Bassein will be fitted each with a 12-pounder
howitzer.

9. The Governor-General in Council proceeds now to advert
to the recommendation of Major Fytche, that a police corps
should be raised. The Government is of course desirous to
observe due economy in the new province. But a necessary outlay for the preservation of peace, and for the security of person
and property, in the first beginning of our authority, is the best
and truest economy. The Governor-General in Council is quite
ready, therefore, to sanction the embodiment for the present of
600 armed police in the Bassein district to obviate the necessity
for those detachments of regular troops which are detailed in the
11th para. of Major Fytche's despatch. His Lordship in Council
authorises you to give effect to this measure at once, or if you
should still be absent on the northern frontier, the Deputy-Commissioner is authorised to act upon the permission herein conveyed. A copy of this communication will be sent to Major
Fytche.

— — —

*From Major A. Fytche, Deputy Commissioner, Bassein, to Captain
A. P. Phayre, Commissioner and Governor-General's Agent
in Pegu, Rangoon, No. 263, Judicial, dated Bassein, 5th
August, 1854.*

In continuation of my last letter to your address No. 215, of
the 7th ultimo, I have the honour to inform you that the police
corps ordered to be raised in the Bassein district, under the
authority of Government, conveyed in letter No. 2,090, dated
10th May, 1854, from the Secretary to the Government of India,
Foreign Department, to your address, is now complete in men.
I have deferred appointing the whole of the commissioned and
non-commissioned officers, waiting to choose the remainder from
those who turn out the most intelligent and smart on trial.

2. I commenced raising the corps in June last. The service is popular. A large number of candidates appeared for enlistment, and the corps could have been completed that month, but I rejected, from policy, men with settled employment, being anxious to absorb those that had been in employ, or were professional dacoits and robbers under the Burmese rule, the majority of whom would never settle down to any honest means of livelihood, but still continue the practice of extortion and robbery for subsistence, until purchased or otherwise disposed of. About three-fourths of the men now enlisted are of this stamp, and the commissioned and non-commissioned officers already appointed, men of influence, who brought in large bands of their followers with them for enlistment. One of these, for instance, was one of the most active chiefs under Myat-htoon, and he has brought in with him some eighty picked men, who were with Myat-htoon up to the final defeat and dispersion of his band at Kywn-ka-dzeng.

3. This absorption will be a very great relief to the country, and these " Ishmaelites of Society " will gradually fall under control, and be turned to good account, if properly handled at the commencement. But their management for some time to come will be a source of anxiety,* and demand the whole of my leisure time in drilling and disciplining them. Such material requires a peculiar course of discipline, and I would, with due deference, recommend that I be appointed their commandant, and that they be taught for the present to look to me alone for their rewards and punishments. I would also recommend that the corps had some distinctive name, such as Bassein Rangers. Many of the chiefs who have joined are of true Burmese spirit ; an empty name or title has great weight with them, and would tend much to establish an *esprit de corps.*

4. I enclose herewith a sketch of the uniform I propose for the corps. The cloth shown on the private, and pantaloons of the others, is American drill dyed with indigo, and the jackets of the commissioned and non-commissioned officers, dark broadcloth.

---

* I have already had to flog and imprison 3 men for highway robbery and 3 for theft.

The helmet is a Burmese pattern, and composed of leather covered with theet-tsee (the bright black varnish of the country). Until these are made up, I propose a red turban to be worn (*vide margin of sketch*). The scarf shown across the breast of the private in heavy marching order is the Burmese tsoung, or sheet in which the Burmese cover themselves while sleeping. Wrapped up in this and suspended at the back will be carried a bag (shaped like a large sausage bag) containing four or five days' food. Clothed in an easy dress of this description, and carrying thirty rounds each of ammunition in pouch, they will be able to march some thirty or forty miles a day, and no baggage or commissariat whatever required to accompany them.

5. I propose that two companies of the corps be stationed at Nga-thaing-khyoung under the Assistant Commissioner there, and as soon as the men are drilled, small detachments of them should be distributed under the Myo-okes of the most troublesome townships, and relieved every six months from head-quarters. I will report to you more fully hereafter on this subject. The detachment of the 10th Bengal Native Infantry has already been withdrawn from Nga-thaing-khyoung, and the removal of the company of the 30th Madras Native Infantry, still there, will, I have every hope, be able to be effected within the next six or eight months, which will leave no regular troops whatever detached in the interior of the Bassein district. I would recommend that the Burmese terms,

For Subadar.... .. Tat-moo.
,, Jemadar ... Shwe-thouk-gyee.
,, Havildar .. Akyat-gyee.
,, Naick ...... Akyat-ngay.
,, Bugler .... Khaya-hmok-thama.
,, Sepahi...... Tat-tha.

as per margin, be used in the corps instead of the Hindustanee denominations.

6. The two European non-commissioned officers are absolutely indispensable at present to aid me in drilling the corps. I have not as yet fixed upon two men for these appointments. But I hope, with the assistance of the officer commanding the detachment of H.M.'s 29th Regiment at this station, who has written to the head-quarters of his regiment concerning them, to be enabled to do so shortly, when I will inform you of the matter, in order that steps may be taken for their being transferred.

As Deputy Commissioner of Bassein.

From G. F. Edmonstone, Esq., Secretary to the Government of India, to Major Phayre, Commissioner and Governor-General's Agent in Pegu, dated Fort William, 22nd September, 1854.

I have received and laid before the Governor-General of India in Council your letter dated the 31st ultimo, No. 4, forwarding copy of a letter from Major Fytche, Deputy Commissioner of Bassein, reporting that the police corps, ordered to be raised in that district, is complete in men.

2. I reply I am directed by His Lordship in Council to acquaint you that the rapid organisation of this corps is satisfactory to the Government, and highly creditable to the exertions of Major Fytche.

3. Major Fytche states that he rejected men of settled employment from policy, and that three-fourths of the corps consist of men who were "professional dacoits and robbers under the Burmese rule." The policy of absorbing such persons no doubt will be effectual in some respects. But it will be necessary to exercise a very close watch and a very severe control over characters such as these, lest the authority given and the opportunity afforded them as police officers should be turned to the same purposes of extortion by which they have hitherto subsisted. The dress of the corps is approved.

From Major Phayre, Commissioner and Governor-General's Agent in Pegu, to Major Fytche, Deputy Commissioner, Bassein, dated Prome, 9th February, 1854.

During the last visit of the Most Noble the Governor-General of India to the Province of Pegu, I was requested to prepare a report on the conduct and qualities of the several officers under my orders. This report having been submitted, I have now been directed to convey to you the approbation of His Lordship at the efficient manner in which you have conducted the duties of your office, and the energy and skill with which you have managed the affairs of the country under your jurisdiction.

From Major Phayre, Commissioner and Governor-General's Agent in Pegu, to Major Fytche, Deputy Commissioner of Bassein, No. 62, dated Rangoon, June 6th, 1855.

I have much satisfaction in forwarding to you extract of letter to my address, No. 73, dated the 2nd April last, from the Secretary to the Government of India, containing the orders of His Lordship on your revenue statements for the year 1853–54. " On the whole His Lordship is of opinion that the general results of the revenue administration, as exhibited in this report, are satisfactory, and reflect credit on the district officers, who, it is clear, have laboured under great disadvantages, and he desires that you will express to Major Fytche, Mr. O'Riley, Captain Sparks, and Lieutenant Ardagh, *especially to the two former*, his approbation of the manner in which they have performed their duties.

From G. F. Edmonstone, Esq., Secretary to the Government of India, to Major Phayre, Commissioner and Governor-General's Agent in Pegu, dated Fort William, 14th April, 1857.

With reference to the letter to your address, dated 11th February last, from Major Fytche, Deputy Commissioner of Bassein, dated the 11th February last, No. 37 (a copy of which has been sent direct by that officer for the information of Government), submitting a report of the breaking out of a Karen rebellion in that district, I am directed by the Governor-General of India in

Council to state that the account given by Major Fytche of the manner in which this sudden and not contemptible outbreak has been dealt with, is very creditable to all concerned. The movements of the force at Major Fytche's disposal were planned by him with excellent judgment and executed with great courage and perseverance.

2. The exertions and endurance of the men and officers of the Bassein police corps deserve the marked thanks of the Governor-General in Council, which Major Fytche should be instructed to convey to Lieut. Cox and to Sergeant-Major Gorman. He should also receive an entire approval of his own conduct.

3. It is to be regretted that the leader of the rebellion has escaped, for whoever he may be, and from wherever he may come, it is clear that he has much power of mischief. His Lordship in Council desires me to draw your attention to the statement in Major Fytche's letter regarding the proceedings of the King of Ava's steamer.

4. A copy of this letter has been sent for the information of Major Fytche.

From Major Phayre, Commissioner and Governor-General's Agent in Pegu, to Major Fytche, Deputy Commissioner of Bassein, dated Henzadah, 17th May, 1855.

I have the honour to acknowledge the receipt of your letter No. 36, dated 12th instant. It is with deep regret I learn that the state of your health renders it necessary for you to proceed to Europe on sick certificate. You will leave the district of Bassein profoundly quiet, a district which you reduced to order in a style which earned for you the marked approbation of the Government of India, and the distinction of an honorary reward for distinguished service from Her Majesty's Government. I shall feel keenly the loss of your co-operation both as regards the district generally and the foundation of the new city of Dalhousie, but if it be finally determined that you must seek* health in your native land, you carry my very best wishes for a speedy recovery.

From the Secretary to the Government of India to the Commissioner and Governor-General's Agent in Pegu, No. 2,170, dated Fort William, the 8th May, 1857.

I have the honour to acknowledge the receipt of your letter, No. 34, dated 31st March last, and its enclosure, reporting the occurrence of a fire at Bassein, by which the Records of the Court and Treasury were destroyed, and the Treasure defaced.

2. In reply I am directed to request that you will convey the thanks of the Governor-General of India in Council to Major Fytche, for his exertions on the occasion of this formidable conflagration at Bassein.

3. With reference to the loss which Major Fytche has sustained in the destruction of all his private property, while attempting to save the property of Government, I am directed to request that you will call upon that officer to submit a detailed list of all the property destroyed, with its value, showing at the same time what might have been saved had not Major Fytche's attention been wholly directed to saving the property of Government.

* Major Fytche recovered his health somewhat, and did not leave India on sick leave at that time; but was obliged to do so two and a half years afterwards.

From Colonel W. E. Baker, Secretary to the Government of
Public Works Department. *India, to the Commissioner and Governor-*
(Military.) *General's Agent in Pegu, dated Fort*
William, the 30th June, 1857.

With reference to the correspondence noted in the margin, I am

Commissioner of Pegu, No. 53, directed to forward for your information,
dated 28th February, 1856.
Reply No. 1454, dated 4th and for communication to Major Fytche,
April, 1856. an extract from the Honourable the

Extract from Para. 36 of a Despatch from the Honourable the Court Court of Di-
of Directors to the Government of India, in the Military Department, Letter dated 10th October, 1856, No. 11. "We notice with rectors, No.
great satisfaction, the economical and effective measures taken by
Major Fytche, Deputy Commissioner of Bassein, in constructing the 56, dated 1st
magazine of permanent materials." April last, ap-

proving of the economical and effective manner in which that
officer constructed a magazine for the ammunition of the Bassein
Police Corps.

APPENDIX C.

NARRATIVE

MISSION TO MANDALAY IN 1867.

*From Colonel Albert Fytche, Chief Commissioner of British Burmah
and Agent to the Governor-General, to the Secretary to the
Government of India, Foreign Department,—No. 214A., dated
Rangoon, the 8th November, 1867.*

I HAVE the honour to forward herewith the Narrative of my
Mission to Mandalay as Envoy from his Excellency the Viceroy
and Governor-General.

NARRATIVE OF THE MISSION TO MANDALAY IN 1867.

The party consisted of the Envoy Colonel Fytche, Chief Com-
missioner of British Burmah, Captain Duncan, Inspector-General
of Police, Mr. Edwards, Collector of Customs, Rangoon, the
Reverend H. W. Crofton, Chaplain of Rangoon, and the Officers
of the Military Escort, *viz.*, Captain Surplice, Mr. Assistant-
Surgeon Douglas, and Lieutenants Younghusband, Williams, and
Randolph, Mr. Assistant-Surgeon Douglas, 2-24th Regiment, and
Lieutenant Rolland, Royal Artillery. Captain Hannen, Royal
Artillery, was also of the party, being on leave; and Mrs. Fytche
and Mrs. Lloyd accompanied the Mission. The escort consisted
of 72 men of all ranks of the 2-24th Regiment and 12 men of the

Royal Artillery. The party was conveyed by the Steamers *Nemesis* and *Colonel Phayre*, the latter having a flat in tow.

Leaving Rangoon on the morning of Friday, the 20th September, the Mission reached Prome on the afternoon of the 23rd, and, starting early next day, passed the frontier station of Thayetmyo on the 24th, anchored that evening on the frontier line about 15 miles above Thayetmyo. On the 25th while proceeding up the river the engines of the *Nemesis* got out of order, and the distance travelled was only about twenty miles, when the town of Tsingboungway was reached, where anchor was cast for the night.

This small town of 400 houses is the residence of the Meeaday Won, or Governor of the Burmese frontier, that is, of that portion of it which extends eastward from the Irawadi to the Tonghoo hills, the watershed of the Irawadi and Sittang Rivers. He, however, was not present, having gone to Menhla, as it had not been intended that the Mission should stop at Tsingboungway.

On the 26th but little progress was made, and after having got over about eighteen miles, the steamers anchored at dusk opposite the pretty village of Melloon, on the left bank, about four miles short of Menhla. Early the next morning, the 27th, four war-boats, with some of the deputation who had been sent from Mandalay to meet the Chief Commissioner, came to the steamers to welcome the Mission, when it was arranged that the Chief Commissioner should receive them at Menhla.

Accordingly, having reached Menhla at 10 A. M,, the full deputation was received on board the *Nemesis*. The quarter-deck had been arranged and decorated with flags, and chairs were placed for the reception of the visitors. A guard of honour was drawn up on either side of the deck, all officers were present in uniform, and the scene altogether presented a handsome and dignified appearance, with sufficient formality to give due importance to the occasion of the first meeting of the British Envoy with the Royal Deputies.

The Burmese officials who came on board were—the Paopa Wondouk, the head of the Mission from Mandalay, a venerable and well-affected gentleman, who bore his part with much self-composure and dignity; the Padein Won, also from the capital, a young intelligent Burman, who spoke English well, having been educated in Calcutta; lastly, the Ex-Won of Tsingo, an elderly and pleasant-mannered officer of the Court, who had frequently been employed on like duties. He similarly received the first Mission to the Court of Ava, in 1855, and had accompanied the Burmese Ambassadors to Calcutta when they visited Lord Dalhousie.

With these three officials, who had been specially deputed from the capital, came also the Tseetkay of Menhla, and the Meeaday Won referred to before. The Menhla Tseetkay has wide jurisdiction over the whole valley of the Irawadi below Mandalay, the frontier Won being under his orders and control. He is a shrewd, intelligent, and determined officer, somewhat grim and severe in countenance, and stately and stiff in manners, but manifestly a man of much force of character. He occupied the same position during the rebellion of 1866, and defended and protected the King's interests with much vigour and resolution. The Meeaday Won had until the rebellion been frequently employed as supercargo of the King's steamers running between Mandalay and Rangoon, and had consequently acquired an easier (or, one might say, commoner) manner than the others; he is quick and good-natured. The old Wondouk was met at the gangway by Mr. Edwards, and, followed by the other officials, was led up to the Chief Commissioner, and after shaking hands with him was seated on his right, the other officials being seated alternately with officers of the suite to the right and left. After a friendly conversation of half an hour, the deputation left with every mark of satisfaction at their reception.

The officers remarked that they had been at Menhla for more than a month. This was in consequence of a reference to Mandalay being necessary, which had not been anticipated. They said that at certain halting-places on the river preparations had been made and supplies laid in, and they asked that the Mission should visit each of these. They were ten in number from Menhla to Mandalay, giving an average distance between each of fifteen miles. As the war-boats were to accompany the steamer to the capital, these stages were considered of fair length, the river running with much strength in parts of its course. There were altogether eight war-boats, each having a crew of forty men, while the principal official, the Wondouk, had for his use a large barge, which was, however, taken in tow by the steamer.

The town of Menhla has about 700 houses, and was clean, and neatly kept; the houses, however, were poorly constructed, mostly with bamboo, some of them with untrimmed wooden pole supports, but scarcely any of dressed timber. There were a few pieces of ordnance in a shed near the Tseetkay's house—a six-pounder brass gun, a small iron three-pounder ship's gun apparently, and four or five small iron pieces or boat's guns, of small bore and rough manufacture. In the Court-house, near at hand, there were seventy stand of flint muskets, much out of order and damaged at the muzzle; it was noticed that there was no ammunition in the pouches.

A Pooay, or Burmese play, was going on all day, which the Chief Commissioner and his suite visited after dinner, and met there the Burmese deputation.

On the morning of the 28th, the steamers, escorted by the war-boats, passed upwards to Magwé, a distance of ten miles. It was impossible to reach the town itself, owing to an island opposite to it, which leaves but a narrow and shallow channel between it and the eastern bank. The steamers stopped at a small village about three miles below Magwé, built on a pretty grassy bank over a pebbly beach. Here a small mandat, or temporary shed, had been built, in which a Pooay was going on from the time of the arrival of the steamers (3 P. M.). The village consisted of some thirty or forty houses, each in its own enclosure, fenced in by a cactus hedge. There were here also some good monasteries and pagodas, the latter encircled by some fine specimens of petrified wood stuck up as posts.

The town of Magwé, having 800 houses, and a population of 4,000 souls, which, as before stated, was three miles further up the river, was almost entirely burnt down during the rebellion by the Toungdwengyee Meng-gyee. Yule, writing in 1855, says the number of houses was given as 3,000, and he reckoned the population at 8,000 or 9,000. In the evening the Chief Commissioner rode up to the town of Magwé, and some of the party went out shooting. Rain came on and stopped the Pooay. From this place the Menhla Tseetkay returned to Menhla, having accompanied the Mission on this day's journey. The war-boats lay by the steamers all night, and on the morning of the 29th all again moved on eighteen miles to Yaynankhyoung, which is on the eastern or left bank. Shortly after starting we passed the pretty town of Memboo on the western bank, with spurs of hills crowned by numerous pagodas in the back ground. On the east bank, opposite Memboo, is Magwé, seemingly a busy place, with a good many boats. Approaching Yaynankhyoung, the country on the east bank was strikingly picturesque ; the banks mostly bluffs, broken with small ravines running up straight from the river ; above the bluffs the country stretching away in park-like uplands, with here and there clumps of light timber. The whole formed a striking contrast to the heavy luxuriant foliage on the banks of the river on its lower portion in British territory. The steamers reached Yaynankhyoung at 3-30 P. M.; when about two or three miles below the town the Mission was met by seven or eight loungs, or long canoes, each paddled by from twenty to thirty men : these accompanied us till the steamers anchored. The usual Pooay was going on, and some fifty ponies were in readiness for the use of the Mission. Yaynankhyoung was burned down by the Toungdwengyee Meng-gyee last year, and now the houses are very poor ; most are constructed of bamboo : there is not one good wooden house in the town. There are 1,300 houses in the town, it is said, with a population of 6,500, but it looks only half the size which this number would make it.

On the morning of the 30th, the Chief Commissioner accompanied by the Burmese officials, visited the earth oil (yaynan) or petroleum wells : these are fully described in Yule's " Mission to Ava." At 9 A. M. the steamers left for Pakhan-ngé, the next stopping place, and just after starting were met by the *Yaynantsekyah*, one of the King's steamers sent down to meet the Mission and to accompany it to the capital.

At Yaynankhyoung, as at the other halting-places, the greatest desire was shown to consult and meet the wishes of the Mission ; large presents of grain, vegetables, and fruit were brought to the steamers, and the procession of boats which escorted us in was evidently intended as a remark of respect. On leaving, the Paopa Wondouk and the Tsengoon Won came on board the *Colonel Phayre* and *Panlang* flat to make the acquaintance of the officers of the escort. The Wondouk's barge, which had been towed by the *Nemesis* heretofore, was this day in tow of the *Colonel Phayre*, so that the Burmese officials might spend the day in company with the English officers. The Wondouk went over both vessels, and after some conversation returned to his barge for breakfast. The Tsengoon Won breakfasted with the officers of the escort, and entered readily and with much intelligence into general subjects of conversation. The halting-place was nominally at Pakhan-ngé, but really about two miles below it, at a small village where the reception shed, &c., had been erected ; this was reached at 4 P. M. The King's steamer had accompanied the Mission during the day ; in her were eight guns, six of them 24lb. howitzers, iron, and two much smaller guns, also of iron ; besides these there were fifty stand of flint muskets, clean and apparently in good order. There were on board about one hundred and fifty men, some in red and some in green uniforms, which consisted of a short jacket and short loose trowsers. During the evening there was the usual Pooay, the performers being the ones who had played the previous night.

On the 1st October the Mission moved on eight or nine miles only to Tsillémyo, arriving there at 11-30 A. M. The Wondouk's boat was taken in tow by the King's steamer. Tsillémyo is prettily situated on a point of high land on the eastern bank, the houses running up the face of the hill, which is surmounted with pagodas.   On the approach of the steamers a dozen loungs (pulling boats) came out a short distance to welcome and escort the party.   Considerable preparations had been made, the reception-room was handsomer and larger, with a made road leading up from the river.   Under temporary barracks (sheds) there were 150 of the King's troops armed with muskets, which were clean and in fair order.   There is at present a Myo-ok in charge of the town and circle.   The town was burned down last year by the Myeen-gon Prince, and there are now only 150 houses in it, all poor, bamboo and mat constructions.   The pagodas are numerous and handsome.   The principal occupation of the inhabitants is the manufacture of lacquered boxes and cotton cloths (Tsoungs). We saw the former in its different stages : first a box in the shape required, of fine bamboo basket work, this is dipped into Thittsee (wood-oil) and buried for five or six days, or until the lacquer is properly set on the bamboo, again dipped and buried, and for a third time the process is repeated.   The frame is thus covered with a good coating of the lacquer.   On this is traced the pattern which it is intended to produce, in red tracing say.   The red pigment is then rubbed over the whole, but bites where the tracing has been made only.   After being allowed to remain a few days the superfluous red pigment is rubbed off.   There is then traced out the pattern which it may be intended to produce in yellow, and the above process is repeated with yellow pigment, and so on until all the tracing is done and coloured.   The whole is then put on a lathe and polished with fine charcoal.   The pattern is traced by a little iron style, and by the eye entirely. The workers were much interested when we promised to let them have some new designs, and readily undertook to produce them on the boxes.   In this way, with a little trouble, monograms or any design could be obtained on the boxes.   In the evening, by the particular desire of the Wondouk, the party visited the Pooay, the Myo-ok having taken great trouble in erecting a suitable building.   On passing the temporary barracks at about 11-30 P. M., on returning to the steamer, the soldiery were observed to be on the alert, each man sitting behind his musket, which, upright, was resting on a frame before him.

On the 2nd October the day's journey was to Pagan, a distance of twenty-four miles, the steamers starting at about 6 A. M. At about 8 o'clock the two largest of the Pagan pagodas were distinctly visible up the river. Pagan was reached at 3-30 P. M. The Tseetkay, or Governor of the district, came down some miles with several pulling boats to meet us. The pagodas of Pagan (fully described by Yule) were visited by the Chief Commissioner and some of the Mission. The roads through the town had all been swept and cleaned, and low pathways cut through the low shrub and jungle to the principal places of interest. Guides were furnished to all who desired to visit the temples, and the greatest civility was shown. The town escaped the fate of Magwé and other towns lower down, and was not burned down by the rebels last year, although a contribution was levied from it by the Myeen-gon Prince. There are 300 houses in the town, but none of any pretension. The King's steamer, which was occupied by the Burmese officials, was late in coming up, and the Wondouk wished to halt here for a day or two, as the war-boats could not well keep up. The Envoy, however, declined to agree to this, and, in fact, the stages were short and easy, and there could have been no real difficulty in the boats keeping up, assisted as they were by the steamer; besides the programme, which was accepted at Menhla, did not provide for any halts, and it was thought better to adhere to it as originally agreed upon.

In the evening the Pooay was visited by the Envoy and several officers of the suite; some trouble had been taken in preparing the building, and the performance consisted of a play by marionettes instead of by actors as previously.

On the 3rd October the steamers started early. After a run of about four miles to Nyoungoo they stopped for about an hour to allow of the purchase of some of the lacquer-ware of the finer sort, for which the place is celebrated throughout Burma. The little town is prettily situated, having wide streets, all of which were very clean and in good order. At 9 A. M. the steamers again started, and reached Koonkwa, a small town on the right bank of the river, at about 3·30 P. M. The usual party of boats came down to meet the Mission, and a good reception-house, with a Pooay, attracted some of the party on shore. Letters were dispatched to Captain Sladen, the Chief Commissioner's Agent at Mandalay, announcing that the Mission would be at Kyouktalon on the 5th.

From Koonkwa the Mission proceeded on the morning of the 4th, passing the lower opening of the Kyeng-dweng River to the westward at about 8 A. M. At 11 the steamers passed the large town of Myeeng-yan on the left bank, the most populous and busiest place seen since the frontier was crossed. It is the centre of a district from which a good deal of cotton is exported to British territory and rice to the northward. Myeeng-yan is one of the few towns on the river that supplies freight to the steamers running between Rangoon and Mandalay. Last year the Myeengon Prince made it his head-quarters for a month and a half while in rebellion against his father the King, and it was here that he was attacked in October last by the two King's steamers which came up from British territory. He made no stand, but at once fled to the frontier. It was particularly noticed that as we passed the town hardly any of the inhabitants were seen on the bank. The place seemed deserted, and so unusual an occurrence could only have been caused by some order. The steamers reached Tsameet Kywn at 3·30 P. M. and remained there that night, the run having been of about twenty-five miles. The village is on the left bank, and consists of about 150 houses only, having one narrow and irregular street, flanked with, generally speaking, poor-looking houses : there were one or two, however, of wood. This place is noted for its manufacture of saltpetre. In the neighbourhood there is a considerable plain, consisting mainly of rice fields. The usual fleet of row boats met the Mission on its approach, and the usual Pooay was provided. The steamers left at about 6 A. M. on the 5th and passed the upper mouth of the Kyeng-dweng. From this point the Irawadi visibly narrowed, but still remained a wide and noble stream. About 10 A. M. a large village (probably the Moowa of Yule's map) on the right bank was passed, and the Mandalay Hills came in sight. At about 11 Kyouktalon, the next halting-place, could be seen, and it was reached at about 2 P. M. No boats came out, nor were the people on the banks ; there was no Pooay, but a shed had been prepared. The village is a small one.

On the 6th October, after starting, the *Nemesis* got aground on a sand bank. The day was spent in unsuccessful efforts to get her off. On the morning of the 7th the *Colonel Phayre* dragged her off, and at 10 A. M. the two steamers proceeded up the river again. Previously, at 9 A. M., Captain Sladen, accompanied by several war-boats, had arrived from Mandalay and came on board the *Nemesis.* The fleet of war-boats accompanied the steamers on their way up.

Tsagain was passed without stopping, and Mandalay was reached at about 3 P. M. Mandalay itself is about two miles inland from the river, but at the landing-place there is a considerable village, occupied principally by natives of India and Munipúrees (Cathays). Lying here was one of the King's steamers, and one of his flats, and a second flat belonging to the Flotilla Company. On the bank was a guard of about thirty men of the King's troops in green jackets and red striped putsoes (kilts), with red helmets. The Wondouk who accompanied us was much disappointed that we had not stopped at Tsagain, where great preparations had been made.

It was arranged that the Ministers should visit the Chief Commissioner next day, and that the Mission should land the day afterwards. Some of the gentlemen living at Mandalay came off in the evening.

After breakfast on the 8th all collected on board the *Nemesis,* which had been arranged as at Menhla, and at about midday the deputation from the King came down to the river. It consisted of the Yaynankhyoung Mengyee, Oo Tso, and the Keng Wondouk, with a number of Secretaries and minor officials. Oo

Tso's son, a lad of fourteen, came with his father. The conversation was lively and entirely about the journey, and whether it had been a pleasant one or not. Inquiry was made regarding the dimensions of the *Nemesis*, and whether it could go on the sea; and questions, numerous enough, were asked as to the *personnel* of the Mission. The Burmese officials went over the steamer, and shortly afterwards went on shore again. It had been requested of the English officers that none would go to the city until the formal entry had been made; the party was, therefore, confined to short strolls on the bank of the river.

Early on the morning of the 9th the march to the Residency was commenced. The order being as follows :—First about fifty of the King's troops in uniform, then Mrs. Fytche in a handsome gilded litter sent to her by the Queen, followed by the Paopa Wondouk on an elephant; then the Chief Commissioner followed by Mrs. Lloyd, and in due order the officers composing the suite of the Envoy, all on elephants, followed by the escort of British Infantry and Artillery on foot. About a mile and a half from the river a creek was crossed by boats, of which a great number were collected. At his point the procession was met by the Keng Wondouk and a number of minor officials, when the march was resumed, the procession being headed by the newly-arrived officials and accompanied by about 500 cavalry, and probably 3,000 foot soldiers. The cavalry were generally in red jackets and trowsers, a few wearing a red jerkin over these, and still fewer dressed in the full uniform of the cavalry, shoulder-pieces, gilt helmet, with ear-pieces and embroidered jerkin; all had the white saddle-flap and high-peaked pummel and cantle. The men were armed with a spear and a sword each, the latter being, as a rule, the Burmese dha, but some few had a sword of European shape with a scabbard of brass or steel. The infantry had only the white jacket worn by the ordinary population; all had flint muskets. These troops accompanied the *cortège* through the suburbs of the town to the Residency. This suburb was that called Kulah-dan, or foreign quarter. It is traversed by a handsome broad and clean street, at least half a mile in length, planted with tamarind trees of good growth, considering that the town was only commenced in 1856. The sun was hot, and the Residency was not reached until 10 A. M. The distance altogether was not three and a half miles, but the pace was slow and the halts frequent.

At the Residency the Envoy was received by the Yaynan-khyoung Meng-gyee and a large party of officials. The whole morning's proceeding went off very well indeed.

The Agency compound has been enclosed by a good strong post and mat fence, and within this enclosure all the buildings for the Mission had been erected.

During the 10th Captain Sladen visited the King, and His Majesty consented to receive the Envoy next day. This early reception was considered as a mark of condescension, as it has been the custom of the Court to require a much longer interval before receiving an Embassy, but it was important that it should thus be granted, as the 11th was the full moon, during which day religious ceremonies prevent all business, and the 12th, 13th, and 14th were to be festival days, during which the Kadaus, or Royal presents, are presented to His Majesty by his subjects; they are frequently called "beg-pardon days," as the offerings are intended to propitiate His Majesty and to obtain forgiveness for any faults committed. It would have been unbecoming for the British Envoy to have had his audience on one of these days; and as no business can be transacted until after the formal reception by the King, a considerable delay would have taken place had this ceremony been put off until the festival was over.

During the day Burmese plays were going on continually within in the enclosure. The Envoy received visits from the European gentlemen resident in Mandalay.

On the morning of the 11th the Envoy and suite proceeded to the palace, starting at about 10 A. M. The order of the procession was as follows :—Leading the way, a considerable distance in front, was the Myo Won, or Governor of the city of Mandalay.

He was followed by the escort of European Infantry on foot,
then the British flag was borne aloft carried by ship's lascars ;
after which came the Envoy, Colonel Fytche, attended by two
golden umbrellas.   He was followed by Captain Sladen, Captain
Duncan, Mr. Edwards, the Paopa Wondouk, and the officers of
the escort and some officers on leave at Mandalay from the frontier
station of Thayetmyo.   The same number of Burmese troops that
escorted the Mission from the steamers to the Agency accompanied the *cortège* on this occasion, and on entering the chief gate
it was found that the road leading from it to the Palace Gate
was lined with men bearing arms, probably about 5,000 men.
They had the common white jacket, were manifestly untrained to
the use of arms, and seemed to be people called out merely for
the occasion.   About one-fifth were armed with spears, the
remainder with muskets, a similar proportion, *viz.*, one-fifth, were
old men or young boys, unfitted for military duties.   The procession entered the city by the western gate, and then moved
round the palace to its eastern gate : there the party dismounted,
and swords and umbrellas were dispensed with.   The palace is
enclosed first by a strong wooden stockade, then, at an interval
of 100 feet, by a brick wall, and at a further interval of 100 feet
by another brick wall.   Between the two walls some pieces of
ordnance with their field carriages were placed, lining the road ;
and just outside the inner wall was placed the Hlwotdau, or
Supreme Court.   Here were stationed the Pakhan Meng-gyee and
the Yaynankhyoung Meng-gyees with some other officials ; the
Envoy stopped and spoke to them, but did not enter the Hlwot.
At the side of the gate of the inner wall there was a wicket
through which the embassy passed.   About twenty yards intervened between this wicket and the steps of the palace, where the
party took off their shoes and were then led through the Myaynan,
or principal Hall of Audience, in which is the throne.   Leaving
the throne to the left, and passing out of the Myaynan, a
smaller chamber just behind the throne was reached : here it was
that the audience was given.   It was an open hall or portico,
supported by white chunammed pillars, and was about thirty feet

square; at the western side, before a golden folding-door, was placed a low couch for His Majesty; immediately in front of this, at a distance of four or five yards, the Envoy and party sat down. They were flanked by numerous Burmese officials, who, on either side, reached up close to his Majesty's couch. At its side on the left were four of the King's grown-up sons—the Thonzai, Nyoungyan, Mek-ka-ra, and Myeengon Princes. Behind them were some more of the royal children. Some fifteen or twenty minutes elapsed, and then the doors were thrown open. The King was seen approaching from a considerable distance up a vista of gilded doors of various succeeding chambers. He was preceded by two officers carrying dhas, and accompanied by a little child of five or six years of age, one of his little daughters. He took off his shoes at the further side of the couch and sat down reclining on one side. Silence prevailed for some time, and then the King opened the conversation, which proceeded as follows :—

King.—Is the English Ruler well?

Envoy.—The English Ruler is well, your Majesty.

King.—How many days is it since you left Rangoon?

Envoy.—Nineteen days, your Majesty.

Here the list of presents from the Viceroy to His Majesty was read out.

King.—I trust you have found everything prepared in accordance with the friendship existing between the Governments.

Envoy.—We have received every possible attention on our way through your royal dominions, and I beg to thank your Majesty for the kind treatment we have experienced.

No reply.

Envoy.—I have been surprised and pleased to see how fine a city Mandalay is, seeing that it was only founded a few years ago.

King.—It is not finished yet, but next time you come it will be in a still better state. What is the age of the Envoy?

Envoy.—Forty-four years, your Majesty.

Here the King said something in a low voice to his sons, and a nephew of His Majesty brought to the Envoy on a golden salver a small packet, which when opened was found to contain a collar of the Burmese order of the Tsalwé of the first grade. The Burmese Minister, on a motion from His Majesty, said, "invest the Envoy," and Captain Sladen put it over the Envoy's left shoulder. Colonel Fytche bowed, and thanked His Majesty for the honour conferred on him.

Envoy.—The house which your Majesty has prepared for us here is very handsome and commodious, and we are grateful for the trouble that has been taken in getting it ready.

King.—It has been constructed mainly through the activity of Sladen.

Captain Sladen.—And also, your Majesty, with the assistance of the officials you were pleased to direct to help me.

King.—Sladen is a good man, and has done all he can to advance the interests of both the British and the Burmese Governments.

Envoy.—I have every confidence that he has done so.

King.—Sladen is an honest man. It is from honest men being in such a position as his that good friendship is preserved between Governments.

Envoy.—I am glad to learn your Majesty's good opinion of Captain Sladen, and I shall report to His Excellency the Viceroy all that you have been pleased to say concerning him.

Captain Sladen.—I feel highly honoured, your Majesty, by your royal approbation, and I shall never forget this public expression of it.

King.—Sladen must visit me daily while the Envoy is here : (addressing him) you must come every day, come with the Kulah-won (Mr. Manook, the official through whom the King communicates with all foreigners).

Having said this the King got off the couch and stood up with his back to the audience. The doors were opened, he passed out, and they were at once closed. During the interview the King spoke in a quite low tone. His Majesty had a pair of opera-glasses through which he frequently looked at the members of the embassy.

After the departure of the King considerable general conversation ensued between the officers of the Mission and the numerous Burmese officials present. The audience was quite an open one, and it was found that all the servants of the officers, who had accompanied them to the palace, had been present, seated at the back. Sweetmeats and cakes in great profusion were brought in. There were fried locusts also, which were pressed on the visitors as delicacies. After a short time passed in trying the various dishes and talking the while on sundry subjects, the Envoy left. Shoes were resumed at the foot of the palace steps. The Meng-yees again greeted the party at the steps of the Hlwot-dau, and the Wondouk and other officials accompanied it to the gates of the palace, whence the return to the Agency was quickly effected on elephants, the troops still lining the streets as before and the cavalry accompanying the *cortège*. The Agency was reached at 2 P. M.

To-day a boat arrived with letters for the Chief Commissioner which had left Thayetmyo on the 4th instant.

On the 12th no business of a public nature was transacted, as it was the day of the full moon, during which the Burmese have certain religious observances to attend to. And so also on the 13th, which, besides being Sunday, was a festival day with the Burmese.

On the 14th Mrs. Fytche and Mrs. Lloyd visited the palace, having interviews with the principal Queen (who is also the King's half-sister) and with her mother, and the second Queen, or Alaynandau Phura. It was also arranged that the King should receive the Envoy, attended by Captain Sladen, Captain Duncan, and Mr. Edwards, on the 16th at a private audience, when business would be commenced, the object of the Mission officially announced, and permission asked to discuss matters with the Ministers. It was hoped that the official visits to the Ministers might take place the same day. On the 15th Captain Sladen saw the King, and informed him of the communications which would be made to him next day, and His Majesty expressed his readiness to receive them from the Envoy. On the 16th, however, Captain Sladen was so unwell as to be unable to attend with the Envoy at the palace. Information to this effect was conveyed to His Majesty, and he was asked whether it would be agreeable to him to receive the Envoy and other officers without Captain Sladen, or whether His Majesty would prefer to wait for a day or two for Captain Sladen's recovery. His Majesty suggested that the audience should be postponed till the 18th, and the Ministers at the same time sent to the Envoy requesting he would pay his visits to them also on the 18th. The delay in seeing the King did not really interfere with the transaction of business, and none could have been gone into with the Ministers until after they had been visited.

On the 18th the visits were again postponed until the 19th, when the Envoy had what was called a private audience with His Majesty. Colonel Fytche was accompanied by Captain Sladen, Captain Duncan, and Mr. Edwards. The reception took place in the southern garden in a summer-house. There were present the Keng Wondouk, the Paopa Wondouk, an Atwen Won, and the Kulah-won, Mr. Manook. The following conversation took place :—

King.—I hope you continue well and comfortable.

Envoy.—Everything is most comfortable. I already had the honour of thanking your Majesty publicly for the reception and accommodation afforded us, and I beg now to repeat the same. It will give me much pleasure on my approaching visit to Calcutta to inform the Viceroy and Governor-General of India of the kindness and consideration your Majesty has shown.

Pause.

Colonel Fytche.—The water in the river is now falling fast, and I should be glad if your Majesty would give me an opportunity of concluding the business upon which I have come.

King.—Do you mean the business you have written about and which Sladen has conducted with me?

Colonel Fytche.—Yes, your Majesty.

King.—That is arranged : nothing remains but to meet the Wongyees and conclude matters with them.

Colonel Fytche.—I had great pleasure, before leaving Rangoon, in writing to inform the Viceroy of your Majesty's assent to the several Treaty propositions which were laid before you by Captain Sladen. On my return to Rangoon it is my intention to proceed to Calcutta to visit the Viceroy.

King.—When you visit Calcutta there is one thing I wish you to mention to the Viceroy, *viz.*, that he would give you permission to visit me once a year at least.

Colonel Fytche.—I shall do so, your Majesty.

King.—I see Mr. Edwards ; (to Mr. Edwards) Edwards you never get old ; what is your age? (To Colonel Fytche.) Be kind to Mr. Edwards ; he has served Government faithfully for a number of years. (To Mr. Edwards.) Edwards, when the British Government cease to employ you, come to me, and I will keep you here. I shall not expect you to work, but I shall keep you in comfort.

Pause.

King.—There is no state or condition of life which is not made more perfect by a good friendly understanding. I wish for sincere friendship with you, Colonel Fytche. When I make a request you must not think that I wish merely for my own personal interests. I look to the interests of both countries. In return, any requests which you may have to make of me should have reference to mutual advantages ; our friendship will then be complete. But there are certain ways in which friendship will be completely broken off and utterly destroyed. No more effectual means exists than listening to the idle stories of evil-minded men. Even the most affectionate couple, as husband and wife, brother and sister, father and son, may soon be made to hate each other by reports from intriguers. Lately, for instance, before you came, there were people who told me you were a bad man, and that I might expect the worst from your visit : I now see how false were these words. They also tried to make me believe that you were no friend of Sladen's.

Colonel Fytche.—I have every confidence in Captain Sladen. He has been known to me for many years, and served directly under me when I was Commissioner of Tenasserim.

King.—A man like Sladen is rare even among foreigners. You will do well to give him your confidence. He works for the interests of both countries. He is as much in my confidence as any of my own Ministers, and I often say more to him than I would to them. Sladen, you know the duties of a Ruler; what is the first duty ?

Captain Sladen.—That he should have patience (or self-restraint), your Majesty.

King (laughing).—Exactly, a Ruler should never lose his temper ; he should listen to all sides of a question, but never allow himself to be angry, &c., &c.

Pause.

King.—I wish you, Colonel Fytche, to see my hospitals for the sick and old; they will interest you. I myself derive much satisfaction from being able to exercise charity towards the afflicted and the priests, besides which I thereby lay up for myself future reward ; but I am not supposed to keep all this to myself. There is no gift of gold or silver which can be compared to the priceless one of a share in the reward or merit of good actions. I want you, Colonel Fytche, to say you will accept what I have of that to give you.

Colonel Fytche.—I do so, your Majesty. The tenets of the Buddhist faith resemble those of the Christian religion in this and in many other respects.—" He that hath pity on the poor lendeth unto the Lord ; what he layeth out it shall be paid him again."

King.—Then I admit you to share the merit of my charitable works. I cannot make you a greater offering than this. I have long known you by report, and have got your portrait, which I have had for some years. Although we have known one another personally for a short time only, you must still consider that we have long been friends. Who is that sitting near the Envoy?

Colonel Fytche.—It is the Inspector-General of Police, Captain Duncan.

King (to Captain Duncan).—Do you understand Burmese?

Captain Duncan.—I do, your Majesty.

King.—Then I hope you will remember all I have been saying.

Colonel Fytche.—Captain Sladen under my instructions spoke to your Majesty a day or two ago regarding the exploring expedition which the Viceroy proposes to send from Bhamo to China. I wish to write on the subject to your Majesty.

King.—Do so by all means. I will sanction the expedition (literally, I will give permission for the party to go); when will it start, where will it go?

Colonel Fytche.—It will leave this in December and proceed from Bhamo to China.

King.—Who is to go with the party? If you send Sladen, I will assist him throughout to China, and send my own people with him.

Colonel Fytche.—It is my intention to send Captain Sladen, but arrangements will have to be made for any business which may have to be transacted here during his absence.

King.—Sladen will only be away a short time. It will be better not to appoint any one here in his absence. I shall order my Won-gyees to communicate direct with you in Rangoon on business matters.

Colonel Fytche.—I am glad to inform your Majesty that brigandage has decreased on the frontier since your Majesty deputed a special officer from Mandalay to reside with a guard at Shazeebo.

King.—I am glad to hear this; I have attended to your wishes in respect to this appointment. My desire is to put down brigandage and marauding. It is by thus having a due regard to mutual advantages that we shall continue to get on well together.

Our officers on the frontier should understand each other and co-operate in the apprehension of offenders.

Colonel Fytche.—My officers report that they and the Burmese officer (Boh Moungalay) work in close concert, and they speak highly of his energy.

King.—Do you know Moung Toung Boh, the present Governor of Meeaday? He is a good man, and gets on well with English officials. Several bad characters ran away from this during the rebellion and are now congregated in British territory where they will scheme for evil; keep a good watch on them.

Colonel Fytche.—We have lists of the refugees your Majesty refers to, and they are under observation.

The King here pointed out to Colonel Fytche the Keng Wondouk, and said he wished Colonel Fytche to know him and like him : he (the King) had reared the Wondouk from the time he was a child. Colonel Fytche replied that he had met the Keng Wondouk once or twice since his arrival, and had liked him from the first. His Majesty also pointed out the Padein Won, Shwé Beng (a young Burman who received an English education in Calcutta), and requested Colonel Fytche to look on him as his son. Colonel Fytche mentioned to the King that the Paopa Wondouk (who was present) had been most attentive since the Mission had entered Burmese territory. The King replied that the Wondouk was an old officer of Government, and served his father years ago.

King.—Regarding the Myeen-gon Prince, although he is my son he has given me a great deal of trouble. I now maintain 8,000 men in the Shan States to watch him. What are the last accounts you have heard of him?

Colonel Fytche.—By the latest accounts he was in a very poor condition, with but few followers in Kyaypogyee's country. The eastern and western Karennees are fighting amongst themselves, but do not countenance the Prince.

King.—Do all you can to induce the Prince to come into you. The Karennees are assisting him, and he is trying to raise the Shans. He has been issuing circulars to the people to join his standard and fight. I can send you one of his proclamations, which was sent me by a Mahomedan trader from near Tonghoo.

Colonel Fytche.—I have written to Kyaypogyee, expressing dissatisfaction at any assistance he may give to the Prince. Strict orders have also been issued to the Shan Chiefs who are in our territory that they are not on any account to cross the frontier or to give any aid to the Prince.

King.—I am aware of that, but the Shans are a foolish people, and they would listen to evil advice. Burmans are foolish, too ; a small spark soon kindles into a flame. Had you not sent the Myeengondaing Prince away from Rangoon, he also would have created a disturbance.

Colonel Fytche.—About the Myeengondaing Prince I wished to inform your Majesty that he was sent to the Andamans for safety at the time it was necessary to remove him quickly. But as the Andaman Islands are used as a convict colony, it is now proposed to send him to some suitable place in Bengal.

King.—Very good, send him as far away as possible from Burma and all association with Burmese. I should wish to have two river steamers, one of them to be armed. During the rebellion my country was saved by the steamers that came up from Rangoon : as soon as they appeared the rebels dispersed everywhere. Colonel Phayre advised me to have two war steamers, one between this and Bhamo, and the other between this and the frontier. I want your Government to supply me with these steamers ; what would they cost ?

Colonel Fytche.—The steamers can be furnished easily enough, but it will be necessary that your Majesty should furnish details as to the kind of steamer you want, its length, breadth, draught, horse-power, &c., &c. There are so many varieties of steamers suitable for river navigation.

Here ensued a short discussion as to what would be required, and it was eventually arranged that the Burmese Ministers would furnish details regarding the steamers, and Colonel Fytche would make inquiries in Calcutta as to the cost, &c., &c.

King.—I also want 8,000 rifles. You have already assented to my having 2,000, which I am now getting from Dr. Williams; and if you let me have 8,000 more, I shall have 10,000 men well armed with rifles, and they will always remain near me at the capital.

To this Colonel Fytche replied that the rifles could be furnished, but that the kind of rifle wanted should be settled. A conversation ensued regarding smooth-bores, rifles, and breech-loaders, and it was explained to the King that to use rifles or breech-loaders the men had to be well instructed, and then to take great care of their arms. The King replied—" In time no doubt my men would learn all that," and it was arranged that His Majesty should decide and let Colonel Fytche know what kind of arm he desired to have. The King then turned to leave, and turning round on the sofa said—" Sladen, I am sorry you have been sick. I shall send you something to-morrow to make you well," and with that withdrew.

The party then adjourned to an open pavilion, where sweet-meats and fruits were served. Subsequently, the Chief Commissioner, Captain Duncan, and Mr. Edwards visited the Wongyees. The first was the Loungshay Meng-gyee, an officer who had been most severely wounded during the late rebellion, and who is still much disabled. During the visit there was no business discussed, but a friendly conversation lasted for some time. The next visit was to the Yaynankhyoung Meng-gyee, Oo Tso, an old soldier of high repute among the Burmese. He has been engaged in a good many campaigns, and during the rebellion last year re-established the King's authority in all the districts south of Mandalay to the frontier. He received a bullet wound in one of the fights, and indeed the bullet has not been extracted. The Meng-gyee is a man of very quiet and affable manners. Some of the ladies of this family were present. He spoke on general subjects, and only casually adverted to the fact of a Treaty being in negotiation, asking when it would be concluded. He seldom mixes in politics, and his reputation is entirely military. The Pakhan Meng-gyee was next visited. This official may be described as holding the position of Prime Minister; he is the cleverest of the officials now in office, was a fellow-priest with the King before he came to the throne, and has always been employed in political matters. At his house the Keng Wondouk (who has already been frequently mentioned) was present. The visit was a most agreeable one, as they are both men of unusual intelligence. The subjects were general, and no business was referred to. The subjects talked of were some points of the Christian religion, the deluge, the solar system, the duration of night and day in different portions of the globe, &c., &c., all carried on with great vivacity and good humour. At each of the officials' houses refreshments were served up in the English style with plates, knives and forks, glasses, napkins, &c., &c. At the Yaynankhyoung Meng-gyee's house beer and sherry were on the table; at those of the others tea was served.

On the 21st November Colonel Fytche visited the Pakhan Meng-gyee for the purpose of discussing any matters regarding the Treaty. He was accompanied by Captain Sladen, Captain Duncan, and Mr. Edwards. At the Meng-gyee's house was the Keng Wondouk, and Mr. Manook, the Kulah-won; the usual staff of writers also were there to record whatever might pass. The negotiations regarding the Treaty have been elsewhere reported, and it will be unnecessary to give here in detail the course of the discussions. Some corrections were made in the draft Treaty making more clear the provisions of the Articles. The interchange of value lists and their correction, the free import and export of silver and gold, the right of purchase of warlike stores, all came up more or less for desultory discussion; but no important alterations were proposed by the Minister, nor any desire of pressing them shown. The subjects from various aspects were dilated upon, but throughout the whole day's conversation no opposition on either side became necessary. The conclusion was that the Treaty generally was finally agreed to, leaving only one clause in the Article regarding the jurisdiction of the Agent for reference to His Majesty the King. As soon as business was over, lunch was over, and a long general conversation ensued.

Next day (the 22nd) the Pakhan Meng-gyee and the Keng Won-douk visited the Chief Commissioner. It was only towards the close that a further discussion regarding the jurisdiction Article ensued; they had not yet received the orders of the King, and were themselves somewhat opposed to the Article: this led them again to bring up some of the terms of the other Articles, but there was a manifest desire to avoid coming to a direct difference of opinion. The orders of His Majesty were to be received by them that evening.

On the 23rd the entire Mission visited the palace on the invitation of His Majesty to see a sort of amateur ballet performed by the young ladies attached to the households of the Queens. The reception took place in the same building in which the last interview took place. A large circular shed had been constructed as for a native play; at one side was a raised alcove with a low railing, within which was the couch for His Majesty. Immediately in front of the alcove there was a rough attempt at scenery, forming the background to a troop of professional actors and actresses who were in attendance. To the right of the King's position sat several of his officials and the officers of the Mission. To the left were seated Mrs. Fytche and Mrs. Lloyd, and the wives of the Burmese Ministers. After a short delay, the King entered, and took his place on the couch. He made a few remarks to the effect that he wished the English officers to visit his gardens and any other objects of interest in the palace, and concluded by asking whether we wished to see the ordinary play by the professionals or the ballet. A preference was expressed for the latter, when he called attention to the fact that the players on the drums, gongs, and clarionets were all women.

The performance commenced by the entrance of about 30 young girls in single file, who arranged themselves in a semi-circle, and kneeling down, bowed to His Majesty. They wore the ordinary hta-mein, or Burmese petticoat, but the jacket was more of the fashion of that worn by Princes in the plays. The hta-meins were all red and green, the jackets white satin, with circular pieces of silver stitched on, so as somewhat to resemble armour. On the head the girls wore peaked helmets, also usually worn by male performers in the ordinary plays. The girls rising, first performed a slow, graceful dance round the theatre to the accompaniment of the band, varying the step and pace from time to time, and again knelt down; one of the number taking up her position in the centre, then sang and chanted in a rich contralto voice a slow hymn in honour of His Majesty, describing his greatness and goodness. This was acknowledged to be one of the most effective exhibitions ever witnessed in the East by any of the English party. The dead silence of the whole assembly, the clear and exceedingly sweet tone of the solo, and the peculiar measure of the air, half-recitative, half-sang, made the whole scene most striking and beautiful. The hymn consisted of three verses; at the end of each the girls, still kneeling, bowed low to His Majesty. They then resumed the dance, which they accompanied with a low chant, and varied it by beating time with two ornamental sticks which they now carried. This, too, being ended, the King rose and left. During the performance, the Nama-daw Phura, or principal Queen, accompanied by a considerable retinue of ladies, entered, and seated herself close to His Majesty on a sofa placed for her reception. A considerable retinue of ladies accompanied her, but as they were seated at the back of the alcove, it was difficult to see who they were.

On the departure of His Majesty, the Mission were served with fruit and sweetmeats in an open arbour, and afterwards proceeded to visit the so-called white elephant. The animal is a small specimen, and can only by great courtesy be called white. In reality, he has light points, and the hair is not so coarse as in the ordinary elephant; it may be more truly described as brownish; the lighter tint being more observable from a very black female elephant being assigned him as a companion in his stable. From this the party visited the stone-cutters, now busily engaged in engraving on marble slabs the entire Pitagât, or Burmese scriptures. These are to be placed round the King's temple in the neighbourhood of Mandalay. After a cursory look at some of the ordnance, the Mint was visited, where the coinage of rupees was going on. The machinery was procured from Birmingham, but, although the engine is under the charge of an African, the actual operations of smelting and coining are performed by Burmans. They state that they can coin about rupees 15,000 per diem, but this seemed a large out-turn for so small a machine, there being only one die at work.

On leaving the palace, all returned to the Agency, with the exception of Colonel Fytche, Captain Sladen, Captain Duncan, and Mr. Edwards, who paid another visit to the Pakhan Meng-gyee. The Treaty was again discussed, and the final alterations in the jurisdiction Article agreed to. It was arranged that the document should be fairly written out next day, and signed on the 25th, when, also, the farewell visit was to be paid to the King.

On the 24th no visits were interchanged by the Envoy.

On the 25th the Mission went in procession to the palace in much the same order as on the occasion of the first visit to the King. On arriving at the Hlwotdan, or Supreme Court, the officers took off their shoes at the steps, and entering the building, joined the Pakhan and Yaynankhyoung Meng-gyees, who were there seated; there were also present the Keng Wondouk, the Kulah-won, and some secretaries. The Treaty was prepared on large sheets of parchment, and the two Burmese copies were read over and compared. The English copies were read over carefully by the Padien Won (who understands English), and all being found correct, they were signed and sealed. The Mission then entered the palace building, and were conducted to the reception-room where the first interview was held. The same arrangements had been made as on that occasion, but there was only one of the King's sons present.

After taking his seat, as usual, His Majesty first observed that the weather was very hot, to which remark, no doubt, all silently assented, as the heat had for some days been very great. The King then said that he wished the officers to visit his gardens

before they left, mentioning to his officers the particular places
to which they should be taken. Then followed a short conversation.

King.—When is it proposed that the Envoy should return to
Rangoon?

Colonel Fytche.—On the 3rd day after this, your Majesty, we
propose going on board the steamers, and the next day we will
start down the river.

King.—Will the Envoy then go to Calcutta, and who of the
party will go with him?

Colonel Fytche.—Yes; I am to pay a visit to His Excellency
the Viceroy and Governor-General as soon as I can after reaching
Rangoon, but none of the other officers will go.

King.—You will, I hope, remember to ask leave to visit me
once a year.

Colonel Fytche.—I shall certainly do so, your Majesty, and in
the next occasion I should wish, with your permission, to visit the
capital in a quiet and informal manner.

King.—Among foreigners (Kulahs) there are many deceitful and
wicked men. I trust you will be careful regarding such.

The King then directed that the presents should be brought in.
These consisted of a gold cup and silk putsoe to each member of
the Mission, and, in addition to these, two rings (a ruby and a
sapphire) were given to Colonel Fytche.

King.—I understand that you have an English clergyman
here?

Colonel Fytche.—Yes, your Majesty (pointing to the Rev. Mr.
Crofton); this is the Chaplain of Rangoon.

King.—Is that the Inspector-General of Police sitting near
you?

Colonel Fytche.—It is, your Majesty.

King.—Where is he generally stationed in the British territory?
In Rangoon?

Colonel Fytche.—Yes; his head-quarters are at Rangoon, but
he has to visit all the districts in Arakan and Tenasserim as
well.

King.—I understand that you wish for some wormwood seed, which I have procured for you (it was here brought in). Now I think you would like to visit the garden, and with these words His Majesty rose and went off.

The Envoy and the officers of the suit then visited the gardens inside the palace, and were served with sweetmeats, &c., &c. After this they proceeded to the house of Mr. Manook, the Kulah-won, to lunch. This officer, who is the official medium between the King and foreigners generally, had been most attentive to the Mission from the time of its arrival, and all were much in-debted to him for the constant anxiety he showed to make the visit agreeable.

The 26th and 27th were passed without official business of any interest, and on the 28th, the day fixed for our departure, the Ministers came to bid Colonel Fytche good-bye; their visit was a lengthy one, and of the most friendly and agreeable kind. His Majesty sent to the Envoy a small Whitworth gun, with field carriage, which had been made in his arsenal. It carries a one pound shot, and was made from a small Whitworth presented to the King two or three years ago by a gentleman from England, who visited Mandalay regarding the construction of a railway.

In the afternoon the members of the Mission embarked on board the steamers, and next day proceeded down the river, accompanied by the Paopa Wondouk and other officials, as far as Kyouktalon, in one of the King's steamers.

A Secretary and a Commissariat Officer came on in our steamer to Menhla, which was reached on the 1st November. Here the Tseetkay of Menhla came on board, and after a short interview the journey was continued, and the frontier crossed that after-noon.

The foregoing short description of the Mission to Mandalay of the Chief Commissioner of British Burma, as Envoy from the Viceroy and Governor-General of India, will have shown how satisfactorily all the circumstances connected with it passed off. The position of affairs anterior to the visit was such as to give exceptional importance to the event. Just one year previously, the Court of Ava had declined to enter into further Treaty engagements with the British Government, which were considered essential to a proper carrying out of the spirit of the Treaty of 1852, and which were no less necessary to meet the growing requirements of the large commercial relations of the two countries.

The dissatisfaction felt by the Government of India at the course pursued by the Court of Ava was communicated to His Majesty the King, and the disappointment of the public generally at the narrow policy thus displayed led to a strong expression of resentment against the Burmese Government.

Negotiations were re-opened by the desire of His Majesty, and eventuated in the visit of the Chief Commissioner for the purpose of concluding a subsidiary Treaty. Some significance, therefore, was necessarily attached to the manner in which the Mission might be received, irrespective of the result, whether that might be successful or not. On this point there can be no two opinions as to the reception of the Envoy and his suite. From the time the party crossed the frontier, until it left Mandalay, there was the most manifest desire to show every consideration and respect towards the representative of His Excellency the Viceroy and Governor-General. During the progress up the river, every provision was made for the comfort and convenience of the party. At the capital, the accommodation provided was exceptionally handsome and commodious. In all the details connected with the interviews with His Majesty, measures were taken to show the importance attached by the Court to a fitting reception at the palace ; and in the more direct and personal communication with His Majesty and with his Ministers, the most friendly tone prevailed. Frequent expression was given to the desire for a lasting and close friendship between the respective Governments.

Further, the Treaty was agreed to and concluded. Its terms, which provide for greater freedom in the trade of the two countries, and greater security for British interests in the Burmese territory, are eminently calculated to develope the commercial relations of the two nations. If the same appreciation of its value which has led the Burmese Court to conclude this Treaty will also induce it to carry out its provisions cordially and liberally, we may hope for the best results in the increased prosperity of the Burmese kingdom.

(Sd.)   ALBERT FYTCHE, Col.,

Chief Commissioner of British Burma, Agent
to His Excellency the Viceroy and Governor-
General.

Rangoon,
The 8th Nov., 1867.

APPENDIX.

Treaty concluded on 25th October, 1867 *A.D., corresponding with* 13*th day of the waning moon Tha-den-gyoot* 1229 *B. E., by Colonel Albert Fytche, Chief Commissioner of British Burma, in virtue of full power vested in him by His Excellency the Right Hon'ble Sir John Laird Mair Lawrence, Bart., G.C.B., G.C.S.I., Viceroy and Governor-General of India, and by His Excellency the Pakhan Woongyee, Men-Thudo-Mengyee Maha-Menhla See-Thoo, in virtue of full power vested in him by His Majesty the King of Burma.*

ARTICLE I.

Save and except Earth Oil, Timber, and Precious Stones, which are hereby reserved as Royal Monopolies, all goods and merchandise passing between British and Burmese territory shall be liable, at the Burmese Customs Houses, to the payment of a uniform Import and Export Duty of five per cent. *ad valorem* for a period of ten years, commencing from the first day of the Burmese year 1229, corresponding with 15th April, 1867. No indirect dues or payments of any kind shall be levied or demanded on such goods over and above the five per cent. *ad valorem* duty.

ARTICLE II.

But after the expiration of ten years, during which Customs Duties will be collected as provided for above in Article I., it shall be optional with the Burmese Government, whilst estimating the capabilities and requirements of trade, either to increase or decrease the existing five per cent. Import and Export Duties, so that the increase shall at no time exceed (10) ten, or the decrease to be reduced below a three (3) per cent. *ad valorem* rate on any particular article of commerce. Three months' notice shall be given of any intention to increase or decrease the rates of Customs Duty as above, previous to the commencement of the year in which such increase or decrease shall have effect.

ARTICLE III.

The British Government hereby stipulates that it will adhere to the abolition of Frontier Customs Duty, as expressed in Article VIII. of the treaty of 1862, during such time as the Burmese Government shall collect five per cent. *ad valorem* duties, or a lesser rate as provided for in Articles I. and II. of this Treaty.

ARTICLE IV.

Both Governments further stipulate to furnish each other annually with price lists, showing the market value of all goods, imported and exported under Articles I. and II. Such price lists shall be furnished two months before the commencement of the year during which they are to have effect, and may be corrected from time to time as found necessary, by the mutual consent of both Governments through their respective Political Agents.

ARTICLE V.

The British Government is hereby privileged to establish a Resident or Political Agent in Burmese territory, with full and final jurisdiction in all Civil suits arising between Registered British subjects at the capital. Civil cases between Burmese subjects and Registered British subjects shall be heard and finally decided by a mixed Court composed of the British Political Agent and a suitable Burmese Officer of high rank. The Burmese Government reserves to itself the right of establishing a Resident or Political Agent in British territory whenever it may choose to do so.

ARTICLE VI.

The British Government is further allowed the right of appointing British officials to reside at any or each of the stations in Burmese territory at which Customs Duty may be leviable. Such officials shall watch and inquire into all cases affecting trade, in its relation to Customs Duty ; and may purchase land and build suitable dwelling-houses at any town or station where they may be appointed to reside.

ARTICLE VII.

In like manner the Burmese Government is also allowed the right of appointing Burmese officials to reside at any or each of the stations in British Burma at which Customs Duty may be leviable. Such officials shall watch and inquire into all cases affecting trade, in its relation to Customs Duty ; and may purchase land and build suitable dwelling-houses at any town or station where they may be appointed to reside.

ARTICLE VIII.

In accordance with the great friendship which exists between the two Governments, the subjects of either shall be allowed free trade in the import and export of gold and silver bullion between the two countries, without let or hindrance of any kind, on due declaration being made at the time of import or export. The Burmese Government shall further be allowed permission to purchase arms, ammunition, and war materials generally in British territory, subject only to the consent and approval in each case of the Chief Commissioner of British Burma and Agent to the Governor-General.

ARTICLE IX.

Persons found in British territory, being Burmese subjects, charged with having committed any of the following offences, *viz.*, murder, robbery, dacoity, or theft, in Burmese territory, may be apprehended and delivered up to the Burmese Government for trial, on due demand being made by the Government, provided that the charge on which the demand is made shall have been investigated by the proper Burmese Officers in the presence of the British Political Agent : and provided also the British Political Agent shall consider that sufficient cause exists under British Law procedure to justify the said demand, and place the accused persons on their trial. The demand and delivery in each case shall be made through the British Political Agent at the Capital.

ARTICLE X.

Persons found in Burmese territory, being British subjects, charged with having committed any of the following offences, *viz.*, murder, robbery, dacoity, or theft, in British territory, may be apprehended and delivered up to the British Government for trial, on due demand being made by that Government, provided that the charge on which the demand is made shall have been investigated by the proper British Officers, in the presence of the Burmese Political Agent ; and provided also that the Burmese Political Agent shall be satisfied that sufficient cause exists under Burmese Law Procedure to justify the said demand and put the accused persons on their trial. The demand and delivery in each case shall be made through the Burmese Political Agent in British territory.

ARTICLE XI.

Persons found in Burmese territory, being Burmese subjects, charged with having committed any of the following offences, *viz.*, murder, robbery, dacoity, or theft, in British territory, shall, on apprehension, be tried and punished in accordance with Burmese Law and custom. A special Officer may be appointed by the British Government to watch the proceedings on the trial of all persons apprehended under this Article.

ARTICLE XII.

Persons found in British territory, being British subjects, charged with having committed any of the following offences, *viz.*, murder, robbery, dacoity, or theft, in Burmese territory, shall, on apprehension, be tried and punished in accordance with British Law and custom. A special Officer may be appointed by the Burmese Government to watch the proceedings on the trial of all persons apprehended under this Article.

ARTICLE XIII.

The Treaty which was concluded on the 10th November, 1862, shall remain in full force : the stipulations now made and agreed to in the above Articles being deemed as subsidiary only, and as in no way affecting the several provisions of that Treaty.

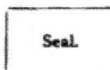

	(Sd.)	ALBERT FYTCHE, COLONEL,

Seal.

Chief Commissioner, British Burma ;
and
Aent to the Viceroy and Governor-General of India.

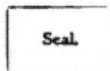

Seal.   Signed in Burmese.

Ratified by the Viceroy and Governor-General of India in Council this day, the 26th November, 1867.

     (Sd.)   JOHN LAWRENCE,
            Viceroy and Governor-General.

FORT WILLIAM,
The 26th November, 1867.

APPENDIX D.

MEMORANDUM

ON THE

COMPARATIVE PROGRESS OF THE PROVINCES, NOW FORMING BRITISH BURMA UNDER BRITISH AND NATIVE RULE.

Dated Rangoon, 23rd August, 1867.

It may be premised, that the following paper has been drawn up on the understanding, that, *data* should be furnished showing, as clearly as possible, the material progress of British Burma under British Administration, as compared with its condition under Native Rule, or with the condition of existing neighbouring States and Powers : and that, no discussion or argument is desired as to the popularity of our rule, or the advantages which it may possess, except, so far as these are to be assumed, from the Statements indicative of the comparative progress of the people under our Government.

2. British Burma affords means of drawing a fair comparison between British and Native Administration—because it has in immediate contact with it, as a Government, the very power from whose dominions the Province was obtained. In 1826, the Provinces of Arakan and Tenasserim were annexed to the British Territories from the Burmese power, still leaving to the King of Ava the whole of the Northern portion of his dominions, as well as the important Province of Pegu, formed of the lower portion of the valley of the Irawadi River, and its delta. We thus obtained possession of the least productive portion of the Burmese Kingdom, while the King retained the magnificent lands of Pegu, with

the valuable outlet of Rangoon, to which point foreign trade had solely been drawn.

3. A reference to the map will show, that the Province of Pegu was fairly interposed between the newly-acquired districts, in a position easily to withdraw from them both population and trade, provided Native rule had proved more attractive to either. These conditions then, seem to furnish a fair test—only that the presumption was in favour of the Native Dynasty in virtue of it holding a far richer, and more accessible country.

4. As it is required that the endeavour to compare the result of British and of Native Rule, in these countries, is to be made on specific data, it is necessary to select some one element of advancement as a standard, from which can be deduced the many numerous conditions, which go to make up material progress. If this be not done, the comparison must spread out into an examination too minute and extended to be satisfactorily disposed of within a reasonable compass—and the difficulty is increased from the impossibility of obtaining in detail, the items which constituted the Revenue, taxes, and trade of British Burma, previous to our occupation, in such a shape as would enable individual comparison with the fiscal arrangements now in force.

5. In the East, there is probably no better general test of the advancement of a country, than the rise or fall, the ebb or flow, of its population. A steady increase in the population indicates in fact a prosperous people, a firm and staple Government, and an absence of oppression. It produces, especially where the proportion is not in excess of the capabilities of the soil, extended cultivation, and increased trade. If then, it can be fairly shown, *that*, the population of the Provinces composing British Burma, has increased at a rate which far exceeds the numbers to be obtained from natural increase, and must be attributed to immigration; *that*, in one instance where the locality, whence the immigration was drawn, became British, the exodus ceased; while the flow from Native states into British districts more accessible, continued; and *that*, where detailed statistics are available, it will be seen our frontier Districts have increased at the highest ratio, then we may

conclude that British Administration in Burma has proved its
superiority over Native Rule.   In British Burma the population
returns are fairly reliable, because they are susceptible of easy
check from the Capitation Tax in force in these Provinces.   This
tax is levied from all male adults, and the revenue received there
from,—actual money paid into the Treasury at fixed rates per
head, has shown a proportional increase, corresponding with the
rise in population.

6. It is well known that when Arakan and Tenasserim first
came into our possession, in 1826, they were almost depopulated,
and were so unproductive, that it was seriously deliberated whether
they should not be restored to Burma.   The following figures will
show how much these apparently unprofitable acquirements pros-
pered under our Administration.

7. In 1826 the Province of Arakan, with an area of 18,630
square miles, had a population of only 100,000 souls, these were
the indigenous population.   In 1835 this had risen to 211,536, of
whom not more than 6,000 were foreigners.   In 1845 the population numbered 309,608, an increase of fifty per cent. in the decade,
and in 1855 reached 366,310, or fifteen per cent. in the decade,
but in 1852 Pegu had become a British possession, the effect of
which was immediately felt in Arakan, still the total increase in
Arakan during the twenty nine years, was 250 per cent. of the
indigenous population, or an average of fifty per cent. in each
decade.

8. Now turning to Tenasserim, we find that in 1829, three
years after the annexation, the population in a province with an
area of 28,000 square miles, was estimated at a little over 70,000
souls.   In 1835 it had risen to 84,917, or twenty-one per cent. in
six years.   In 1845 to 127,455, or fifty per cent. in the decade.
In 1855 to 213,692, or sixty-nine per cent. in the decade.   In
other words it had increased by 200 per cent. in 26 years.   The
actual increase in the home population of England and Wales
(after the loss from Emigration) has been about twelve per cent.
in each decade of the last fifty years.

9. To support the above returns, we will give the Statistics of

revenue and assessed cultivation during the same period. The Revenue of Arakan which in 1826 was £23,225 rose as follows:—In 1835 to £52,832: in 1845 to £68,455: and in 1855 to £127,729. The area of assessed cultivation, commencing in 1830 with 66,227 acres, advanced in 1835 to 133,952: in 1845 to 233,769: and in 1855 to 353,885 acres, while the value of the entire trade in the same year amounted to £1,876,998.

10. In Tenasserim the first year's Revenue in 1825-26 was £2,676. In 1835-36 it had risen to £33,953. In 1845-46, £52,525, and in 1855-56 had reached £83,300: while the total trade amounted to £836,305. Land under cultivation was not assessed by area in the earlier years of our occupation, and we have no returns on that head, until 1843, when 100,657 acres were assessed. This in 1845 had increased to 119,869, and in 1855-56, to 181,681.

11. Now from 1826 until 1852, these Provinces of Arakan and Tenasserim had, as a competitor both for trade and population, the Burman territories with a frontier of some 800 miles, across which our subjects were free to go, as far as we were concerned; but not free to come, because the Burman authorities strongly opposed emigration, and put serious obstacles in the way of any of their people migrating to our territories. Yet the immense increase of population shows that very large numbers were attracted to our rule.

12. As to the trade, there are no reliable data available to show what it could have been under Burmese rule, for say, the half century before we occupied the provinces, but we know from the absence of any seaport towns of importance, and from the small number of vessels which ever visited these provinces from other countries, that, at the time they came into our possession, there was scarcely any external trade at all. During the years, however, which have now been described, Maulmain, in the Tenasserim Provinces, became from a fishing village, a city of 60,000 inhabitants; and Akyab, in Arakan, similarly sprung into existence, and reached a population of 20,000 souls.

13. So far has been traced the progress of these Provinces up

to 1855, but in 1852, the Province of Pegu, including the rich
delta of the Irawadi, had been annexed to our territory, the
three Provinces eventually forming British Burma ; and we have
brought the older two Provinces up to 1855, because from that
date a carefully prepared statement of the statistics of the whole
three, provides a ready reference on all points of their material
progress, as well as because in the first few years of our occupation
of Pegu, the returns are necessarily not so reliable as when the
Administration was completely organized.

14. Pegu came into our possession in 1852, with an estimated
population of 500,000 souls, and an area of 33,400 square miles,
or a ratio of 15 persons to the square mile. In 1855 it is returned
at 631,640 souls, or nearly 19 to the square mile. It will be
remembered that Arakan commencing in 1826, with a ratio of $5\frac{1}{2}$
persons to the square mile, had risen in 1855 to a ratio of 20
persons ; and Tenasserim, from a ratio of $2\frac{1}{3}$ persons in 1829, had
increased to 7 persons per square mile in 1855. But it would
seem that in the beginning of the century, the population of the
true Burman Empire (that is, Upper Burma, as now constituted,
Pegu and Martaban) was estimated by various authorities at from
20 to 23 persons the square mile, and if this were the general
average, it may be concluded that the fertile Province of Pegu
containing the valley of the Irawadi, with that river as the
highway from the seaport town of Rangoon to Ava, the Capital of
the Empire, must have had a higher rate than the remainder of
the country.

15. But taking the population of Pegu at 23 persons the square
mile in 1826, we can then compare the position of the territories
British and Native after 29 years of mutual contact, thus :—

			1826. Population.	1855. Population.
NATIVE	. .	Pegu . .	. 769,120	719,640
BRITISH .	. .	{ Arakan .	. . 100,000	341,310*
		{ Tenasserim .	. 70,000	213,692
		Total .	. 939,320	1,274,642

* Not including foreigners.

Now we know that the gross increase in Arakan and Tenasserim in these 29 years was 385,000 souls, from which, allowing the natural increase during that period to have been 75 per cent. on the original population, we may deduct 127,500 on that account, and this will leave us 257,500 souls, as the emigration from Pegu and the other native Burman States into British Territory; and if we compare Pegu (including Martaban) fairly estimated in 1826, with Pegu (including Martaban) even in 1855 (three years after it came into our possession, during which period its population is believed to have risen from 588,000 to 719,640), we find it with nearly 50,000 less population at the latter than at the former period. This is an astonishing result when placed against the immense progress of the British territories in its immediate neighbourhood.

16. The very scanty ratio of population to area, which it is believed Burma has, within historical periods, always had under native rule, is almost certain proof that the actual natural increase is very low, or rather has been very low; yet it has very great capacity for supporting human life; and we have been able in tracing the British occupation of Arakan and Tenasserim, far less productive countries, to provide for a natural increase in them of 75 per cent. in 29 years, and even then have a large surplus population. Had Pegu during the same period, with its greater advantages, increased at the same proportion, it should have been possessed of a population of more than one million souls when it came into our hands. Instead of this, we find its population to have retrograded, and there can be no reasonable doubt that the people who should have enriched the Native State were drawn into British Territory.

17. Having thus brought up these Provinces to 1855, we shall now trace their progress since that period. The Province of Pegu, as has been said, came into our possession in 1852, but making allowances for the distressed condition of a country after a campaign, and for the imperfect returns, accidental to a newly-organized Administration, we may pass over the years up to 1855, and from that date commence our deductions.

18. Now as to the Province of Pegu, it faces, with a perfectly open frontier of (say) 200 miles, the still existing Burmese territories under the King of Ava, so that it is fairly pitted against the possibly superior attractions of Native Rule. From our territories, any subject of ours is free to move into Upper Burma whenever he desires, whereas there is a steady opposition shown to any emigration from the King's dominions into ours. So strong is this, that when families of cultivators wish to cross they are frequently obliged to do so by stealth at night, bringing possibly their cattle and carts, but abandoning their houses and much property. They send intelligence constantly to our Police Stations on the frontier to announce that they are coming, asking at the same time that a guard may meet them on the frontier, to protect them from the pursuing Burmese officials ; and again and again are our Police Stations flanked by the camps of whole villages, who have bodily moved into our territories, and taken shelter there until they had selected their future fields.

19. In the face of these difficulties, then, we find that Pegu, first a separate Province, now a Division of British Burma, had in 1855 a population of 631,640 souls, which in 1865 had risen to 1,350,989. That is, had more than doubled itself in ten years, the exact increase being 113 per cent. The proportion of population to area had increased from 19 to 40 per square mile. If we allow a natural increase of 25 per cent. during the decade in question, we may deduct 157,910 on that account ; and 20,000, the number of foreigners, from 719,349, which is the total gross increase ; and these deductions will leave us an immigration of the indigenous population, into our territories, of the enormous number of 561,439 souls in the ten years from 1855 to 1865.

20. Further, if we look to the increase of individual Districts during the same period, it will appear that their ratio of increase is strangely in accordance with their propinquity to foreign territory, and their consequent facility for absorbing emigrants. Thus the Prome District, which in its Northern aspect forms our frontier in the valley of the Irawadi, has increased its population by no less than 156 per cent. in these ten years. The

Toungoo District, which is our frontier in the valley of the Sittang (also facing Upper Burma), has had its population augmented in the same period 115 per cent. The Myanoung District, which adjoins Prome to the south, shows an increase of 81 per cent. The Bassein District, which has drawn, as will be shown hereafter, from Arakan as well as Upper Burma, has raised its population by 113 per cent. While the Rangoon District, which is the most southerly and removed from our frontier, has increased by 70 per cent. in the same decade.

21. The population returns from the other two divisions extending over the same ten years, 1855-56 to 1865-66, fully support the conclusion that they formerly drew their additional population from Upper Burma, and from Pegu, so long as it was under Native rule, and that when the latter came under British Administration the transfer ceased. Thus intercommunication between Arakan and the Pegu Division is comparatively easy along their mutual boundary, but when we reach the Northern Frontier of the Pegu Division, running athwart the valley of the Irawadi, then the passage from Upper Burma (Native) above that line to the Arakan Division is one of considerable difficulty ; in fact, the Aeng Pass is the only really feasible route leading through the broad range of mountains there separating Arakan from Burma Proper. We have shown that while Arakan under British Administration had to compete with Pegu under Native Rule, its population increased at an average of 50 per cent. each decade ; but when it has Pegu under British management, as its neighbour, and physical obstacles prevent a supply being drawn from Burma, as has been the case from 1855-56 to 1865-66, we find the population has only increased from 366,310 to 414,640, or 13 per cent. We have already pointed out that the Bassein District of the Pegu Division, which immediately adjoins Arakan, has during this period increased 113 per cent., and this is probably in some degree due to the reflux of those who had, while Pegu was under Native Rule, moved into the Province of Arakan. Tenasserim, on the other hand, has many routes by which she can draw population from the Native States, and we find that in the period from 1855-56 to

1865-66, this Division has increased its population from 254,605 to 430,551, or 68 per cent., a decennial rate as high as any it had attained since its occupation.

22. The foregoing data seem to establish beyond any doubt that during the whole period of British Administration of the Provinces of Arakan, Tenasserim, and Pegu, they have, in addition to an allowed natural increase of population, far higher than we have any historical authority for supposing they ever reached under Native Rule, withdrawn and absorbed enormous numbers of people from the neighbouring Native States, which may be summarised as follows :

Into Tenasserim and Arakan, 1826 to 1855 .	.	257,500
,, Pegu from 1855 to 1865 . . .	.	561,439
,, Tenasserim from 1855 to 1865 . .	.	113,295
Total .	.	932,234

23. Now looking to specific marks of material progress, to see whether they support the conclusions we would wish to draw, we find that in the Pegu Division during the decade 1855-56 to 1865-66, the area of assessed cultivation has increased from 539,808 to 991,102 acres, or 83 per cent. Customs from £56,281 to £151,088. The total revenue from £297,753 to £646,462 ; while the entire trade rose from £2,143,100 to £7,300,224. These results fully bear out our argument that increased population and increased prosperity in a country situated and constituted as Burma is run hand in hand together.

24. Tenasserim also in the past decade has progressed satisfactorily, in accordance with the increase in its population. The assessed area has risen from 181, 681, to 273,289 acres, customs from £7,796 to £13,517. The total revenue from £106,609 to £193,566, while the entire trade has increased from £836,305 to £1,712,307.

25. Arakan, on the other hand, shows the effect on her prosperity of having a British instead of a Native Administration to contend with as a neighbour. It has been indicated already that physical obstacles stand between Arakan and Upper Burma,

which do not, and did not, between it and Pegu. We have given the rapid increase in the population and prosperity of Arakan up to 1855, but in the decade to 1865 there is a marked falling off. Assessed lands increased from 353,885 to 377,012 acres, revenue from £127,429 to £190,032, while trade has fallen from £1,876,998 to £1,395,580.

26. We have hitherto been concerned only to show the undoubted fact, that the countries under British Administration have possessed advantages so manifest to the population of neighbouring Native States, that a steady emigration from them into our territories has continued ever since our Government was established among the Indo-Chinese nations, the original ratio of population to area being very low, while the life-supporting capacity of the soil is very high. This rapid increase of population has produced a remarkable progress in all the elements which go to make up the material prosperity of the country.

27. And when we look to those native powers which have been our competitors during this period the picture is reversed. In the dominions of the King of Burma, including the tributary Shan States, we find everywhere signs of progressive decay; a discontented people abandoning his territory; a decreasing revenue; the area of cultivation lessening yearly; and the weakness of the Government shown in the rebellions and outbreaks which so regularly occur. During this year (1867), had it not been for the rich granaries of Pegu that supplied Upper Burma with rice, a famine would have succeeded the Civil War which raged last year. The natives of Upper Burma themselves indicate truly the process now being undergone by the British and native dominions. "Here," they say, "in British Burma your villages are becoming towns, but with us in Upper Burma our towns are becoming villages."

ALBERT FYTCHE, Colonel,
Chief Commissioner, British Burma; and
Agent to the Governor-General.

APPENDIX E.

—·—

MEMORANDUM

ON THE

PANTHAYS, OR MAHOMMEDAN POPULATION OF YUNNAN.

By COLONEL ALBERT FYTCHE,

CHIEF COMMISSIONER BRITISH BURMA, AND AGENT TO HIS EXCELLENCY
THE VICEROY AND GOVERNOR-GENERAL OF INDIA.

———— ——

Dated Rangoon, July 15th, 1867.

CONSIDERABLE difficulties exist in procuring correct intelligence of the Panthays, or Mahommedan population of Yunnan. In the first place, they are not inclined themselves to be communicative ; but rather assume a studied ignorance of their own affairs :— Secondly, communication can only be ordinarily held with them through Chinese Merchants and Brokers, residents of Burma Proper, who speak the Burmese language ; and who, in addition to their own private and self-interested motives, for preventing free intercourse, with traders from Yunnan, are moreover in the pay, or subject to the influence of the King of Burma. They well understand the Royal policy of exclusiveness, and have been made acquainted with the several indirect orders which have from time to time been issued by that Government, in order to restrict, as effectually as possible, every means of intercourse between Panthays and foreigners of all nations. The little information, therefore, which it has been possible to collect from the above sources furnished me by Captain Sladen, and also from a few Panthays who visited Moulmain with a Shan Caravan, when I was Commissioner of the Tenasserim and Martaban Provinces in 1861, is vague and meagre; but such as it is, I will now briefly record.

A paper has been published in the Russian Military Journal for August, 1866, on the late rising of the Dungens, or Mussulman population in Western China. I am of opinion that no Political affinity exists between the Dungens of the North Western, and the Panthays of the South Western Provinces of China; or rather, that the present rising of the Dungens on the North, bears no relation to the former rebellion of the Panthays on the South; or to any subsequent movement of the Southern Mussulman populalation of Yunnan, to throw off the Chinese yoke; such movement having commenced as early as the year 1855.

This opinion must be understood, however, to have reference only to the present attitude and circumstances of the Panthays in Yunnan; without any speculative allusion to causes, or the possibility of future combination, for the Panthays of Yunnan and the Dugens are, after all, of the same race and religion, and are merely divided from each other by the Province of Sechuen; and a general struggle for independence, if it really exists, and is able to make head against the Chinese Government, will certainly include, at no great distance of time, the whole of the Mahommedan population in China wherever found. The first sign of a combination between Panthays and Dungens will be manifested by the fall of Sechuen, and the news of such an event would soon reach this Province.

The term Dungen or Turgen is not known or comprehended by either Panthays or Burmese. The Mahommedans of the North Western Provinces of China are known to the Panthays, by the same denomination as they call themselves, "Mooselin," and to the Burmese as "Tharet." The word Panthay, or as it is sometimes pronounced Panzee, is of Burmese origin, and is a mere corruption of the Burmese word "Puthee," which signifies, or distinguishes Mahommedans from persons of other religions in Burma. The Chinese call the Panthays "Quayzse."[*] What they term the Mahommedans of Kansoo, I am not aware—possibly it may be Dungen or Turgen. The Mahommedans of Kansoo are said to have lately achieved their independence, and occupy that Province under a Chief named Abdool Jaffir.

The Mahommedans of Yunnan are merely a remnant, I should imagine, of the great wave of Mahommedan aggression, which under Mahomed of Ghuznee, Mahomed Ghori, and Jenghis Khan,[†] overran Persia, India, and a portion of Northern China: their ingress and progress in China is separately given, or accounted for by Chinese and Panthays. The Panthay account is somewhat mythical, and assumes at once the superiority of their race. The Chinese version deals less in mystery, and is more in bearing with supposed historical facts. They are as follows :—

Panthay version.—Once upon a time, China was subjected to a plague of evil spirits, who desolated the whole country, and in fact put a stop to the regular course of nature. The sun ceased to show itself, excepting now and then, in obscure and fitful gleams ; and the land refused to produce or yield fruit in due season. During this calamitous state of affairs, the Emperor " dreamed a dream," in which a form was prominently revealed to him, in the dress of an Arab ; but indicating at the same time, every appearance of peace and friendly goodwill. Astrologers and Experts in such matters interpreted the Emperor's dream to

[*] This term *Quayzse,* the late Mr. J. W. S. Wylie, in an article on this Memorandum, published in the "Edinburgh Review," (No. cxxvii., p. 357), conjectures to be identical with *Hoai-hoai,* the generic term applied to the Chinese to all Mahomedans. But Dr. John Anderson, in an article published in the "Journal of the Anthropological Institute" on the same paper, correctly points out, I think, that *Quayzse* means a foreigner, and that *Hoaisse* is the term applied by the Chinese to the Panthays, and other Mahomedans independent of Chinese authority, *Hoai* meaning Mahomedan, and *Zse* independent.

[†] The conquest of China by Jenghis Khan was the means, no doubt, of introducing a considerable Mahomedan population into China, particularly of the Osijour and Turganee tribes. The former tribe had abjured Buddhism upwards of two centuries before the time of Jenghis Khan.

signify, that the plague of evil spirits would cease, on the appearance of a force of Mahommedan Arabs, who were well known to be a source of terror to evil spirits and devils of every description. The Emperor was convinced, and sent a mission direct to the Prophet Mahomed, in which he begged the assistance of a few of the Prophet's followers. Mahomed sent 360 men, who, in due time, reached China. By virtue of their presence, the evil spirits vanished, and the country was restored to its former prosperity. The Arabs were treated with becoming honour, and allowed to settle, and establish themselves, in the vicinity of the Royal Capital. But in course of time their numbers increased to such an extent that the Chinese Government became anxious about its own safety; and an arrangement was effected, by which the Arab population near Pekin was broken up, and sent in small parties to the confines of the empire; where they have since established themselves, more or less firmly, and in some instances proclaimed their independence.

Chinese version.—About a thousand years ago, there was a great rebellion in China, and the Government was in danger. The reigning Sovereign at the time was Oung-lo-show; and being in tribulation, he sent for assistance to a certain King, named Razzee or Khazee, who ruled over the countries to the west of China. A Mahommedan contingent of 10,000 men was sent, and with their assistance, the rebellion was suppressed, and the services of the contingent dispensed with. But a difficulty now arose, as to the return of the Mahommedans to their own country. They had been greatly reduced in numbers, and their inclination to stay where they were, and settle down in China, was encouraged by reports, which reached them, to the effect that a return to their own country was forbidden owing to long residence abroad, and their pollution as Mahommedans by contact with swine, and other abominations, which were known to abound in China. The remnant of the contingent was finally located in Yunnan, and settling down there, became peaceful subjects of the Emperor of China.

It is to be inferred that the Mahommedan population in Yunnan

was for some centuries, at least, loyally disposed towards the
Chinese Government ; for no particular mention is made of them
in Chinese History as far as is known, after their domestication
in Yunnan, until the year 1855, when they rebelled and successfully threw off the Chinese yoke.

The rebellion is stated to have originated and been carried out
in this wise. The Panthays in Yunnan had multiplied and become a flourishing and distinct community. They preserved
their separate nationality and customs, but were nevertheless
obedient to the Chinese laws. The Chinese and Tartar officials
are said to have been oppressive, and the foreign population was
specially marked out for the exercise of more than ordinary
severity. Their industrious habits, and general aptitude, made
the Mahommedans profitable subjects ; whilst it rendered them at
the same time victims to unjust and extortionate masters. Then
a feeling of enmity and hate was engendered, with the usual
results. The Loosonphoo Silver Mines of Yunnan were worked
by Panthays, under the superintendence of Chinese officers.
On a certain day a dispute arose at the mines, and the miners,
exasperated by unjust treatment, had recourse to force, and
murdered every Chinese officer they could find. The revolt of
the miners was at once followed by a general armed rising of the
Panthays throughout Yunnan. Being far inferior in number to
the Chinese, they at first took to the woods and mountain fast-
nesses, from thence they carried on a fierce guerilla warfare.
Meeting everywhere with success, they were soon joined by large
numbers of the neighbouring semi-independent hill tribes of Shans,
Kakhyens,* and others, when they soon extended their operations
to the plains, and to the siege of large towns ; and the local
government receiving no assistance from Pekin finally succumbed,
the insurgents became supreme, and a separate Panthay Govern-

---

* The Kakhyens above alluded to are a portion of the vast horde of
Singphoos that inhabit the mountainous districts of Northern Assam, and
stretch round the north of Burma into Western China. They extend not only
all along the northern frontier, but dip down southward whenever the mountain ranges lead them, and nearly as far south as the latitude of Mandalay.

ment was established with its Head-quarters at Tali or Talifoo ;
then only a city of secondary importance, but where the Mahomedan element had always been very strong. Feeble attempts have
since been made from time to time to recover the lost province,
by the despatch of Imperial troops from the capital ; but the
Chinese Government has never been able to make head against
the Panthays ; and the troops sent have generally been repulsed,
before they could even penetrate within the Yunnan frontier.

The present Mahommedan Government of Yunnan, is presided
over by a military chief styled Sooleman by the Panthays, and
Tuwintsen by the Chinese. He has assumed the insignia of
Royalty, by formal installation on the Guddee, and by the exclusive and prerogatived use of yellow clothing and appurtenances.
This Chief or King is assisted by four military and four civil
ministers, the principal one of whom is established at Momein, a
large town close to the Shan frontier, west of Yunnan. There
appears to be little departure in the matter of administration, from the
old form of Chinese Government, except being more military in
its character. Taxation is extremely light, being restricted as far
as can be understood, to a moderate assessment on land.

The Panthays are Mahommedans of the Soonee sect, and pride
themselves on their Arab descent ; many of them are able to con-
verse in Arabic, and their prayers are all in this language. They
have Mosques or Musjids, of the true moslem type and are fana-
tical and strict in their religious performances ; as far as I have
been able to ascertain, however, there is no trace of any religious
zeal, or motive, as the origin or pretext for the present rising of
the Panthays against Chinese rule. The Chinese are generally
tolerant of all religious persuasions, and unlikely to cause irritation
to the Mahommedans by any interference with their religion. The
Buddhist wherever found is untrammelled by conventional dogma,
and far less imbued with the odium theologicum, or that contemptuous abhorrence of all creeds and customs other than their
own, than is the case with other natives of the East, of whatever
creed or denomination. The dress of the Panthays is in accordance, for the most part, with Chinese habit : though many of

them cut their hair to a certain length, and allow it to fall back on the nape of the neck. They also wear, in many instances, a distinctive turban, of more ample form than in use amongst Chinese. They are fair, tall, and strongly built men, are an interesting race, or community of people : and after twelve years of absolute government in Yunnan, it is not improbable to suppose that their future independence is secure.

Panthay traders say, that during the past year, an Embassy was received from the Emperor of China, in which the Imperial Government sued for a cessation of hostilities, and volunteered to cede Yunnan to the Panthays, provided they would come to terms, and commit no further acts of aggression on neighbouring provinces. The offer it is said was indignantly refused, and the Embassy was obliged to return to Pekin, without accomplishing its object.

This, if true, bodes evil to our future intercourse with China through Yunnan by railway or otherwise. The trade viâ Bamo between China and Upper Burma, amounted in 1854 (the year before the Mahommedan insurrection) to half a million of pounds sterling. No caravans of Sechien or other provinces of China, since the establishment of Mahommedan rule, have passed through Yunnan ; and trade by this route has almost altogether ceased. But with Yunnan alone, a large trade was formerly carried on, and it is hoped that the caravan route, at any rate, may be again shortly re-opened. It possesses the unusual advantage of having been used for centuries as a line of traffic, and has maintained its vitality heretofore, among all the disturbing influences of the flow and ebb of the Chinese and Burmese power, and is a cogent proof of the necessity for interchange of commodities between the respective countries.

An apparent interminable feud has doubtless arisen between the Manchur dynasty, and the Mahommedan population, of China, which may probably, combined with other numerous causes, ultimately end disastrously to that dynasty. How long it will take for the Chinese Government to disintegrate and re-appear under a new form ; what effect such a change would have on the independent Mahommedan population of the Western Provinces ; and will the change be brought about by them, are questions which may probably affect a future generation ; but are nevertheless full of interest to neighbouring governments, and political speculators of the present day.

ALBERT FYTCHE, Colonel,

Chief Commissioner, British Burma ; and
Agent to His Excellency the Viceroy
and Governor-General of India.

APPENDIX F.

LETTER of APOLOGY from the EMPEROR of CHINA,

AND

CREDENTIALS OF THE ENVOY KUO SUNG-TAO,
ON HIS MISSION TO GREAT BRITAIN.

DATED OCTOBER, 1876.

(Translation.)

*The Emperor of China salutes the Queen of England and
Empress of India.*

HAVING become inheritor of the great estate by the mandate of
Heaven, and reverently continued the succession to our great
estate, we have borne in affectionate remembrance the States in
amity with us and [have desired] to consolidate for ever relations
of friendship and concord.

In the first moon of the first year of the reign of Kwang Sü
(February, 1875), the official interpreter of your Majesty's Government, Ma Kia-li (Mr. Margary) by name, whilst travelling under
passport from Burma, and on having reached the frontier region
of the province of Yunnan, was murdered, and his companion,
Colonel Browne, was attacked and driven back.

We made special appointment of Li Han-chang, Governor-
General of the Hu Kusang provinces, to proceed to Yunnan for
the purpose of instituting inquiry and taking action in conformity
with the principles of justice ; and we furthermore issued a Decree
enjoining upon the Governors-General and Governors of all the

provinces that they should give instructions to all local authorities within their jurisdiction to the effect that the provisions of the Treaties must be duly fulfilled with reference to all persons travelling under passport in the places under their authority.

Li Hun-chang having completed his investigation, memorialised us requesting that the military officer, Li Chêu-kwoh, and others might be severally punished for their offences.

In the month of August last, we further specially appointed Li Hun-chang, a Senior Grand Secretary, Governor-General of the Province of Chihli, of the first class of the Third Order of Nobility, to proceed as High Minister Plenipotentiary to Chefoo, in the Province of Shantung, to act there with your Majesty's Special Envoy, Wei Toma (Sir Thomas Wade), in arranging the terms of a settlement of this case. Li Hun-chang has memorialised us, in reply, stating that your Majesty's Envoy, Sir Thomas Wade, had expressed the opinion that security for the future was to be preferred to punishment of the past; and we issued thereupon a special rescript in reply, according to the request that was made, granting, as an act of grace, remission of the penalties that had been incurred by Li Chêu-kwoh and the others involved with him, and still further enjoining upon the high authorities of all the provinces implicit obedience to the commands of last year, that protection should be afforded in conformity with the Treaty stipulations. We have also commanded the Yamên of Foreign Affairs to draw up a Proclamation and to forward a copy of the draft to each Provincial Government to be acted upon, to the end that tranquillity may prevail in the relations between China and foreigners.

That Mr. Margary, whilst travelling under passport within the frontier of Yunnan, should have lamentably been murdered, is a fact which not alone involves the question of a loss of life, but which also has gone near to disturb our relations of amity and concord. We profoundly regret and lament it. We have now made special appointment of Kwoh Sung-tao, an acting Senior Vice-President of the Board of Ceremonies, and one of the Ministers of the Office of Foreign Affairs, as Envoy Extraordinary, to proceed to your Majesty's country to give utterance, on our behalf, to the sentiments we have at heart, as a proof of our genuine desire of amity and concord.

We know Kwoh Sung-tao to be an officer of capacity and experience, of loyalty and truthfulness, who is in disposition amiable and just, and far reaching in intelligence. He has acquired great familiarity in the treatment of affairs between Chinese and foreign Powers. We would ask that sincere confidence be reposed in him, to the end that blessings of friendly concord may for ever be experienced in the highest degree, and that all alike may enjoy the happiness of a state of peace. This, we doubt not, will be greatly to the satisfaction [of your Majesty].

APPENDIX G.

—•—

MEMORANDUM

ON

FOUR YEARS' ADMINISTRATION OF BRITISH BURMA, 1867—1871.

BY MAJOR-GEN. A. FYTCHE, C.S.L, CHIEF COMMISSIONER.

———— ————

BEFORE taking my departure from the province of British Burma on a furlough to Europe, from which perchance I may never return, it may not be out of place if I put upon record for the information of my successor, and the public generally, a few particulars respecting the past history of this administration, and its progress throughout the four years during which it has been entrusted to my care. This task was in some measure undertaken by my eminent predecessor Sir Arthur Phayre, who previous to his departure from Burma submitted to the Government of India statistical tables of the progress of the province during the period of his administration prior to 1867; and if I venture to enter upon a more comprehensive review I may be pardoned from the consideration that the main portion of my life has been spent in this country, and that for more than thirty years I have been serving in one or other of the three divisions of Arakan, Pegu, and Tenasserim.

When I first landed in Burma in 1841, and joined the old Arakan local battalion, British territory only com-

Reasons for reviewing the administration. 1867-1871.

Statistical tables for ten years submitted by Sir Arthur Phayre.

British Burma in 1841.

prised the strips of sea-board known as Arakan and
Tenasserim ; Arakan being separated from Tenasserim
by the important Burmese province of Pegu.   In those
days when the Government of India was contemplating
the occupation of Affghanistan, Burma was so little cared
for that a withdrawal from the country was more than
once seriously contemplated.   Our rule was popular with
the people, but the revenue was insufficient to meet the
expenditure, and indeed the country had only recently
begun to recover from the devastating wars, which for
centuries had been desolating the entire region from
Chittagong to Siam.   Meantime the whole of the fertile
valley of the Irawadi, from the sea-coast upward to the
wild tribes which intervene between Burma and China,
was in the hands of a cruel and barbarous despot, utterly
ignorant of the great world around him, and consequently unrestrained by the public opinion of civilised
countries.

Early
history of
British
occupation.

Here I would take the opportunity ot glancing very
briefly at the early history of the British occupation of
Burma, inasmuch as it will clear away much of the misapprehension which at present prevails respecting the
Burmese wars of 1825 and 1852, and will establish beyond all further doubt the vast superiority of British
administration over Native rule.

First Bur-
mese war
forced upon
the British
Government,
1825–26.

The first Burmese war, namely that of 1825–26, was
fairly forced upon the British Government.   For nearly
forty years the Government of India had endured indig-
nities, which Great Britain would never have suffered for
a moment ; but the Indian Government was already engaged in expensive wars against the Mahrattas, Ghoorkas,
and Pindarrees, and was reluctant to engage in further
hostilities which might provoke the enemies of the old
East India Company to renew their attacks upon the

Aggressions
of Burmese
officials.

trading monopoly.   At length, however, the Burmese
officials seized an island belonging to the British Govern-

ment, and invaded territory which was under British protection. To submit to such aggressions was clearly out of the question and could only have led to further insults. Accordingly, the British Government was dragged into a war which terminated, as already stated, in the annexation of Arakan and Tenasserim.

When these provinces came into British possession in 1826, they were so depopulated and impoverished that the restoration of Burma to the Court of Ava, although opposed to all sound principles of imperial policy, recommended itself to favour on financial grounds. But during the quarter of a century that intervened between the first Burmese war of 1826 and the second Burmese war of 1852, Arakan and Tenasserim had attained a prosperity which is scarcely credible when the general immobility of Asiatic races is taken into consideration. In Arakan the population had increased from a hundred thousand souls to more than three hundred thousand. The revenue had quadrupled, being less than £25,000 in 1826, and at least £100,000 in 1852. The area of cultivation had increased from less than 70,000 acres in 1826 to more than 300,000 acres in 1852. In Tenasserim it will suffice to say that the ratio of progression was nearly the same.

Rapid improvement of Arakan and Tenasserim under British administration.

During the first ten years of my residence in Burma, the fertile province of Pegu, which intervened between the two British provinces of Arakan and Tenasserim, was under Burmese rule; and I need scarcely add that it failed to exhibit any one of those signs of progress and prosperity, which characterised the adjoining parts und e British administration. Stagnation and squalor were the order of the day. The King who then filled the throne was rather a favourable type of a Burmese sovereign, and his reign is still regarded as a golden era. Indeed the name of King Tharawadi is still familiar to every Burman, and to every European residing in this country,

State of Pegu under native rule, 1841 -1852.

although it is but little known to the outer world; yet this potentate was a tyrannical despot, who stabbed and shot his ministers with his own hands, and who not only repudiated the treaty which had been concluded with his predecessor, but openly insulted the British Resident at his capital, and defied the British Government to do its worst.

Second Burmese war 1852.

Such provocations would have again stirred up any European power excepting our own; but we continued to endure them, and they were naturally succeeded by outrages on British subjects and war-like demonstrations against British territory. At length, after many years of arrogant insolence on the part of the Burmese officials and vain remonstrance on the part of the British Government, the latter was compelled, by a sense of its own dignity, and the very instinct of self-preservation, to send an expedition up the Irawadi, which terminated in the annexation of the important province of Pegu.

Importance of the annexation of Pegu.

It is difficult to overrate the value of this acquisition to the British Government, and the increased prosperity which has thereby accrued to the people of the country. The two strips of sea-board, known as Arakan and Tenasserim, have been consolidated and strengthened by the annexation of the territory on the lower Irawadi, and the three divisions now form a compact province, occupying an uninterrupted line of sea-coast of nearly a thousand miles in length, and a water communication with the distant interior, more easily navigable than the Ganges, and which promises to open up a trade route of nearly equal importance to British commerce and manufactures. Indeed it may be safely asserted that without Pegu our possessions in Burma are of comparatively small value; but that with Pegu our territory in Burma has become one of the most prosperous provinces of our Eastern empire.

These results are due to the policy initiated by the far-seeing genius of Lord Dalhousie, who took the liveliest interest in British Burma, and was the first, and up to this date, the only Governor-General that ever visited these shores. I may however add that at least an equal interest in this province has been taken by His Excellency Lord Mayo ; and it is a cause of sincere regret that his Lordship's visit to Rangoon, which was seriously contemplated last year, and which I had hoped would have taken place during my tenure of office, has now been indefinitely postponed. Interest of Lord Dalhousie in Burma.

Upon one point only does the action taken by the Government of India in 1852 appear to me to have been open to question ; and even in this direction it has been generally supposed that Lord Dalhousie acted under pressure from home. I allude to the premature withdrawal of the expedition in 1852. Had that force been allowed to remain a few weeks longer, our political relations with the Court of Ava might have been established on a lasting basis, which would have proved beneficial to both states. Fortunately this result has been in a great measure achieved in later years, partly by diplomatic action, and partly by a spontaneous display of friendship and confidence on the part of His Majesty the King of Ava, which was previously unknown. Premature cessation of hostilities in 1852.

Within a period of little more than eighteen years British Burma has thus attained a prosperity which can be favourably compared with that of any province in India ; and in the latter part of 1866, or commencement of 1867, my predecessor submitted the statistical tables already mentioned, which showed that during the ten years from 1855–56 to 1864–65 the revenue had increased from Rs. 53,17,922, per annum, to Rs. 103,00,620. At the same time the population had increased from 1,252,555, to 2,196,180; the export trade from Rs. Subsequent prosperity of British Burma.

232,41,866, to Rs. 555,55,595 ; and the import trade from Rs. 262,22,219, to Rs. 481,25,559.

It is scarcely necessary for me to dilate upon these gratifying results ; but I venture to allude prominently to the important increase in the population, respecting which some misapprehension might otherwise arise. The leading feature in the past and present condition of British Burma is the vast excess of culturable land over land actually under cultivation. I have reason to believe that speaking in round figures there are thirty thousand square miles of culturable land in this province, which are lying waste from want of cultivators ; whilst there are not above three thousand square miles which are under cultivation. At the same time the population has already increased from about one million, at which it apparently stood at the introduction of our rule, to nearly two and a half millions. It would thus appear *à priori* that if nearly two millions and a half of people can be supported by the cultivation of three thousand square miles of land, the cultivation of the entire area of culturable waste would maintain ten times that amount of population, or about twenty-five millions of people ; whilst the great increase in the population of British Burma proves that there is a yearly immigration of Burmese, Shans, Chinese, and other cognate races into British Burma, driven out from their own countries by the exactions and oppressions of native rule, who are eager to cultivate new lands under the peace, protection, and personal liberty, which they may enjoy under British administration, and which cannot be found elsewhere throughout the Malacca peninsula.

If I now refer to the various measures which have been carried out, and the advance which has been made in the progress of the province since the departure of Sir Arthur Phayre in the early part of 1867, it is not so much for the sake of self-gratulation, or for the purpose of bestowing praise, however richly deserved, upon the

officers under my administration; but as an encouragement to my successors, to show how much has been
done within the last four years; and how much, I regret
to say, still remains to be accomplished before full justice is done to this province, and it is in a position to
work out for itself the important problem of its future
prosperity.

I will now endeavour to review, as rapidly as may be,
the main features of my administration during the past
four years under the several heads of foreign policy,
internal administration, and public works. Under the
head of foreign policy I propose to review the progress
of our relations with the Court of Ava, and all the
countries upon our frontier; under that of internal administration I will endeavour to indicate the progress
which has been made, and the measures which have
been undertaken in connection with trade, mail service,
revenue, local funds, police, military defences and education. Public Works, being a most important subject
in this province, I will notice under a separate heading.

Distinction between foreign policy and internal administration.

1.—FOREIGN POLICY.

As regards foreign policy, I will in the first instance
notice the progress of diplomatic relations with the Court
of Ava. The expedition of 1852, as already intimated,
was brought to a premature close without the conclusion
of such a formal peace, as would have established our
political relations with Ava upon an intelligible and permanent basis. In 1862, however, ten years after the
war, my predecessor, Sir Arthur Phayre, concluded a
treaty with the Court of Mandalay; but this treaty,
admirable as it was in itself, and gratifying as the first
step in opening up friendly and political relations with
the King of Ava, proved to be of little or no advantage
to British interests and trade. The Burmese officials
were alike ignorant of our ways and suspicious of our

Progress of diplomatic relations with Ava.

Treaty of 1862.

intentions. Commerce was obstructed, injurious monopolies were retained by the King, and justice for British
subjects was practically unattainable in Burmese territory.

Rebellion of 1860. In 1866 a rebellion broke out in Mandalay, which well
nigh proved successful, and was only effectually sup-
pressed by the friendly action of the British Government.
At its conclusion a favourable opportunity appeared to
present itself for concluding a more satisfactory treaty
with the King, which should really open up his territories
to British commerce, and provide for the stipulations of
the treaty of 1862 being carried out in a spirit of sincerity
Failure of Sir Arthur Phayre to conclude a treaty. and friendship by the two governments. Sir Arthur
Phayre, however, was prevented by adverse circum-
stances, which need not be specified, from bringing the
negotiations to a satisfactory conclusion, and consequently no treaty was executed.

Measures of 1867. When I was entrusted with the charge of the Chief
Commissionership in the early part of 1867, one of my
first objects was to open up a friendly intercourse with the
King, and to endeavour through Major Sladen, who was
at that time my assistant at the Court of Mandalay, to
remove all suspicions from the mind of His Majesty, and
to convince the Burmese Government that the only
object of the British Government was to promote the
material interests of the two states, by mutual concessions. At that time so little had been accomplished in
the way of developing the trade with Upper Burma under
the treaty of 1862, that during the whole interval that
had elapsed between that year and the date of my
taking charge of this administration in the early part of
1867, only four merchant steamers had made their way
to Mandalay.

Improved communica- tions with Ava. One of my earliest measures was to provide for a
more rapid and regular communication, not only be-
tween Rangoon and the frontier town of Thayetmyo, but
between Thayetmyo and Mandalay, the capital of Ava,

and with the stations in the Ava territory still further inland, as far as the remote and decaying commercial city of Bhamo. The details of these measures will be found more at length under the head of internal administration, and are only mentioned here on account of their political bearing; and it will suffice to say that the subject has been one of grave importance, politically and commercially. In the first instance I was contented with tentative measures which will be noticed hereafter; but I am now happy to say that after much consideration and correspondence, arrangements have been concluded under which a weekly steamer is despatched to Mandalay, whilst a monthly steamer is despatched to the more remote station of Bhamo, with the view of opening up the old trade route with Western China, and encouraging the influx of population into British territory.

Having prepared the way by diplomacy and improved communications for opening up more direct negotiations with the King, I proceeded to Mandalay in October, 1867; and after considerable discussion I succeeded in concluding the treaty which forms the basis of our present political relations with the Court of Mandalay. This treaty provided for the utmost freedom as regards commercial intercourse between the people of the two countries; for the permanent residence of a political agent at the Court of Mandalay, who is the medium of all official communications between the British Government and the King of Ava and his ministers; and for the establishment of a court, in which the political agent has the power to adjudicate in all such cases in which British subjects are alone concerned, and in which a Burman official of high rank sits on the same bench for the adjudication of all civil cases in which both Burmese and British subjects are concerned. Moreover under this treaty the King has given up his more oppressive monopolies, and measures have been carried out for

Conclusion
of the treaty
of 1867.

re-opening the old trade route with Western China, by
which in former years a considerable trade had been
carried on between Burma and Yunnan.

The measures so far as they refer to the re-opening of
the old trade route with Western China, perhaps require
more detailed notice, inasmuch as they are calculated to
exercise a permanent effect upon British commerce.   In
the northern part of the dominions of the King of Ava is
the old commercial city of Bhamo.   Prior to 1852 this
place was an emporium of trade.   Caravans of Chinese
and Shans arrived every year at Bhamo with the products of Western China ; whilst a variety of goods,
European and Burmese, found their way to the same
place up the Irawadi river.   Between, however, 1852 and
1855, this trade was brought to a somewhat sudden conclusion by a war which broke out between some Mussulman subjects of the emperor of China and the surrounding
Chinese population ; and whilst these hostilities were in
progress the route over the Kakhyen hills towards the
city of Talifu in Western China was closed by banditti.
Of late years this war has been dying out, and I considered the opportunity a favourable one for attempting
to open up communications with the Mussulman and
Chinese authorities, with a view of diverting the trade to
its former channel.   Accordingly in 1868, at my urgent
request, Major Sladen was sent with some other officers
on an expedition, which succeeded not only in visiting
Bhamo, but in penetrating the Kakhyen hills as far as
Momein, and exchanging letters with the Mussulman
governor of Talifu.   The reports of this expedition have
already been published at considerable length, and it
will suffice to state here that its success was even larger
than I had anticipated.   Some obstructions may have
been shown in the first instance by those of the Burmese
officials who may have been suspicious of our real
object ; but all such difficulties have now entirely dis-

appeared before the cordial assistance which has been granted by the King, and the real interest which His Majesty has displayed in measures which are quite as much calculated to promote the prosperity of his own country as the interests of commerce generally. Since the latter part of 1869, Captain Strover has continued to reside at Bhamo as assistant political agent; and has succeeded in establishing the most friendly terms with the Burmese officials, as well as with the Kakhyen hill chiefs; and every mail steamer from Bhamo brings additional proofs of the important trade which is fast springing up in that quarter.

Meantime the bonds of relation between the British Government and the Court of Ava, are drawing the two countries into closer communciation than could have been anticipated at any previous period. The King has sent several young Burmese to Europe to be educated, whilst he welcomes any European merchant or official, who may pay a visit to his capital.

Another country whose frontier is conterminous with that of British territory is Siam. Our relations with Siam have it is believed always been satisfactory, but from some reason which I confess I cannot understand, all diplomatic intercourse between the British Government and the Court of Siam is carried on between Her Majesty's Secretary of State for Foreign Affairs in London and a British Consul residing at Bankok, the capital of Siam. For forty years, however, the question of the frontier between Siam and British territory has never been finally settled; and in 1864, when I was Commissioner of Tenasserim, I was appointed to negotiate the matter with some Siamese officials of rank who had been especially nominated by the King of Siam to discuss with me upon the subject. I accordingly proceeded to the Pak-chan river, where I met the Siamese officers; and after a lengthy negotiation it was agreed that the Pakchan

and Thoungyeen rivers should be accepted as the
boundaries on the south and north ; whilst the watershed
of the central mountain range on the east was to form
the boundary in that direction.   At the same time an
amicable arrangement was made as regards the Islands.
Since then this line of frontier has been surveyed and
demarcated by Captain A. H. Bagge, R.E., and duly
ratified by a treaty between the Government of India
and the King of Siam.   I regret to state that since this
memorandum was under consideration the news has
arrived that Captain Bagge is no more ; and the premature death of this efficient and popular young officer
will not only be deplored by his friends, but will be
deeply felt by this Administration and the British
Government.

The other questions connected with what may be
called Foreign policy refer to our dealings with the hill
tribes on the Arakan frontier, and similar wild tribes on
the upper valley of the Salween river.

The tribes on the Arakan frontier and region beyond,
are a wild savage race of a very primitive type.   They
go by different names, but their general characteristics
are the same.   They cultivate the jungle by clearing
away some available slope with fire, and then sow the
grain and use the ashes for manure.   As the same spot
can only be cultivated under this system about once in
ten years, the people of a hill village often find it necessary to emigrate from one site to another, carrying with
them their families, household goods, pigs, and dogs.
They also practise the system of kidnapping and slavery
amongst themselves, which this Administration has done
its best to suppress, but which still prevails in the more
inaccessible hills, and leads to frequent raids.   At my
recommendation the Government of India have appointed a European superintendent to reside in these
hills, and much good has been effected by this measure

in maintaining a check upon the tribes; but the climate is unfortunately very unhealthy during a large portion of the year, and few European constitutions are impervious to its effects. Other measures are under consideration, which I have no doubt will tend to solve the questions connected with the administration and political control of these remote regions.

The tribes on the upper course of the Salween river, and in the unknown countries beyond, have also engaged my attention. The most important of these half-savage people are known as the Red Karens and the Zimmay Shans; and they inflicted considerable injury upon the timber trade on the upper Salween by their occasional raids. The Red Karens are virtually independent, but the western chiefs have more than once requested the British Government to take them under its protection, which, however, has not been hitherto deemed expedient. The chief of the Zimmay Shans is practically almost as independent, but he owes a nominal allegiance to the King of Siam. Under Burmese rule all these tribes were treated as though they were wild beasts of the jungle; and Burmese officials have been too often engaged in hunting the people down, burning their villages, killing all who resisted and reducing all the rest to slavery. Of late years their condition has been much ameliorated, but the lawless condition of their territories has been much aggravated by a fierce dispute between the Zimmay Shans and the eastern Karennees respecting a tract of forest land lying on the left bank of the Salween; and the frequent hostilities employed in connection with this dispute has brought the timber trade almost to a standstill. At my recommendation the Government of India has sanctioned my sending Captain Lowdnes on a mission to the Zimmay chief, in the hope of being able to settle the difficulties which impede the timber trade, and bring about, if possible, a reconciliation

between that chief and the chiefs of Eastern Karennee.
Other measures are also under consideration which it is
hoped will effect the main objects in view.

II.—INTERNAL ADMINISTRATION.

Heads of internal administration. The internal administration of British Burma may now
be considered under the several sections of trade, mail
service, local funds, police, military defences, and education.

Large increase of trade, 1867 to 1871. *Trade.*—It affords me great gratification to notice the
large increase in the trade of this province, which is
especially noticeable in the year 1868–69. This commercial progress is no doubt due in great measure to the
new markets which were opened up in Upper Burma in
consequence of the privileges conceded by the Court of
Mandalay under the treaty which I had the honour of
concluding in 1867. It will be seen that after adding an
additional month to the official year 1866–67, which in
consequence of changing the close of the official year
from 30th April to 31st March, consisted of eleven
months only, the increase in the gross internal and external trade of the province in 1868–69 amounted to twenty-
three per cent. over 1866–67, being more than ten millions
and a half sterling in 1868–69 against eight millions and
Inland trade. a half sterling in 1866–67. In the inland trade this
increase is especially observable ; for in 1866–67 it was
only one million forty thousand sterling, whilst in 1867–
68 it had increased to more than two millions and a half
sterling. In 1868–69 it fell slightly to two millions and
a hundred thousand sterling ; but in 1869–70 it rose
again to two millions and two hundred thousand sterling.
Customs. The customs show a still more decided increase in
revenue. In 1866–67 the amount collected under this
head was about one hundred and nineteen thousand
pounds. In 1867–68 it rose to nearly two hundred
thousand ; in 1868–69 it further rose to two hundred

and eighty-seven thousand. In 1869–70 it fell slightly, but still a sum of over two hundred thousand pounds was collected. Some of this increase is no doubt due to the enhanced rate levied on grain; but still a large proportion is to be ascribed to the general increase of trade.

There is perhaps no necessity for overloading the present memorandum with statistics, which will be found fully given in an appendix, but I may be permitted to notice the remarkable increase in the export trade in cutch, jade, rice, paddy, and timber. In 1866–67 the exports of cutch only amounted to £40,000; in 1867–68 they amounted to £125,000, in 1868–69 to £181,000, and in 1869–70 to more than £193,000. In 1866–67 the exports of jade only amounted to £6,400; in 1867–68 they amounted to £36,400, in 1868–69 to £42,200, in 1869–70 there was a falling off, but still they amounted to nearly £21,000. In rice, paddy, and timber the increase has been steady but not quite so perceptible. *Export trade.*

There has also been a marked increase in imports, especially in those of cotton-twist and yarn, and piece-goods in silk and cotton. The imports in cotton-twist and yarn have risen from three hundred and ten thousand sterling in 1866–67 to three hundred and eighty thousand in 1867–68, and three hundred and seventy-five thousand in 1868–69. Cotton piece-goods have risen from five hundred and ten thousand sterling in 1866–67 to six hundred and sixty thousand in 1867–68, and six hundred and eighty thousand in 1868–69. Silk piece-goods have increased, but the increase has not been so well maintained. In 1866–67 they amounted to two hundred and ten thousand sterling; in 1867–68 and again in 1868–69 they rose to two hundred and sixty thousand, but in 1869–70 they fell to two hundred and twenty-seven thousand. In treaty goods the increase has been *Imports of piece goods* the most marked of all. In 1866–67 the gross amount did not reach six hundred pounds; in 1867–68 it was five thousand six hundred pounds; in 1868–69 it was fifty-two thousand four hundred; in 1869–70 the aggregate amount was one hundred and forty thousand. These figures represent pretty fairly the fluctuations of trade in Burma during the four years of my administration. The treaty of 1867 naturally led to a large increase of trade, and no doubt to some over speculation. The consequence was that though a large margin of increase continued to be maintained, yet there was a decided falling off in 1869–70 in the amount of trade; but the year 1870–71 shows, I am happy to say, a decided increase, which will I trust continue to characterise the trade returns of this province for an unlimited period.

The export duties on rice have naturally excited much public discussion; and without attempting to decide a point which is still a vexed question with political economists, I will simply review the facts. Prior to March, 1867, the export duty on rice, both husked and unhusked, was seven shillings per ton. On the 20th of that month a revised Customs Act was brought into force under which the duty was raised to ten shillings and sixpence per ton. This enhanced duty had no effect in checking the exports of rice, for in the year following the introduction of the act, the exports increased by about one-third, and in 1868–69 were nearly doubled. In 1869–70 the exports were not quite so large, but still about one-third in excess of what they were in the year before the rice duty was increased; and during the year now closing they have been very large, but I am unable as yet to give the actual figures.

Meantime the East India and China Association in England, and the Chamber of Commerce at Rangoon, complained that the rice of British Burma was being

driven out of the home markets, by the produce of
Cochin China and Siam ; but this has proved to some
extent fallacious, as most of the rice of these countries is
carried to China, where it is in considerable demand.
The consequence is, that the agitation has for some time
subsided, and I have been assured by some of the leading merchants of Rangoon, that the reduction of the
duty, as far as husked rice is concerned, will have little
or no effect upon the trade, beyond swelling the profits
of the brokers, or middlemen, between the European
merchants and the cultivator. I am, however, inclined
to think that the duty on unhusked rice, commonly
called paddy, might be reduced with advantage.

Mail Service.—The improvement of the mail service
on the Irawadi is so closely associated with the development of trade in Burma, that I am happy to say it has
received every consideration during my tenure of office,
and has eventuated in an arrangement which I have
reason to believe will prove as satisfactory to the British
Government as to the public at large. I allude to the
extension and improvement of the mail service between
Rangoon and the different stations on the upper Irawadi.
From the acquisition of Pegu in 1852 until the year 1864,
all the mails were carried up the river by Government
steamers, and it was only on very rare occasions that any
of these vessels proceeded beyond the frontier town of
Thayetmyo. About 1862–63 all the Government steamers
and plant were sold to Messrs. Todd, Findlay, and Company, of Rangoon ; and in 1864 the first contract for a
mail service was concluded with that firm, under which
the mails were to be carried once a month to Thayetmyo
in return for a subsidy of £75 per trip, or £150 per
mensem. When I assumed the administration of this
province in the early part of 1867, the mail service was
not in a satisfactory state. Messrs. Todd, Findlay, and
Company complained that they had made a bad bargain ;

Extension
and improve
ment of the
mail service.

that the treaty concluded by my predecessor, Sir Arthur Phayre, in 1862, had not led to any increase of trade with Upper Burma; and they desired that the subsidy of £75 per trip should be raised to £200. The British Government was also dissatisfied that no better results had followed the conclusion of the treaty of 1862, and that no sustained efforts had been made to open up a trade with Upper Burma; and I found on taking charge of the province that not a single steamer had been sent to Bhamo, and that only five trips had been made beyond the British frontier. I need not review the steps I took to remedy this state of things. It will suffice to say that it was in the first instance found necessary to increase the subsidy from £75 per trip, to £150 per trip, or £300 per mensem; but such was the increase of trade in the years immediately following, in consequence of the treaty of 1867, that, in 1869, Messrs. Todd, Findlay, and Company agreed to send a mail steamer three times every month for a subsidy of £100 per mensem, or about £33 per trip, not merely to the frontier station at Thayetmyo, but to the city of Mandalay, which is at present the capital of the dominions of the King of Ava. More recently I have concluded a contract with Messrs. Todd, Findlay, and Company which is even more satisfactory to all parties. New steamers and flats have been put on the river, and not only is there a weekly communication with Mandalay, but a monthly communication with the remote trading station of Bhamo, which I trust will be found a key to the commerce of western China, which has hitherto been shut out from the European world.

Encouragement of immigration. There is another object promoted by the new mail service, which, if possible, is of even greater importance to the prosperity of this province than the extension of commerce. I have already explained that the crying want of this province is population. At present only three thousand square miles are under cultivation, whilst there are remaining thirty thousand square miles of culturable but uncultivated territory, which is literally abandoned to the swamp and the jungle. Meantime there are beyond our frontier millions of an over-populated and oppressed people; Burmese, Shans, and Chinamen, who are eager to emigrate into British territory; and already bands of eager cultivators are swarming into British territory under special arrangements which have been made with reference to the mail steamers, and will no doubt prove the vanguard of caravans whose arrival may be hereafter anticipated.

Revenue.—As regards the revenue I have but little to say. It has increased during the last four years by about £60,000 per annum; at the same time the population has received an increase of two hundred thousand souls.

Local Funds.—In British Burma, as in other provinces of the Indian empire, there is not only an imperial revenue collected and expended under the supervision of the supreme government, but there are a considerable number of funds which are of a strictly local character, being collected under local supervision, and expended on local purposes under the administration of the province. The disposal of these local funds has largely engaged my attention, and I may, perhaps, take this opportunity to explain in more detail the decisions at which I have arrived as regards their expenditure. *Character of local funds.*

All the local funds in this province may be distributed under three separate heads, *viz.* :— *Distribution.*

1st. Town cesses.
2nd. District funds.
3rd. Five per cent. cess.

The town cesses comprise a number of collections, such as house tax, municipal tax, bazaar rents, boat and cart fees, licenses, slaughter-house fees, which may be summed up under the head of "Municipal fund," and I have decided upon amalgamating them into one fund. *Town cesses.*

Indeed, so long as the collections raised in each town are devoted to the requirements of that town, the amalgamation of the town funds are likely to prove more serviceable than if they were divided into infinitesimal sub-divisions that would cramp the completion of many improvements which might be otherwise made practicable.

District funds. As regards district funds, comprising road and ferry funds, cattle market fees and poundage fees, I have decided upon a similar course, namely, to unite them all in one fund to be expended in the district in which they are collected. In the first instance, this fund should be reserved to meet the expenses connected with the several works in the district under which the tax is collected; and should there be any surplus, it might be devoted to improving the approaches to the chief towns in the districts, or effect such other improvements as would seem most advantageous to the district population, all of whom benefit more or less by the prosperity of their respective systems.

Five per cent. cess. The five per cent. cess is levied for local purposes on land tax, fisheries, and net tax. It is payable in the following proportion for each head :—

Roads . . . 1 per cent.
Education . . 1   „
Daks (Post) . ¼   „
Village Police 2¾   „

Total . . 5 per cent.

I may have entertained some doubts upon the policy of such a cess in a young country like Burma, where it is naturally regarded as a grievance, yet I am happy to say that it has enabled me to establish a male and female training school at Rangoon, for the education of school masters and schoolmistresses for the various government schools about to be created and maintained. The question of education will, however, be treated under a separate head.

Police.—As regards the police of this province, I am proud to say that, during my administration, it has been placed on a more efficient footing than was ever maintained at any previous period. From the first year of the administration of Pegu, a great difficulty has been experienced in sufficiently impressing the supreme government with the idea that Burma is in every way an exceptional province, which in many respects differs very considerably from any province in India, and in nothing more so than the cost of living, and current rates of pay amongst the labouring classes. The coolies, who cannot make in India more than five to seven rupees per mensem, can easily earn from twelve to fifteen rupees per mensem in this province, and during the four months of the rice season can make from thirty to forty rupees. When, however, I received charge of this province in 1867, I found that the police were still paid at rates varying from nine to eleven rupees; and the consequence was, that the police was a kind of refuge for the destitute, and those men only enlisted who were too weak or idle for coolie work, or who, it is feared, maintained a secret understanding with thieves and dacoits, and added the wages of corruption to their small salaries.

After considerable correspondence, the Government of India were induced by my representations to re-consider the questions of police pay, and from the 1st January 1869, the rates of the lower grades of constables and serjeants have been raised nearer to a level with the existing labour rates of the province. The result has been decidedly satisfactory. Recruits are obtained with such facility, that the Superintendents of Police are enabled to weed the incapable or corrupt men from their ranks, and replace them with an efficient force. At the same time a better order of men are attached to the

[marginal notes] Former difficulties in police administration.

Increased pay to constables and serjeants.

force, and no longer throw up their appointments on slight provocation, but look forward to promotion and pension. Above all, violent crime has been rapidly decreasing, and during the past year I am happy to say that there has been a decrease of twenty-seven per cent. in dacoity alone throughout the province of British Burma. I am, however, still of opinion that the pay of the higher class of officers is too low, and that it might be increased with great advantage to that branch of the department.

Frontier police.

In one respect matters are not quite so satisfactory as I should have wished; I mean as regards the border police which is necessary to guard one of the largest and most difficult lines of frontier pertaining in any province in our Indian empire, that of the Punjaub not excepted. The question has been one of long and anxious consideration both on my part, and I believe on the part of the Government of India; but final orders have not as yet been passed on my representations, and therefore I will not further allude to the matter, beyond expressing the hope that measures will soon be in progress which will succeed in effecting the important objects in view. The establishment of the frontier of Thayet as a separate district has, however, already proved of great assistance to the police, inasmuch as it involves the presence of an additional Deputy Commissioner; and thus a close and consequently a better supervision has been maintained by the civil officers over the police in that direction.

Measures necessary.

Military defences.—The military defence of the province has long engaged my attention. Our present friendly relations with the King of Ava, and the undoubted inferiority of any military force which could be assembled beyond our frontier, render it unnecessary to consider the subject from anything like an alarmist point of view; but still certain measures are in my opinion necessary for the protection of the province in the event

of any sudden revolutionary movement in Upper Burma
which might take us by surprise; or in the event of a
European war, like that which has recently agitated
Western Europe, and which might bring a hostile European force to these shores.

On the first point as regards our internal defences, I
need scarcely enter into particulars, beyond stating that
I have been perfectly aware of the importance of opening
up a land communication between Thayetmyo and Toungoo. These are our two northern frontier stations, and
beyond them is Ava territory; but yet there are no overland lines of communication between the two stations,
and those between the two stations and the sea are unsatisfactory. Thayetmyo is situated on the right bank of
the Irawadi river, on the side furthest from Rangoon;
and consequently any force marching up from Rangoon
would have to cross the river before it could reinforce
the station. Under these circumstances it seems necessary that either the garrison should be transferred to the
other bank of the river, or the communication between
both banks should be kept constantly open. Toungoo
is in a still more isolated position. It has a water communication *viâ* the Sittang river, with both Rangoon and
Maulmain, but this is not available for steamers; and
there is at present no available road by which troops
could march from Rangoon to Toungoo during the
south-west monsoon. The position of Shwe-gyeen on
the line of communication with Toungoo, is nearly as
isolated.

The questions connected with this state of affairs have
been brought under the consideration of the highest
authorities, and I have reason to believe that all that is
necessary will speedily be accomplished. Already our
frontier is greatly strengthened by the weekly service of
the mail steamers, and the large increase in the river
traffic, which shows itself in a variety of ways.

Internal defences.

Coast
defences. As regards our coast defences I need say nothing. With the restoration of a financial equilibrium I trust to see a new breakwater at Maulmain ; whilst the presence of H. M.'s corvette the *Cossack* in these waters, by which indeed I take my departure from Rangoon, sufficiently proves that in the event of a European war, we may count upon the presence of a naval force amply sufficient to protect this province against any enemy on the sea.

Importance
of education
in Burma. *Education.*—The subject of education in Burma has been one of peculiar interest on account of the special circumstances pertaining to this province, which differ from anything which is to be found elsewhere.

The schools in Burma must be divided into two distinct classes, *viz* :—

Buddhist
schools. 1st.—Those which are more or less attached to the numerous Buddhist monasteries that are scattered all over the country, and which are devoted exclusively to the education of Burmese children, and until very lately were under no supervision in connection with British administration.

Christian
schools. 2ndly.—Those which have been established more or less for the education of Europeans and Eurasians, and have been either connected with Christian missionaries or have had a Christian object in view. A considerable number of Burmese boys have also attended these schools, for the purpose of acquiring a higher order of education, which should fit them for employment in public and private offices ; and as they were more or less under European supervision and control, and furnished a far higher order of education than the monasteries could possibly have afforded, the British Government has hitherto assisted to support them by the grants of yearly allowances under certain rules known as the grants-in-aid system. In addition to these aided institutions there are four schools which have been directly established

and maintained by Government, namely, one at Moulmain, a second at Akyab, a third at Prome, and a fourth at Kyouk Phyoo.

Such, then, is the present basis of educational progress in Burma, and it will be seen that all measures for improvement have had to be devoted to two distinct objects, namely :—

First, the efficiency of monastic schools which are exclusively Burmese.

Secondly, the efficiency of those schools which are more or less under European supervision.

Shortly before I took over charge of the province, my predecessor Sir Arthur Phayre had drawn attention to the large number of monastic schools, and suggested that they might be made the basis of a national system of education. The idea was one which recommended itself in every way. There is not a village in Burma which has not a school, either in connection with a Buddhist monastery, or established as an act of piety by some enthusiastic layman. There is consequently scarcely a Burman to be found, who cannot read, write, and cypher in the vernacular. Nothing was apparently wanting but the co-operation of the Buddhist monks or priests, who are known as phoongyees, to extend and elevate the course of study pursued in these schools, and thus to erect a superstructure of European education and training on a national basis. I must confess that I have always been favourable to this scheme, and am still anxious that every effort should be made to utilize these indigenous schools, and incorporate them in the Government system. At the same time increased knowledge of these schools derived from the personal inspection of those officers in my administration, who have had the largest educational experience, have opened my eyes to difficulties which do not appear to have presented themselves to Sir Arthur Phayre ; and although I am not pre-

Objects to be attained.

Nature and character of Buddhist schools.

pared to admit that they are insurmountable, yet still I
feel bound to mention them for the guidance of my
successor.

Formation
of an educa-
tional de-
partment.

From statistics which have been recently collected, it
is known that there are at least four thousand of these
schools in British Burma, in which at least fifty or sixty
thousand children are educated.   To effect an improvement in these schools an educational department was
formed in 1866, consisting of a director of public instruction and four circuit teachers ; and it was hoped
that with this staff something could be done towards im-
parting a higher knowledge of grammar, arithmetic, and
land-measuring in the monastic schools without hurting
the prejudices of the religious inmates of the building.
Mr. Hough, the first director, commenced his task with
considerable enthusiasm, and although he was shortly
afterwards compelled to leave Burma on account of his
health, yet before he left he succeeded in introducing the
four circuit teachers into some of the monastic schools.
Since then Mr. Hordern, who was especially selected for
the post of director from the officers of the educational
department in Bengal, has devoted considerable attention
to this all-important work, and has devised a scheme
which is now under trial, and which it is hoped may do
something towards effecting the great object in view.

Internal life
of Buddhist
monastic
schools.

Before describing the scheme which Mr. Hordern is
now carrying out, it will be necessary to glance at the
internal life and discipline of a Buddhist monastery, in
order to apprehend the real difficulties against which all
educational schemes have to contend.   According to the
peculiar tenet of Buddhism, the grand object of all
human souls ought to be to escape from the turmoil of
the passions and the vortex of successive existences, and
to find deliverance in the eternal repose of Neibban or
Nirvâna.   To effect this object the individual endeavours
to rise to a higher state of existence by performing acts

of merit in excess of his acts of demerit; and finally passes a life in the seclusion of a monastery, freed from all the cares and turmoils of the outer world, and supported by the voluntary contributions of the community at large. The education of boys has thus been regarded as an act of merit; whilst making offerings of food and clothes to the priests, or phoongyees, are other acts of merit. Consequently education is never at a standstill in Burma. Phoongyees are always to be found, who are only too glad to relieve the monotony of monastic life by engaging in acts of merit like the education of boys; whilst the voluntary contributions of the laity are never wanting, and are probably given partly as acts of merit, and partly out of gratitude for the education which has been received.

But the one end and object of monastic teaching is religion. The literature that is taught is of a religious character; and should a more studious boy continue to remain in school, and seek to fit himself for the higher life of a phoongyee, he can only do so by the acquisition of the Pali language, and perusal of the vast mass of Buddhist theological and semi-historical works of which Burmese literature is in a great measure composed. Here and there a few phoongyees may be found, like many priests during the revival of letters in the middle ages, who are anxious to acquire some knowledge of European literature, and of the great world without. But there the analogy ends. The ambition of the Buddhist priest is confined to his own monastery, or at any rate to the attainment of a higher ecclesiastical rank. He cannot aspire to political power, like the ecclesiastical statesman who took the lead for centuries in many European cabinet councils; and there can be no doubt that the first effect of English education on a phoongyee is to lead him to throw off his yellow gown and return to the ranks of the laity.

Decay of
monastic
discipline.

Meantime, whilst efforts are being made in one direction to promote a higher education, there is an element at work in the monasteries themselves which has a direct tendency to weaken the stimulus by which the phoongyees of Burma, and especially those of Pegu, were formerly actuated. Under native rule the ecclesiastical hierarchy was encouraged, and the promotion of phoongyees to a higher rank was not only recognized, but the heads were enabled to carry out a discipline of their own irrespective of all civil law or authority. Such spiritual powers are no longer recognized under British administration, and consequently there is a spirit of insubordination abroad, under which considerable laxity and insubordination naturally prevails.

Stimulus to
be furnished
to monastic
schools.

Here, then, rises the question of how a new stimulus is to be introduced into the Buddhist monasteries. In the distribution of grants-in-aid education is largely promoted by a system of payment by results; in other words, the amount of the yearly grant to a school depends upon the results of a yearly examination of the scholars. But it is a fundamental rule of Buddhism that no phoongyee shall ever receive money under any pretence whatever. There are thus only two ways remaining by which a stimulus may be applied, namely, by regulating the grant of books to a monastic school according to the proficiency of the pupils, and to look forward to a rivalry which will probably exist hereafter between the monastery schools conducted by Buddhist Priests, and the primary schools which will be established by the British Government.

Formation
of local
committees.

I have also carried out during the past year a measure from which I have great hope of success. The task of maintaining anything like a supervision or inspection over four thousand monastery schools is palpably impracticable without the appointment of a large staff of inspectors, a measure which cannot be entertained at present from financial considerations; and moreover a sudden influx of strangers would probably prove most distasteful to the phoongyees, as well as to the people at large. I have accordingly sanctioned the appointment of a local committee at the head quarters of every district, the members of which will be known to the phoongyees by their official or social position, and who will thus be enabled to promote the progress of education in their particular district, and maintain as much supervision as is perhaps possible under existing circumstances.

As regards the schools which have been established by Government, or which are aided by yearly grants, I have but little to say. It is however gratifying to me to note that before I leave the province a normal school will have been established at Rangoon for the training of both male and female teachers ; and will accordingly furnish a yearly supply of competent masters and governors to take charge of the primary schools which are about to be created. *Normal school at Rangoon.*

The establishment of a female department to the Government training school has always been to me an object of solicitude; and indeed the progress of female education in this province has ever been regarded by me with watchful care. Female education in Burma is fortunately hampered by none of those caste prejudices and zenana restrictions which impede its progress amongst most eastern countries ; and as it forms the basis of all national development, it has naturally been more prominently considered in Burma than in India, by all who have been interested in the future welfare of the people. I believe that during the period I was Commissioner of Tenasserim, I had the honour of founding the first school in British Burma for the exclusive education of Burmese girls ; and since I have had charge of the province both Mrs. Fytche and myself have humbly endeavoured to promote female education by every means in our power. In addition to the measures which have *Female education.*

been taken to extend female education under a Government system, I think that the Ladies' Association which was founded by Mrs. Fytche at Rangoon last year, in communication with the Society for the Propagation of the Gospels' Home Association of Ladies, will long pursue that course of usefulness which it has most successfully commenced ; and although I shall no longer have the honour of remaining its president, I shall always take the greatest possible interest in its future proceedings.

III.—PUBLIC WORKS.

When I assumed the administration of the province I found the condition of the Public Works as follows :—

1st. Regarding Military Works.—Complete accommodation for the troops existed at Rangoon, though the barracks of the European Infantry were not in a satisfactory condition, owing to their age and the semi-permanent materials with which they had been originally constructed.   Very good barracks had lately been completed for the European regiment at Thayetmyo, though much remained to be done in the way of providing subsidiary accommodation.   Barracks for the remaining troops of the division were in existence and in good order.   At Maulmain, garrisoned by a Native regiment, very good accommodation existed.   At Toungoo, held by both European and Native troops, sufficient barrack accommodation had been provided.   The small detachment from the Native Infantry regiment at Toungoo, holding Shwè-gyeen, was found in old and almost worn-out barracks.

The defences of the province were in a most unsatisfactory condition.   The great pagoda of Rangoon with the arsenal lying to its westward were neither entrenched or rendered secure, though the necessity for the work had been clearly shown by Lord Dalhousie so far back as

1853. Battery Point, situated at the junction of the Rangoon, Pegu, and Puzoondoung rivers, and forming the defence of Rangoon from the seaward, was in such a condition of disrepair as to necessitate the early removal of the heavy guns from the breast work surmounting it. A redoubt at Thayetmyo, on the west bank of the river, was held by a small guard and served to cover the cantonments and native town lying to its southward. A similar work at Toungoo, and kept in good repair, was similarly held. But it could not be said that either of these works, and especially the latter, was in a condition to be made use of should necessity arise. At Shwè-gyeen was a small redoubt, formerly garrisoned by both European and Native troops, but abandoned owing to its reputed unhealthiness. Maulmain, the remaining station held by troops, and the chief seaport of the Tenasserim division, was utterly undefended either by land works or river batteries. Practically it may be said that at the commencement of 1867, the province was, setting aside the presence of the troops, in a defenceless state by sea and by land. With the exception of a near completion of the Rangoon pagoda and arsenal defences, I cannot record that the province is in a more advanced state now *quâ* its defences, than it was four years ago.

But so far as the local administration is concerned, the needful steps have been taken for materially improving the military position of the province. First of all, as before stated, the great pagoda and arsenal of Rangoon have been completely surrounded by a ditch and escarp wall, and further safety has been ensured by shutting off all communication between the pagoda and the arsenal, the latter being now completely entrenched. The wall comprising the whole enclosure is now complete, and all that remains to be done is to make the needful provision for mounting the guns in battery at the bastions. This cannot be done until the orders of the Government of

India have been received, the nature of the ordnance to
be provided being still under the consideration of that
Government.

The needful defensive measures at the Battery point
for the safety of the capital of the province are still in
abeyance. Alternative projects for a battery were submitted so far back as October, 1869, but no orders have
been received regarding them. Beyond putting in
foundations of concrete blocks to meet the twofold
object of a base for the battery and to protect the point
from further erosion nothing has been done.

I have before said that Maulmain is entirely without
defence. About three years ago, the Military department
of the Government of India required a report on the
subject of defending this place. Colonel A. Fraser,
C.B.R.E., the Chief Engineer of the province, with the
assistance of Mr. Prince, drew out a scheme for the
purpose. This scheme, together with a plan, was submitted to the Government of India, but apparently at a
time when the state of the finances would not permit of
such an extensive project being sanctioned.

Complete projects for the proper occupation of the
redoubt at the frontier stations at Thayetmyo and
Toungoo have been prepared by Colonel Fraser. Regarding the Thayetmyo defence scheme it may be noted
that the question regarding the position of this station
generally from a military point of view is, I understand,
under the consideration of His Excellency the Commander-in-Chief in India. The scheme for the defence
of Toungoo is in process of elaboration. There can be
no question but that the redoubt in its present unoc-
cupied state is rather a source of weakness than of
strength.

During 1870, the Madras Government was addressed
relative to the desirableness of again occupying the small
redoubt at Shwè-gyeen. The garrison there is housed

in barracks built of most inflammable materials, which are situated in an exposed and defenceless position, bearing in mind the troublesome nature of the tribes on the eastern frontier of the district, it appears to be highly necessary to take early measures for the proper accommodation of the detachment there. The subject is still under the consideration of the Madras Government.

The general conditions of the military position of the province have been fully set forth by Colonel A. Fraser, the Chief Engineer of the province, in a memorandum dated 5th September, 1870, and which I submitted to the Government of India in the military department. This memorandum will be found to contain a very full description of the position, and indeed I have drawn upon it largely for the foregoing remarks.

I will now address myself to the civil works of the province. And first as to the communications. Early in 1867, there was not one completed road in British Burma. A trunk road running through the valley of the Irawadi from Rangoon to the frontier station of Thayetmyo was under construction; and so was a road leading from Maulmain town to Yeb, Tavoy, and Mergui on the Tenasserim coast. A survey had been made for a road to Amherst, Rangoon, and Pegu. A commencement had been made on a road proposed to connect Maulmain with the Shan states on the N. E. frontier. A road runs between Toungoop in the Akyab district and Padoung on the Irawadi in the Prome district, originally designed by Lord Dalhousie for purely military purposes; it can hardly be called a line of communication for general purposes, there being little or no traffic between the districts on the Irawadi and those in Arakan : and I am satisfied there would be no object in keeping it up except for the convenience of the telegraph department. The question has been referred for the decision of the Government of India.

The backward state of our lines of communication is a matter of great regret to me. Two of the divisions of the province (Arakan and Tenasserim) we have held for 45 years and the third division (Pegu) for 18 years. In Arakan there is not one road with the exception of the incomplete Dacca and Chittagong road. In Tenasserim, the first 37 miles of the projected road to Yeh have now been completed and bridged, and the same may be said of a branch line to Amherst, a village at the mouth of the Maulmain river and the head-quarters of an Assistant Commissionership. The road projected towards the Northern Shan states has been completed for a distance of 6 miles, or to the Gyne river.

In Pegu, fair progress has been made on the Rangoon and frontier trunk road on the east bank of the Irawadi. The whole of the earthwork has been completed, many miles have been metalled and bridged, and the bridges for the remaining distance are under construction. The metalling of this road would ere this have been nearly completed, but that (as I shall show further on) a proposal has been made for laying the rails of the projected railway on it. The Pegu road is fast approaching completion. The earthwork is complete, metalling has been collected, and the whole of the bridges, with the exception of that over the Pegu river, are under construction, and will be shortly completed. A commencement has been made on the first portion of the Pegu and Toungoo frontier road.

I may here refer to certain proposals I set before the Government of India in May, 1869, for the construction of many lines of roads throughout the province. These proposals were put forward by Colonel Fraser, and there can be no reasonable doubt that, if they are acted upon, the result will be most favourable both to the Government and the people. It is much to be regretted that the general scheme has failed to secure any support from the Government of India, though under the present provincial financial arrangements its execution will possibly rest with the local administration. From all points of view, whether military, police, or revenue, it is one of the utmost importance to the province, and indeed without these great lines of communication, any great further increase of revenues cannot be hoped for. On this point I have repeatedly addressed myself to the Government of India, commencing with a letter written in March, 1868, regarding the transfer of road maintenance charges from imperial to local funds.

The question of embankments is one possessing much interest and importance for this province, especially for that portion of it lying in the delta of the Irawadi. There are thousands upon thousands of acres of rich soil only awaiting protection from the floods of the river to render them available for a large population. The density and richness of the vegetation composed of trees and grass are sufficient proof of the adaptability of the soil for all the purposes of cultivation. My predecessor, Sir A. Phayre, recognized fully the urgent necessity for reclaiming a portion at least of this highly favoured valley, and accordingly Colonel Short, of the Bengal Engineers, was deputed in 1863 for the purpose of devising a scheme of embankments for the protection of the land lying to the west of the river. This scheme has been carried out to a great extent; an embankment five feet above the highest known floods having been carried from above Myanoung to Henzadah. The result has been to render available land for cultivation, though other embankments remain to be constructed before the full benefit can be obtained. For one of these a project (that for the Laymethna embankment) has already been submitted to and approved by the Government of India. A project has also been sanctioned for the continuation of the embankment southward as far as Zaloon, but

neither this nor the Laymethna one can be put in hand
until certain statements showing the actual and probable
financial results of the whole of the works can be placed
before the Government of India.

Immediataly after his arrival in British Burma as Chief
Engineer, Colonel Fraser wrote a most valuable note on
the reclamation by embankments, of land on the east of
the Irawadi. He showed that upwards of 800 square
miles of rich land could thereby in process of time be
brought under cultivation, leading to an increase in the
revenues of the province amounting to £80,000 at an
outlay of £90,000. This scheme led to the deputation
of a specially qualified officer in 1869 to make the needful investigation and surveys, the result of which, so far
as they went, show that there is no difficulty in carrying
out the project. Financial difficulties stood in the way
of further inquiry, and so, for the present, the subject is
in abeyance.

The financial returns above referred to may, however,
lead to the execution of the project. In September,
1870, I submitted to the Government of India a note
by Colonel Fraser, with statements attached, which shows
fully the financial results to be expected from a complete
system of embankments on *both* sides of the river. The
following figures explain themselves :—

		Sq. miles.
Area to be protected on west bank	. . .	2,091
,, ,, east ,, . . .		1,200
Total . .		3,291

Total cost of works completed and to be undertaken on west bank	£249,800
Approximate cost of works on east bank . . .	90,000
Total . .	£339,000

Ultimate yearly revenue from land on west bank .	£250,000
Approximate ultimate yearly revenue from land on east bank	80,000
Total .	£330,000

The figures for the eastern bank are doubtless under-estimated, both as regards cost of construction and yearly revenue. But at the same time it will have to be remembered that, from the experience gained in the construction of the *existing* west embankment, we learn that for the eastern side a much less expensive style of construction will answer every purpose, and then even more favourable results may be looked for than those now anticipated.

I think there can be no doubt but that the Government *must* carry out these works if any material increase to our revenues is looked for. Although the area of the country is large, yet the *immediately* available area for purposes of cultivation is small. Out of 93,000 square miles but 3,000 are under cultivation. The greater portion of the remainder is not available for cultivation from want of communication with the rivers, which are at present the trade arteries of the province. There is then an intimate connection between roads and embankments, and to render the latter useful in the highest degree will necessitate early construction of the former. These are points I have repeatedly brought to the notice of the Government of India.

There is not much to he said regarding public buildings. Gaols on approved principles have been erected in almost every station throughout the province, a comprehensive scheme for some of them having been laid before the government by Sir Arthur Phayre. A new gaol is necessary at Tavoy and possibly a district gaol at Henzadah. During my administration a lunatic asylum has been erected in Rangoon, and lock hospitals are under construction in the four principal seaports of the province. Court-houses have been erected in the most important districts, most of them having been put in hand before my assumption of office. And a handsome building was purchased for the chief court and the two secretariats.

It is with much pleasure that I can record during my
administration the completion of many light-houses
around the coast of British Burma. The coast now is
rendered perfectly secure both for local and provincial
navigation. Arrangements are being made for the construction of a light-house on the Oyster reef to the north
of Akyab, and the improvement of the Harbour light on
the " Savage " rocks at Akyab has just been completed.
The name of Colonel Fraser, who made the arrangements
for all these works, must ever be associated with the ease
and safety with which a hitherto dangerous coast may
now be navigated. But his reputation is so high in this
respect, that further comment regarding his services in
connection with the light houses is superfluous.

I have now to speak of the projected Rangoon and
Prome railway. A complete scheme matured by Mr.
Prince after careful surveys has been elaborated and
submitted for the orders of the Government of India.
Here, again, I must record my appreciation for Colonel
Fraser's services, to whom I am indebted for the initiation
of the project. It has been for a considerable period
before the Government of India, but as yet I have
received no instructions regarding it.

In this province the administration of the forests is
conducted in the Public Works Department. They form
a considerable source of revenue to the government, for
which happy results we are mainly indebted to the
valuable services of Dr. Brandis, the present Inspector
General of Forests, who was for many years the Superintendent. With my review of the forest report for
1867–68, I submitted to the Government of India a
statement showing the financial results of twelve years'
administration, from 1856–57 to 1867–68. During that
period teak timber, amounting in quantity to 1,107,695
tons, and in value to £4,984,627, has been either extracted from forests within British territory or brought

from forests in independent states. The cost of extract-
ing the timber and of the maintenance of the foreign
timber revenue stations at Maulmain amounts to
£326,901 ; whilst the gross revenue from all sources
amounts to £823,289. The net revenue is thus
£496,388, a sum which has been poured into the
Imperial treasury without the expenditure of any capital.
This is most satisfactory, and the receipts (net) for
the remaining years 1868–69 to 1870–71 are equally
satisfactory.

A definite scheme for the formation of plantations on
a large scale has also been prepared and sanctioned
by the Government of India. I have always held that
any attempt at reproduction in the forests would not
be successful, but that we must look to plantations,
managed under proper supervision, for our eventual
supplies.

Reservation of certain rich forests as State domains
has also been put actively in hand. There can be no
question but that the stringent nature of the forest rules
regarding the preservation of teak has borne very hardly
upon the inhabitants of the teak-producing tracts. They
have been subject to visits of a most objectionable
character, and their peculiar system of cultivation (called
"toungya") has been materially interfered with. The
reservations now in progress will leave the people free to
cultivate according to customs handed down from time
immemorial. Within the reserved tracts the rights of the
State will be, of course, most jealously guarded.

I am inclined to think that the "toungya" system of
cultivation should be brought under some control, and
with this view I have asked the opinion of the Commissioner of Arakan with regard to the destruction of the
iron wood forests of Arakan by cultivation of this nature.
It will be for my successor to extend the inquiry to the
Pegu and Tenasserim divisions. The matter is one of

some delicacy, as the custom is a deeply rooted one, and any action restricting it is sure to produce some irritation.

In 1869, I directed an inquiry to be made into the condition of the iron wood forests of Arakan with a view to bring them, if needful, under forest conservancy. Doctor Schlich, the officer of the department to whom I entrusted this duty, submitted a most interesting report, which, however, does not advocate any action being taken for the thorough conservancy of the forests. They appear to be of great extent and to contain a large number of trees, but there is no demand for the timber, and therefore I could not recommend any outlay on supervising establishment. I have, however, called for the Commissioner's opinion on the best way of lessening the mischief at present being done to the forests, and it is possible this report may show the advisableness of a small staff being entertained for the purpose.

Having regard to the possible construction of the Prome railway, I ordered certain tracts of forest land to be examined and reserved as fuel reserves. The final report has not yet reached me, the work being now in hand.

A new system of assessing the government dues on timber brought out of government forests have been introduced, and I have no doubt but that it will lead to increase of forest revenue. The system formerly in vogue was simply the charging of a fixed rate per log on all timber above a certain length, and another fixed rate for all timber below that length. Under the system now in force all timber will be paid for at a certain rate per foot in length, the rate being fixed with reference to the girth.

The administration of the funds raised for local purposes throughout the province now demands notice. On my arrival in Rangoon, I found that the control over the expenditure was divided between the civil and public works secretaries, and one result of this was, that neither

secretariat knew what the other was spending. Furthermore the officers most interested in the proper administration of the funds, the Deputy Commisioners of districts,
were kept in total ignorance of the manner in which their
various district funds were being spent by the public
works department. There seemed much room for improvement in this branch of the administration, and the
first step taken to carry out this improvement was to
centralize the entire control of the funds in the civil
secretariat. The next was the early preparation of local
funds' budgets. And the third step was to prohibit any
outlay by the public works department except on definite
grants made by the civil department.

I think improvement has certainly followed on this
system. Civil officers now are brought into full rapport
with the expenditure from local sources ; and so far as
the execution of local works by public works officers is
concerned, the plans and estimates have to be signed by
the civil officers in token of their approval.

CONCLUSION.

In conclusion, I must now express my best thanks to
the officers of the Commission by whom I have been most
ably served, and without whose cordial assistance I could
have achieved but little. I would specially beg to notice
the services performed by the Commissioners of divisions,
Colonels Ardagh, Brown, Stevenson, and Ryan ; those of
my late and present Secretaries, Lieutenant-Colonel
Davies, Captain Spearman, Mr. Wheeler, Captain Fur-
long, and Lieutenant Cooke ; and those of the officers of
the Commission generally. I must also not omit to
mention the services of Majors Duncan and Hamilton,
and Mr. Doyle of the police department.

I have specially to thank Col. A. Fraser, C. B. R. E.,
my Secretary in the Public Works Department and Chief
Engineer, for the great support and zealous assistance he

has rendered me on every occasion, and to congratulate him on the completion of that magnificent series of light-houses which protect the commerce of our coasts, as well as the other works which he has either completed, or else are already in progress. To Mr. Macrone, Assistant Secretary in the same department, my thanks are also due.

A. FYTCHE, MAJOR GENERAL, C.S.I.

Chief Commissioner, British Burma, and Agent to the Viceroy and Governor-General of India.

BRITISH BURMA,
RANGOON.
The 25th March, 1871.

THE END.